Praise for the Book

'Innovation is a western word. In spoken Indian languages, there is no equivalent. The act of innovating is referred to as jugaad, meaning an adaptation or practical solution. Although jugaad sometimes has mildly pejorative overtones, it is used by crores of Indian entrepreneurs to create effective solutions to pressing socio-economic issues. By formalizing the jugaad approach to solving problems speedily and frugally, the authors have conceptualized a platform on which future innovation can develop.'

—R. Gopalakrishnan, Director, Tata Sons Ltd, India

'*Jugaad Innovation* is a must read for all MNC executives who have a long-term vision to be successful in India. Targeting local resource opportunities and being ingeniously innovative, jugaad enables local success, and in many ways, also helps fortify global markets. If one succeeds in emerging markets such as India, you can be successful anywhere in the world; and to succeed in India, you need jugaad!'

—Dr Armin Bruck, Managing Director and CEO, Siemens Ltd,
South Asia Cluster

'Frugal innovation is mission critical at YES BANK. I sincerely believe that Indians are natural leaders in frugal innovation, with our jugaad system of enterprising workable solutions from scarce resources. I firmly believe that jugaad is an entrepreneurial approach to innovation, which has indeed been the cornerstone of success for Indian SMEs. I would like to compliment the authors of *Jugaad Innovation* for creatively showcasing this methodology through inspiring examples of companies which have used this concept to drive growth. This book is an excellent guide for innovative Indian entrepreneurs, and truly provides international validation for many Indian corporate leaders to embrace indigenous solutions.'

—Dr Rana Kapoor, Founder, Managing Director
and CEO, YES BANK

'Powered by demographics and geopolitics, the global economic axis is shifting inexorably eastward. This book highlights innovation in rapidly expanding markets like India where frugality and flexibility are strengths that are being leveraged to drive growth in the 21st century. From transnational corporations to grassroots entrepreneurs, and for manufacturers as well as firms in the creative sector, understanding how to catalyze success through innovation is crucial. For all of them, *Jugaad Innovation* is a must read.'

—Amit Khanna, CEO, Reliance Entertainment

'Frugality, flexibility, and following your instincts are principles we all learned growing up in India, and ones that we must effectively leverage for long term growth—especially in large corporations. The authors of *Jugaad Innovation* have it right: to stay ahead, corporate leaders need to adopt the principles of jugaad innovation. This book is a must read for the corporate sector and entrepreneurs alike.'

—Kishore Biyani, Founder, Future Group

'*Jugaad Innovation* details and provides illustrative examples on ways to transform existing innovation processes to the more fluid art and disruptive culture of jugaad. You'll finish the book with a sense of urgency and a roadmap to go after the organic ingenuity lying within your employees, suppliers and customers, and prepared to tackle the economics of scarcity.'

—Terri Bresenham, President and CEO, GE Healthcare,
South Asia

'Innovation flowers at the intersection of disciplines and cultures. For innovation to be engaging, efficient and breakthrough, companies need to go beyond structured innovation and employ the principles of jugaad which is based on frugality, flexibility, and instinct. Anyone can run a process, but few leaders understand the value of instinct and trust in employees and consumers. *Jugaad Innovation* will help leaders unlock the value of these principles in enabling innovation.'

—D. Shivakumar, Senior Vice President, Nokia—India, Middle East, and Africa

'Structured and planned attempts at innovation rarely drive breakthroughs in technology or business models while ad-hoc, unfocused, random innovation rarely makes it into customers' hands. In India, process culture and jugaad culture live side by side, and their marriage, which I call 'Jugaad 2.0', has incredible potential to drive the breakthroughs required for sustainable growth. *Jugaad Innovation* is the roadmap that will help you get there '

—Dr Wido Menhardt, CEO, Philips Innovation Campus, Bangalore

'With its six intuitive and actionable principles, *Jugaad Innovation* provides a unique recipe for organizations to consistently drive radical innovation. With R&D budgets on the rise, and their returns on the decline, business leaders are questioning whether it's time for the top-down approach to innovation to be traded for a more bottom-up approach. This book provides a crystal clear answer. A must read for all business leaders.'

—V.R. Ferose, Managing Director, SAP Labs India

'In an increasingly resource-starved, volatile, and unpredictable world, conventional approaches to innovation will simply not work. Instead, what is needed is a jugaad mindset—one that is frugal, flexible, and sharply focused on outcomes. *Jugaad Innovation* makes a compelling case for corporations to find ways of encouraging this unique mindset even within their existing organizational processes and ways of working.'

—Nitin Paranjpe, CEO and Managing Director,
Hindustan Unilever

'Emerging markets offer a unique growth opportunity in the 21st century. Demographics, economics, and enabling technologies like mobility, social media, cloud computing, and big data create a fertile basis for innovation in these markets. Jugaad is the dominant approach to innovation in emerging markets. Yet, jugaad is not just a quick and dirty solution; it also builds on the core principles of customer experience, scale, and profitability—all critical determinants of success. Using powerful examples, this book shows how you can drive frugal innovation of high quality.'

—N. Chandrasekaran, CEO, Tata Consultancy Services

'The authors bring new life to the concept of jugaad. In the face of immense adversity are born some of the best ideas, and it is heartening to see credit given in this book to the spectacular flexibility and resilience that Indian entrepreneurs demonstrate every day. Read this book to understand why the concept of jugaad innovation must be integrated with the processes of both Indian and Western corporations in order to continuously create the world's best products and services.'

—Tulsi Tanti, Chairman, Suzlon Group

'Need a new roadmap? Fresh inspiration? Accessible tools? It's all in this remarkable book, *Jugaad Innovation*. Get a copy for yourself and every member of your team today'

—Kevin Roberts, CEO Worldwide, Saatchi & Saatchi

JUGAAD

INNOVATION

A FRUGAL AND FLEXIBLE APPROACH
TO INNOVATION FOR THE 21ST CENTURY

NAVI RADJOU, JAIDEEP PRABHU & SIMONE AHUJA

RANDOM HOUSE INDIA

Published by Random House India in 2012
Seventh impression in 2013

First published by Jossey-Bass, A Wiley Imprint
One Montgomery Street, Suite 1200, San Francisco, CA 94104-4594
www.josseybass.com

Random House Publishers India Private Limited
Windsor IT Park, 7th Floor, Tower-B
A-1, Sector-125, Noida-201301, UP

Random House Group Limited
20 Vauxhall Bridge Road
London SW1V 2SA
United Kingdom

978 81 8400 205 8

Typeset in Sabon by InoSoft Systems, Noida

Printed and bound in India by Replika Press Pvt. Ltd

For sale in the Indian Subcontinent only

To our parents, who taught us to be frugal and flexible, and encouraged us to follow our hearts

Contents

Foreword

C ompanies worldwide face a business environment presenting unprecedented challenges. Resource constraint, which is a norm in emerging markets, is becoming a reality even in the advanced economies, given the exigencies of climate change. Market conditions everywhere are fluid, complex, fast paced, and volatile because of the information boom and the rise of the social media.

In the circumstances, it is a truism that innovation will perhaps be the key differentiator that will demarcate the winners and the also-rans. They key questions are: what kind of innovation do companies need so as to enhance and sustain their competitiveness and how do companies embed that kind of innovation in their organizations?

These are such key questions facing business today that the shelves are full of business books addressing those very questions. This is one more such book but it strikes a chord because it is different in its approach and content, while retaining its relevance as a mainstream management treatise.

Jugaad is a Hindi word which does not have an exact English translation, partly because it is derived from the common Indian experience of innovating frugal, homespun, and simple solutions to the myriad problems that beset everyday life in India. The authors have sought to extend this mindset, which embodies survival and competitiveness at perhaps their most primeval manifestations, into a way of life for businesses not just in emerging markets like India but also in advanced economies, so as to forge a growth strategy in today's troubled times.

In the West, the authors point out, innovation is done in structured R&D departments, which has its strengths of scale and rigour. The authors draw on examples of companies from the BRIC countries and other emerging markets, mostly, but also from richer countries to establish how in the current challenging business environment companies could find themselves short if they do not complement their structured and expensive R&D model with more flexible, frugal, and instinct-driven innovation that a jugaad mindset represents.

This book's other distinctiveness is that it is a 'How To' book for CEOs and entrepreneurs in all economies, as it offers a coherent and cohesive framework for embedding the jugaad mindset in companies using six well-defined and proven principles. These principles—Seek opportunity in adversity; Do more with less; Think and act flexibly; Keep it simple; Include the margin; and Follow your heart—seem commonsensical when heard in isolation but come alive in the book.

It goes without saying that the book has a special significance for India, which needs a high rate of growth which is also as equitable as it is sustained. This book gives the examples of several Indian companies using jugaad innovation to come up with practical solutions—across sectors like agriculture, healthcare, energy, financial services—that are affordable and accessible to the masses. These frugal solutions address the needs—rather than the desires—of the masses and represent business models that are inclusive and sustainable and allow companies to do well while doing good.

As the authors of the book argue, India's need is to scale up its solutions, rapidly and widely. To do this, Indian business needs to spread the culture of business innovation through the jugaad mindset into many other areas of the economy. Also, the authors correctly note, Indian business needs to integrate the structured Western R&D model of innovation with their free-flowing jugaad model to create a dynamic balance between both approaches in their organizations.

Corporate leaders and entrepreneurs who want to succeed and grow not just in complex and resource-constrained markets like India but in markets all over will find this book more than a useful read.

R.N. Tata
Chairman, Tata Group

Introduction

Innovation is going to be critical for India—not only for growth and competitive advantage, but also to ensure that our future development is sustainable and inclusive. Our country faces a range of unmet needs related to critical areas such as health, education, agriculture, energy, and skills. It also faces immense challenges related to *demography*, with 55 crore below the age of 25 for whom opportunities must be provided; *disparity*, driven by the multiple deprivations of class, caste, gender, and region; and the challenge of *development*, with the urgent need to lift crores of citizens out of dire poverty. Innovation is going to be central to providing answers to these most pressing challenges and for creating opportunity structures for sharing the benefits of the emerging knowledge economy. Affordable solutions, innovative business models, or processes which ease delivery of services to citizens will allow more people to join the development process and also enable looking beyond the conventional way of doing things.

However, our unique needs call for a new model of innovation that focuses on affordability and inclusive growth and lifts people at the bottom of the pyramid out of poverty and deprivation. For decades, the trajectory of innovation has reflected the priorities of the developed world: focusing more on the desires of the rich, and directing ecosystems of talent and capital to satisfy them. India cannot follow that path. Our innovation must instead focus on the poor, and their most essential wants. The old consumption-intensive approaches cannot work, given the sheer scale of our needs and our vast population: instead, our innovation needs to be frugal with scare resources, affordable for our poorest citizens, and environmentally sustainable. The work of India's National Innovation Council reflects this thinking. Our effort has been aimed at creating an *Indian Model of Innovation*, of the people, by the people, and for the people. Only through this inclusive approach where people are beneficiaries in knowledge creation and generation can we hope to create more sustainable models of development. The Council, through its various initiatives, has been working towards an approach to innovation that goes beyond an R&D intensive paradigm to include innovation in processes, organisational and service delivery models. Our strategy also remains focused on parameters of sustainability, affordability, durability, quality, global competitiveness, and local need. I believe these drivers apply to more than just government policy and will define the agenda of any individual or organisation seeking to successfully innovate in this country.

We also have to be mindful of the fact that today we are a nation of a billion connected people and this connectivity, coupled with ICT talent, is changing the nature of processes, business, industry, governance, education, and delivery systems. Our innovation thinking also has to leverage the unprecedented advantages provided by this changing landscape of connectivity and collaboration.

A new model requires a new mindset: and here, this book makes a particularly vital contribution. Jugaad reflects a rich Indian tradition of ingenuity in the face of challenge. It demonstrates the day-to-day ability of ordinary Indians to solve problems under conditions of constraint and scarcity, and to seize opportunities in the most challenging circumstances. What this book offers its readers is a way of institutionalising this approach in their organisations, and of being systematic about innovating frugally. This is critically important, if inclusive innovation is to be scaled and replicated. Significantly, this book is about more than India. The condition of scarcity, the imperative of inclusiveness, the urgency of basic needs among poorer citizens—these can be found in developing countries around the world. Indian models could inspire innovation well beyond our shores. Navi, Jaideep, and Simone offer not just the analytical clarity needed to incorporate this culture of flexible, frugal innovation into wider programmes—they also offer a range of compelling, practical examples illustrating how these are achieved. Their work is an important step towards creating a new culture of innovation, one that is better suited to our needs and our time.

Sam Pitroda
Adviser to the Prime Minister of India
on Public Information Infrastructure and Innovations;
Chairman, National Innovation Council

Chapter 1

Jugaad: A Breakthrough Growth Strategy

'Any intelligent fool can make things bigger, more complex, and more violent. It takes a touch of genius—and a lot of courage—to move in the opposite direction.'

—ALBERT EINSTEIN

We reached Ramakrishna Nagar, a village in the desert of Gujarat, after travelling 402.3 kilometres from Ahmedabad. Our team—a Silicon Valley management consultant, a business school professor from the University of Cambridge, and the founder of a Minneapolis advisory boutique and media firm—had set out a few months earlier on an extensive research and travel project. Our mission: to discover new approaches to innovation in emerging markets such as India that could help corporate leaders worldwide take on the complexity of our tough and turbulent times.

We came to Gujarat to meet with Professor Anil Gupta at the Indian Institute of Management (IIM) in Ahmedabad.[1] Professor Gupta runs Honey Bee Network, a non-profit organization that identifies and cross-pollinates grassroots innovation all across India. Over more than two decades, Honey Bee has populated a database of over ten thousand inventions of grassroots entrepreneurs who have created ingenious solutions for pressing socio-economic problems in their local communities. Professor Gupta suggested we meet with one of these rural entrepreneurs.

As we left an arrow-straight concrete highway to follow narrower and increasingly cratered gravel roads, the temperature rose to a debilitating 50 degrees. Stepping out of our air-conditioned jeep, we could feel the weight of the desert's oppressive heat. Mansukh Prajapati greeted us warmly outside his workshop.[2] A potter by trade, Prajapati had for years been experimenting with clay to produce a variety of durable goods, many of which were on display in the office outside his lab. We were parched—and grateful—when he asked us if we wanted water. We had run out of bottled water, and there wasn't any sign of a store or kiosk nearby to restock. He reached around to a faucet, handed us cups, and, beaming with pride, said, 'Please, have this cold water—from my fridge.'

Baffled, we looked more closely at the terracotta box in front of us. It was made entirely of clay, except for a glass door and a plastic faucet at the bottom. While sipping the refreshingly cool water, we looked around and found no electrical cord, no battery—just clay. Amused by our expressions, Prajapati explained how this clay fridge—the Mitticool (mitti meaning earth)—works: water from an upper chamber seeps through the side walls, cooling the lower food chamber through evaporation. The fridge consumes no electricity, is 100 percent biodegradable, and produces zero waste during its lifetime. An ingenious invention!

But this inventor and his personal story are even more impressive. Prajapati doesn't work for NASA or Whirlpool, and he doesn't have a PhD in quantum physics or an MBA from Harvard. In fact, he didn't even finish high school. His R&D lab—a simple open-air room with clay in various stages arrayed on the floor and an oven tucked in the corner—is a far cry from the sprawling campuses of GE and Whirlpool, which swarm with hundreds of engineers and scientists.

In 2001, an earthquake had devastated Prajapati's village and the surrounding area. Reading a report of the devastation in the local newspaper, he noticed a photo caption: 'Poor man's fridge broken!' The photo featured a smashed earthen pot commonly used by villagers to fetch water and keep it cool. And though the newspaper had called it a fridge in jest, it triggered Prajapati's first eureka moment. *Why not use clay*, he thought, *to make a real fridge for villagers—one that looks like a typical fridge, but is more affordable and doesn't need electricity?* Over 50 crore Indians live without reliable electricity, including most of the people in Prajapati's village.[3] The positive health and lifestyle benefits of owning a fridge in a desert village where fruit, vegetables, and dairy are available only intermittently would be tremendous.

Prajapati's training as a potter, coupled with his intuition, told him that he was on to something. He experimented for several months and eventually had a viable version of the Mitticool that he began selling to people in his own village. The fridge—which costs around ₹ 2,000—was a hit. Prajapati worked tirelessly on design improvements, and began selling Mitticools across India first, and then internationally. He couldn't keep up with the rising demand and had to find ways to scale up—fast.

Then he had a second eureka moment. *Why not transform pottery from an artisanal craft to an industrial process?* He leveraged his traditional knowledge of pottery to mass-produce goods that met modern consumer needs. Prajapati first developed an entirely new and more efficient method of working with clay. Then he began training women in his village in these industrial pottery techniques and finally hired them to work in his new factory. Soon a 'mini' Industrial Revolution in pottery was launched in this remote Indian village.

Mitticool was the first product that Prajapati mass-produced in his factory. He soon built other products from clay, such as a non-stick frying pan that retains heat longer than other frying pans and costs a mere ₹ 100. From one man and one idea, a frugal yet fruitful industry has grown, one that employs large numbers of people in Prajapati's own community and serves consumers in India and abroad. Prajapati's groundbreaking inventions, which deliver more value at less cost, have earned him accolades from all over the world—including the President of India. And *Forbes* magazine recently named him among the most influential rural Indian entrepreneurs, one of few to have made an impact on the lives of so many.[4]

Jugaad: The Gutsy Art of Improvising an Ingenious Solution

The Mitticool, an idea born out of adverse circumstances, shows how a resilient mindset can transform scarcity into opportunity. Combining limited resources and a never-say-die attitude, Prajapati tapped into his empathy and passion for his fellow community members to conjure up an ingenious solution that improved lives in Gujarat and beyond. Not only did he produce a cheap and effective cooling device, but he also created jobs for dozens of undereducated women. In doing so, Prajapati is both driving environmental and socio-economic sustainability in his community and ensuring the financial sustainability of his own business. Prajapati embodies the true spirit of jugaad.

Jugaad is a colloquial Hindi word that roughly translates as 'an innovative fix; an improvised solution born from ingenuity and cleverness'. Jugaad is, quite simply, a unique way of thinking and acting in response to challenges; it is the gutsy art of spotting opportunities in the most adverse circumstances and resourcefully improvising solutions using simple means. Jugaad is about *doing more with less*. (We feature articles and videos on jugaad on our companion website: jugaadinnovation.com)

Jugaad is practised by almost all Indians in their daily lives to make the most of what they have. Jugaad applications include finding new uses for everyday objects—kitchens are replete with empty soft drink or pickle bottles reused as containers for water, spices, or lentils—or inventing new utilitarian tools using everyday objects, like a makeshift truck cobbled together with a diesel engine slapped onto a cart (interestingly, the origin of the word jugaad, in Punjabi, literally describes such makeshift vehicles).

The word jugaad is also applied to any use of an ingenious way to 'game the system'. For instance, crores of cellphone users in India rely on 'missed calls' to communicate messages to each other using a prearranged protocol between the caller and receiver: a form of *free textless* text messaging. For example, your carpooling partner may give you a 'missed call' in the morning indicating he has just left his house and is on his way to pick you up.[5] Hence, the word jugaad carries a slightly negative connotation for some. But by and large, the entrepreneurial spirit of jugaad is practised by crores in India simply to improvise clever—and completely legitimate—solutions to everyday problems.

In this book, we delve into the frugal and flexible mindset of thousands of ingenious entrepreneurs and enterprises practising jugaad to creatively address critical socio-economic issues in their communities. Jugaad innovators like Mansukh Prajapati view severe constraints, such as a lack of electricity, not as a debilitating challenge but as an opportunity to innovate and overcome these very constraints.

The entrepreneurial spirit of jugaad is not limited to India. It is widely practised in other emerging economies such as China and Brazil, where entrepreneurs are also pursuing growth in difficult circumstances. The Brazilians have their own word for this approach: *jeitinho*.[6] The Chinese call it *zizhu chuangxin*.[7] The Kenyans refer to it as *jua kali*.[8] The French have a term too—*Système D*.[9] Throughout this book we profile jugaad entrepreneurs from Argentina, Brazil, China, Costa Rica, India, Kenya, Mexico, the Philippines and elsewhere who have created simple yet effective solutions to address vexing problems that their fellow citizens face. We hope to shed light on how these jugaad innovators think and act and identify the valuable lessons that large companies can learn from them.

Jugaad: A Better Alternative to the Western Innovation Model?

Money can't buy the ingenuity manifested in jugaad—nor can you legislate or 'manage' jugaad innovation. Jugaad happens organically: it's an 'emergent' phenomenon, not a planned activity. Jugaad embodies—to cite Woodrow Wilson, President of the US from 1913 to 1921—'the highest and best form of efficiency (that) is the spontaneous cooperation of free people'. In sum, jugaad represents a bottom-up innovation model that India excels in.[10]

Yet, when we interact with Indian CEOs, they rarely talk about jugaad. Instead, they inquire about what 'innovation strategies' they need to adopt to accelerate their company's growth. They express concern about India's low investment levels in research and development (R&D) compared with arch-rival China (India today invests less than 1 percent of its gross domestic product, or GDP, on R&D whereas China intends to step up its R&D to GDP ratio from 1.76 in 2010 to 2.5 by

2020). There is no doubt that Indian companies need to boost their R&D spending and embrace sound innovation strategies if they are to achieve their potential in the coming 'decade of innovation'. But even as they carry out these top-down R&D initiatives, Indian CEOs should not overlook a key strength of the existing Indian ecosystem: its entrepreneurs' ability to use jugaad to create products and services in an organic, bottom-up fashion using limited resources.

Rather than dismissing jugaad as the 'poor man's approach to innovating', Indian CEOs should recognize that jugaad is a highly effective business tool that can be formalized and help companies innovate faster, better, and cheaper in today's hypercompetitive and volatile environment. Consequently, they should nurture this free-spirited jugaad mindset within their organization—by unleashing and harnessing grassroots, employee- or consumer-led creativity. This is especially vital in large organizations that are process-driven or operate in regulated sectors. Over-emphasizing processes and compliance could lead to a risk-averse culture that can restrain innovation. That's why, as we show later in this book, forward-thinking CEOs of leading Indian firms such as YES BANK, Future Group, Suzlon, Tata Motors and the heads of Indian subsidiaries of GE, Siemens, Philips, and PepsiCo are striving to cultivate a jugaad mindset among their workforce—without sacrificing the efficiencies obtained through structured processes. These visionary leaders are attempting to achieve the right balance between top-down R&D strategies while supporting bottom-up jugaad innovation. In doing so, they are seeking to avoid the mistakes of Western CEOs who are now paying a hefty price for swinging too much in the direction of a top-down, structured R&D model.

To understand the pitfalls of structured innovation and the lessons these hold for Indian corporations, it is useful to explore how Western economies evolved from a context in which frugal and flexible innovation flourished to one in which such an approach was eclipsed by an expensive and structured approach that has now begun to show its limits.

Indeed, jugaad was once a big part of Western innovation too. It was the flexible mindset of jugaad-style innovators that catalyzed growth in Western economies like the US during the Industrial Revolution in the 19th century. Among the many early American jugaad innovators, the best known may well be Benjamin Franklin, one of America's founding fathers, who was born in Boston, Massachusetts, in 1706. Franklin experienced scarcity and learned about the virtue of frugality firsthand, growing up in a large Puritan family of nine brothers and seven sisters.[11] When he was just ten-years-old, Franklin left school and started working in his father's candle and soap shop to help support his family. Early on, Franklin developed a knack for using limited resources to devise ingenious and frugal solutions to tackle everyday problems faced by his contemporaries. Franklin's legendary ingenuity was fueled by his genuine empathy for his fellow citizens. One of his most practical inventions was the Franklin stove.[12] During the 18th century, homes in the US were primarily heated by inefficient fireplaces that spewed smoke as much of the heat they generated escaped up the chimney. They were also hazardous, as their sparks could trigger fires that quickly devoured wood-built homes.

Franklin's jugaad innovation to tackle this problem was a new type of stove with a simple hooded enclosure in the front and an air box in the rear. The new stove and its reconfiguration of the flues enabled a more efficient fire, one that consumed 75 percent less wood and generated twice as much heat.[13] The Franklin stove delivered 'more with less'. An early advocate of open source technology, Franklin turned down the patent offered for his original design, stating that altruism, rather than profit, was his driving motive for developing the efficient stove. He wanted all Americans to benefit from his invention. In fact, Franklin patented *none* of his jugaad inventions. In his autobiography, he wrote that 'as we enjoy great advantages from the inventions of others, we should be glad of an opportunity to serve others by any invention of ours; and this we should do freely and generously'.[14] As a serial jugaad entrepreneur, his approach to innovation was always inclusive: his ingenious but simple inventions—including the lightning rod, bifocals, and a carriage odometer—enhanced lives throughout the colonies.

America's founding fathers, as well its creative farmers, industrial pioneers, and scientific explorers in the 19th and early 20th centuries—from Ben Franklin to Cyrus McCormick to the Wright brothers—were historic practitioners of jugaad in the West. These ingenious entrepreneurs spurred the Industrial Revolution in Western nations, building a strong foundation of economic leadership that lasted for decades. In the twentieth century, however, especially after World War II, Western nations gradually lost touch with this jugaad spirit as they matured into post-industrial economies and became attached to a systematized, predictable way of life and work. Improvised ingenuity—the essence of jugaad—took a back seat to a more formally structured approach to innovation. As North American and European economies expanded, Western corporations began to institutionalize their innovation capabilities, creating dedicated R&D departments and standardizing the business processes needed to take their ideas to market. They focused on *managing* innovation, just as they managed any other business activity. This industrialization of the creative process led to a *structured* approach to innovation with the following key characteristics: big budgets, standardized business processes, and controlled access to knowledge.

But this structured innovation approach, which helped Western firms become highly successful in the second half of the 20th century, has three clear limitations in the fast pace and volatility of the 21st century: it is too expensive and resource consuming, it lacks flexibility, and it is elitist and insular.

THE STRUCTURED APPROACH IS TOO EXPENSIVE AND RESOURCE CONSUMING

Western firms have come to believe that their innovation system—like any industrial system—will generate more output (inventions) if fed more input (resources). As a result, the structured innovation engine is capital intensive. It requires an abundant supply of financial and natural resources at a time when both are increasingly scarce. The approach is designed to deliver 'more with more'—that is, firms charge customers a hefty premium for over-engineered products that are expensive to develop and produce. For instance, the thousand companies in the world that invest the most in innovation—many of which are Western firms—spent a whopping $550,000,000,000 (that's ₹ 27.5 lakh crore!) on R&D in 2010 alone.[15] But what did they get in return for all this expense? Not much, according to research conducted by the management consultancy Booz & Company. They found that the three Western industries that spend the most on R&D—computing and electronics, healthcare, and automotive—struggle to generate a steady stream of groundbreaking inventions, despite their hefty R&D investments. Hence there is *a weak correlation* between how much money your firm spends in R&D and how well it performs in terms of developing and marketing products that generate a significant financial return. To put it bluntly, *money can't buy innovation*. Fittingly, a Booz & Company report carries a photograph of a dejected-looking CEO wearing a T-shirt that reads: 'We spent $2 billion (₹ 10,000 crore) on R&D and all we got was this lousy T-shirt.' The caption illustrates well the frustrations of Western corporate leaders facing, on the one hand, huge financial constraints, and on the other, immense pressures from shareholders to deliver growth.[16]

The pharmaceutical industry is one sector where the 'bigger is better' R&D strategy is clearly running out of steam. Big Pharma's spending on R&D ballooned from $15 billion (₹ 75,000 crore) in 1995 to $45 billion (₹ 225,000 crore) in 2009.[17] Yet the number of new drugs launched annually has dropped by 44 percent since 1997.[18] This is especially bad news for Big Pharma, given that between 2011 and 2016, drugs worth a whopping $139 billion (₹ 695,000 crore) are set to go off patent.[19] To further complicate things, Big Pharma in the US is facing a growing backlash from politicians and the public as healthcare costs spiral out of control, even as 5 crore Americans continue to lack basic health insurance.

The drug industry is not an exception. The US auto sector spent $16 billion (₹ 80,000 crore) on R&D in 2007 alone.[20] But American automakers nevertheless trail their Japanese, Korean, German, and even Chinese and Indian rivals, as frugal consumers worldwide clamor for more compact, fuel-efficient, and environmentally friendly cars. The US market share of the Big Three—Chrysler, General Motors, and Ford—has steadily declined, from 70 percent in 1998 to 44.2 percent in 2009.[21] In December 2008, the cash-strapped automakers asked the US government for a $34 billion (₹ 170,000 crore) bailout to cover employee healthcare expenses and prevent bankruptcy and massive layoffs.[22] Since December 2009, the US government has given $82 billion (₹ 410,000 crore) in aid to the Big Three—including $62 billion (₹ 310,000 crore) to General Motors and Chrysler alone (both carmakers filed for bankruptcy protection).[23]

THE STRUCTURED APPROACH LACKS FLEXIBILITY

With so much money invested in R&D, Western firms have become risk averse in their approach to innovation. They have implemented standardized business processes such as Six Sigma (an integrated set of management techniques designed to decrease production defects and increase operational efficiency by standardizing processes) and 'stage gate analysis' to manage and control their innovation projects. These structured processes were expected to drastically reduce uncertainty—and risk of failure—from the entire innovation process and make R&D projects more predictable in both execution and outcomes. But these structured business processes and methods are unfit to deliver the agility and differentiation that enterprises need in a fast-paced and volatile world.

Take Six Sigma—the well-known management strategy pioneered by Motorola in 1986 and the corporate dogma of leading Fortune 500 firms such as GE and Boeing. Six Sigma is a set of practises designed to improve quality by eliminating defects. With a Six Sigma process implemented, there is a statistical expectation that 99.99966 percent of the products manufactured will be free of defects. Six Sigma works marvellously when you are seeking to institutionalize 'sameness', and this comes in handy when you are mass-producing widgets in a predictable environment. But Six Sigma is like a straitjacket: once you get in, you are stuck, and when things start to change, you can't move (let alone dance).[24]

Built around stable and predictable processes, programmes like Six Sigma cannot enable the rapid change that companies need as they seek to mass customize products and services, satisfy increasingly diverse and finicky customers, and keep up with technology. Worse, the orthodox Six Sigma culture weeds out 'positive deviance'—the uncommon strategies used by those pioneering employees in a company who use unconventional and counter-intuitive methods to solve vexing business problems that can't be addressed using traditional approaches.[25] But, as Malcolm Gladwell points out in *Outliers*, positively deviant behavior and ideas are what actually drive game-changing innovation.[26] That explains why George Buckley, CEO of 3M—where an outlier named Art Fry invented the famous Post-it® Notes by sheer serendipity—rolled back several Six Sigma initiatives at 3M in a bid to revive innovation in the firm. Buckley points out: 'Invention is by its very nature a disorderly process. You can't put a Six Sigma process into that area and say, well, I'm getting behind on invention, so I'm going to schedule myself for three good ideas on Wednesday and two on Friday. That's not how creativity works.'[27]

THE STRUCTURED APPROACH IS ELITIST AND INSULAR

Throughout the 20th century, Western firms built large R&D labs that employed hundreds of top scientists and engineers, based on a belief that 'knowledge is power' and that controlling access to it was key to success. Thus innovation became an elite activity controlled by a few high priests: engineers and scientists working under conditions of secrecy in in-house labs close to headquarters. Only these chosen few were invited into the R&D department and given the resources and permission to innovate. Any new knowledge they generated was closely guarded. Collaboration with other employees—let alone outsiders—was shunned. The assumption was that to dominate markets through innovation one needed two things: top-of-the-line technology and ownership of the best intellectual property, both of which could be bought with enough money. However true that assumption might have been in an earlier industrial era, it is far less valid now. Part of the old belief was that only a bunch of smart PhDs could *invent* new things. But in today's consumer-driven economy, we know that it's more important to *commercialize* technology, which requires knowledge of fields such as design and marketing—skills that engineers and scientists may not necessarily have.[28] As Bob McDonald, CEO of Procter & Gamble, explains: 'For us, innovation is not invention. It's the conversion of a new idea into consumer delight and, ultimately, into revenues and profits. If an idea or technology cannot be successfully commercialized, it's not an innovation.'[29]

Further, in an interconnected world powered by social media, the intellectual property that one can buy isn't the only source of new ideas. Finding, sharing, and integrating globally dispersed knowledge among all levels of employees is just as important, if not more so. Consider this statistic: as of this writing, every Facebook user creates, on an average, ninety pieces of content per month, contributing to more than 3,000 crore pieces of shared content—ranging from family photos to web links to posts—across the Facebook social network.[30] The power of innovation has shifted from the professional class to the masses. Creativity has been democratized—thanks to social media tools like Facebook. As strategy consultant and author Gary Hamel says, 'The underlying principles on the Web of natural hierarchy, transparency, collaboration and all the rest—those characteristics are going to have to invade management. The idea of a hierarchy that fundamentally empowers the few and disempowers the many is more or less dead.'[31]

Yet top-down R&D systems are often unable to open up and integrate such bottom-up input from employees and customers. Younger, creative employees use new technologies like social media in order to brainstorm ideas, creating a virtual watercooler. Structured organizations often find it hard to integrate these methods of innovation into their business model. The chief information officer of a large engineering services firm in India told us, 'Many of our younger employees brainstorm new ideas on Facebook. As a result, Facebook has become the virtual brainstorming place where people gather and hatch ideas. I really don't know how to funnel those ideas back into our corporate R&D systems.'

Bottom line: the structured approach to innovation has become too rigid, insular, and expensive. It consumes a lot of resources and makes a lot of noise, but—for many companies—it produces little of much significance. If this condition of dysfunction continues much longer, it risks crippling firms even as the global economy emerges from tough times and seeks to grow.

It is clear, therefore, that firms around the world need an alternative innovation engine: one that is frugal and flexible and that allows them to innovate faster, better, and cheaper. To do so, firms and their managers must find new sources of inspiration. Emerging markets—such as India—are a great place to start.

Searching for the Holy Grail of Innovation

When we began our research in 2008, we predicted that the so-called BRICs—Brazil, Russia, India, and China—might be a good place to look for a new approach to innovation.[32] We had each come to this realization in our respective professions— academia, consulting, and media—and this interest brought us together in the shared quest that has culminated in this book.

In early 2008, Simone began extensive background research and ethnographic work for a documentary film series exploring innovation in India. During her work she came across Navi, then an analyst at Forrester Research, and asked him to act as an innovation consultant to the film series. Navi had written extensively about—and consulted on—innovation in both

Western and emerging markets. In late 2008, Navi decided to focus all his attention on emerging markets and joined Jaideep at the University of Cambridge's Judge Business School to set up the Centre for India & Global Business. Jaideep, after spending most of his academic career studying innovation in the West, had also begun to turn his attention to the increasingly important role of emerging markets in the global innovation ecosystem.

When we began our quest, the emerging economies had grown in the previous decade from one-sixth to a quarter of the world economy. Even in 2008, at the height of the global recession, India and China were growing at 7 percent and 9 percent, respectively. Goldman Sachs, among others, had predicted that these nations would continue to grow between 3 percent and 5 percent per year until 2050, dominating the world economy for the next forty years.[33]

The BRIC economies' vastness (both geographically and demographically), their diversity, and their pervasive scarcity of resources, all add up to a challenging state of affairs that would trouble even the most seasoned business leaders. However, the very fact that the BRIC nations have been grappling with complexity and instability for so long seems to give them an edge and a kind of immunity in volatile and adverse circumstances. What is in the immune system of these emerging economies that makes them so resilient? And what might business leaders in these countries be able to teach their counterparts in the West?

To find the answers we studied the *mindset* and *principles* of innovators who were driving growth in the BRIC countries. If corporate leaders could acquire a similar mindset and similar principles, then they could potentially develop the same immunity to complexity—and quickly identify emerging business opportunities in their own mature economies.

Among the BRICs, we chose to study India first because, after China, it is the fastest-growing economy in the world. Further, many—including Goldman Sachs and Ernst & Young—predict that India not only will economically outpace China soon but will continue to grow faster than the other BRICs for several decades to come.[34] Most importantly, India is as complex as they come. The country faces scarcity on a grand scale across the board: from water, food, and energy (over 50 crore Indians lack regular electricity) to access to education and healthcare. Its chaotic democracy is characterized by a Kafkaesque bureaucracy and mind-boggling diversity; its population of 120 crore is expanding at 1.3 percent a year.[35] Despite all the chaos and complexity, the Indian economy is growing strongly in challenging economic times. If Indians have managed to grow 'in spite of complexity', then there must be something there worth learning from.

On our many trips to India, we met dozens of grassroots entrepreneurs and visited over a hundred enterprises, large and small. What we saw amazed us. The country is bursting with ingeniously simple yet effective innovations. After more than three years of extensive field research, searching for the holy grail of innovation all over the country, we came to a realization: all the thrifty innovators we encountered shared a unique mindset—the jugaad mindset.

Expanding our research to other countries, we found that the entrepreneurial spirit of jugaad, far from being a purely Indian thing, is really universal. Other emerging markets, from Latin America to Africa to Eastern Europe to Asia, have their own versions of jugaad. (In our companion website, jugaadinnovation. com, we showcase several of these jugaad innovators.) Because these emerging economies share the same adverse conditions that drive jugaad in India, they also excel at this improvisational and frugal art of responding to complexity. What then are the shared, underlying principles of this jugaad mindset?

The Six Principles of Jugaad

We found that jugaad can be distilled into six guiding principles, which anchor the six practises of highly effective innovators in complex settings like emerging economies. The six principles are:

- Seek opportunity in adversity
- Do more with less
- Think and act flexibly
- Keep it simple
- Include the margin
- Follow your heart

Collectively, these six principles of jugaad help drive resilience, frugality, adaptability, simplicity, inclusivity, empathy, and passion, all of which are essential to compete and win in a complex world. Adopting these principles could help firms—anywhere in the world—innovate and grow in a highly volatile, hypercompetitive environment.

SEEK OPPORTUNITY IN ADVERSITY

Jugaad entrepreneurs perceive harsh constraints as an invitation to innovate. Modern-day alchemists, they transform adversity into an opportunity to bring value to themselves and their communities. For instance, Kanak Das, who lives in a remote village in northeast India, grew tired of riding his bicycle on roads full of potholes and bumps. Rather than complaining, he turned this constraint to his advantage by retrofitting his bicycle with a makeshift device that converts the shocks it receives into acceleration energy—allowing his bicycle to run faster on bumpy roads. Similarly, Enrique Gómez Junco, a Mexican engineer turned jugaad entrepreneur who founded Optima Energía, remained unfazed by the skepticism he faced when he first attempted to convince risk-averse companies to buy his sustainable energy solutions. But this adversity motivated him to adapt his business model and come up with a compelling new value proposition, i.e., customers can buy his energy savings solutions with no upfront payments, which enabled him to convert those initially skeptical companies into loyal customers. (You will learn how Junco reframed adversity to achieve a breakthrough in Chapter 2).

This ability to reframe adversity as a source of innovation and growth is vital for any organization to survive and thrive. And as we discovered, some of these alchemists also work for large Western corporations such as 3M. For example, in Chapter 2 we show how 3M is capturing big growth opportunities in an extremely adversarial business environment by rekindling and unleashing the jugaad spirit of all its employees.

DO MORE WITH LESS

Jugaad innovators are highly resourceful in the face of scarcity. Unlike many Silicon Valley entrepreneurs, raising capital is the least of their worries. The practitioners of jugaad work with what they've got. Doing more with less is in striking contrast to the 'bigger is better' R&D approach used in the West. Indeed, this frugal principle can help firms in both emerging and developed economies optimize the use of scarce financial and natural resources while delivering high value to a greater number of customers.

In Chapter 3, you will meet two jugaad entrepreneurs—Gustavo Grobocopatel of Los Grobo (Argentina) and Sunil

Mittal of Bharti Airtel (India)—who have developed frugal business models to cost effectively deliver agricultural and telecom services, respectively, to the masses. Similarly, you will learn how PepsiCo is reinventing its business model as an affordable and sustainable provider of nutritious food and beverage—in a proactive response to the growing consumer demand for healthy food and the scarcity of natural resources like water.

THINK AND ACT FLEXIBLY

Jugaad is in contrast to structured approaches such as Six Sigma. Jugaad entrepreneurs' flexible mindset constantly questions the status quo, keeps all options open, and transforms existing products, services, and business models. Unconstrained by structured processes, jugaad innovators can quickly respond to unexpected changes in their environment. Jugaad innovators don't just think outside the box: they create whole new boxes. Their nonlinear thinking often yields breakthrough ideas that turn conventional wisdom on its head and help to shape entire new markets and industries. As we explain in Chapter 4, that's the case with Ratan Tata, chairman of the Tata Group, who foresaw a big market for extremely affordable cars and went on to successfully launch the ₹ 1 lakh Nano in 2009—proving wrong those skeptics who had belittled his vision as a pipe dream. When the original plans failed to deliver sales, leaders at Tata Motors (the automotive unit of Tata Group) had to think on their feet and improvise new manufacturing, distribution, and marketing strategies for the Nano.

Jugaad innovators also *act* flexibly. In Chapter 4 we describe how Zhang Ruimin, the entrepreneurial CEO of Haier, a fast-growing Chinese appliance manufacturer, has made Haier's organizational structures flat, thus empowering frontline employees to swiftly sense and respond to changes in customer demand and innovate faster, better, and cheaper than rivals. We also explain how the New York Times Company is exhibiting flexible thinking by proactively embracing social media and mobile technologies, rather than being disrupted by them.

KEEP IT SIMPLE

Jugaad isn't about seeking sophistication or perfection by overengineering products, but rather about developing a 'good enough' solution that gets the job done. Creative simplicity is jugaad's key principle. Western firms that are engaged in an 'arms race' to out-innovate each other by cramming more technology and features into their products and services should make simplicity a key tenet of their innovation projects—just as entrepreneurs in emerging markets do. For instance, the open-source software company Ushahidi has developed an elegantly simple solution—the Ushahidi Platform—that relies on mobile SMS (text messaging) to coordinate bottom-up responses to cataclysmic events such as hurricanes, earthquakes, or epidemic outbreaks. The Ushahidi Platform was pioneered in Africa and is now being widely deployed worldwide—including in the US—as a simple yet highly effective crisis management tool. In Chapter 5, you will discover how large Western companies such as GM, Philips, and Siemens, as well as a next-generation companies such as Google and Facebook, are using simplicity to ensure that their solutions are accessible and easy-to-use by a large number of users.

INCLUDE THE MARGIN

While Western firms typically vie to serve mainstream customers, jugaad entrepreneurs intentionally seek out marginal, underserved customers and pull them into the mainstream. Such entrepreneurs conjure up radically affordable solutions to meet the needs of these underserved markets. Their inclusive business models engage low-income and nontraditional communities, not as passive consumers but as active value co-creators. For instance, Dr Liu Jiren, Chairman and CEO of Neusoft, China's largest IT solution and service provider, is concerned about the health of 80 crore Chinese living in rural areas who, says Dr Liu, are going to 'get older and sicker before they get wealthier'.[36] Dr Liu's genuine concern for China's marginal segments led him to develop inclusive technology solutions—such as tele-medicine applications—that deliver affordable healthcare to millions of rural Chinese.

Similarly, Abhi Naha has founded Zone V, a company that seeks to empower the 28.4 crore blind and partially sighted people worldwide by providing them with cellphones specially designed to meet their particular needs. Naha's aspiration is to build a world in which 'lack of sight doesn't mean lack of vision', as he told us.[37] In Chapter 6, we explain why and how Procter & Gamble is fundamentally shifting its business model to serve the 'un-served and underserved consumers'—marginal segments that increasingly include middle-class consumers in the US whose purchasing power is being squeezed by the lack of growth in their earnings over the last decade.

FOLLOW YOUR HEART

Jugaad innovators do not rely on focus groups or formal market research to decide what products to make—nor do they worry how investors will react to their new product strategies. They know their customers and their products intimately—and ultimately, they trust and follow their hearts. Specifically, jugaad entrepreneurs employ intuition, empathy, and passion—

qualities that are increasingly just as important as analytical thinking in navigating a global environment that is ever more diverse, interconnected, and unpredictable. For instance, Kishore Biyani—founder of Big Bazaar, one of India's largest and most successful retail chains—did not use management consultants to validate his idea of launching retail stores that look, feel, and even smell like chaotic street bazaars. When he launched his new store format, he trusted his intuition—fired by his empathy for Indian consumers—more than any analysis. By intuitively sensing the latent needs of consumers in a high-aspiration society like India, Biyani conjured up an innovative retail model that is hard for rivals to replicate.

Similarly, Steve Jobs was the prototypical jugaad innovator in the West. He always heeded his intuition rather than relying on analytical thinking to innovate and grow. The result, as we explain in Chapter 7, was a series of disruptive inventions such as the iPad, a product that consumers, analysts, and media initially were convinced had no market.

The heart is also the seat of passion. Jugaad entrepreneurs such as Diane Geng and Sara Lam, co-founders of the Rural China Education Foundation (RCEF), are motivated not by money or an 'I want to go IPO and become a millionaire' mentality. Rather, as we detail in Chapter 7, Geng and Lam were driven by a deep passion to make a difference in their communities. It was this passion that led them to develop a radically new approach to providing rural youth in China with a quality education. Also, a growing number of Western firms now recognize that the best way to motivate—and retain—knowledge workers is not by giving them bonuses, but by giving them the freedom to pursue projects that they are passionate about. In Chapter 7 we describe how frog, a global design and innovation consultancy, launched an initiative called Centres of Passion that lets its creative workers worldwide initiate or join projects in which they find a deep sense of meaning and purpose—well beyond sheer intellectual or even emotional satisfaction.

Jugaad: A Complement to Structured Innovation

As domestic Indian companies and Western corporations operating in India strive for continued growth, they have much to gain from adopting and practising these six principles of jugaad—seeking opportunity in adversity, doing more with less, thinking and acting flexibly, keeping it simple, including the margin, and following the heart. Companies operating in India must recognize that the structured model of innovation—which dominated the 20th century—has been like an orchestra: top-down, rigid, and driven by upper-level employees. This model worked well in a stable world of plentiful resources. But given the complex and unpredictable business environment that companies are about to face in the coming years, they also need an alternative approach, one more akin to a jazz band: bottom-up, improvisational, fluid, and collaborative while working within a framework of deep knowledge. Jugaad represents that alternative.

It's important to note, however, that jugaad isn't relevant for all situations and contexts. In particular, jugaad shouldn't *replace* the structured approach to innovation; rather, jugaad should *complement* it. In this book, we argue that jugaad is an important tool that companies can add to their existing innovation toolkit. We explore each of the underlying principles of jugaad and show how they can fortify a structured approach to innovation and achieve growth by adding frugality, flexibility, and agility.

In particular, in Chapter 8, we discuss the advantages and limits of jugaad innovation, and the specific contexts in which jugaad is particularly effective (e.g., complex, volatile and resource constrained environments). We describe how companies can mesh the agile and resilient spirit of jugaad with the more structured approach to innovation. For leaders of those companies that are committed to implementing a structured approach to innovation, the idea of also using jugaad may seem daunting. We make that adoption process easier by helping corporate leaders prioritize the specific jugaad principles they need to adopt most urgently. We do this by matching the benefits of each of the six principles with the needs and context of organizations.

To illustrate how firms can combine the use of jugaad with a structured approach to innovation, we describe how a large corporation—GE—is attempting to do precisely that. In sum, we show that jugaad can enrich the innovation toolkit of firms so they can effectively grow and succeed in a world of complexity and scarcity.

In our companion website (jugaadinnovation.com), you will find additional tools and roadmaps for prioritizing—and accelerating—the adoption of jugaad principles within your own organization.

A Groundswell Jugaad Movement is Growing Around the World

Over the last three years, we have drawn on our business experience, academic training, and multimedia expertise to document and understand how emerging market innovators—from grassroots entrepreneurs such as Mansukh Prajapati to pioneering CEOs like Ratan Tata—think and act. We have written extensively about these innovators—and their jugaad principles—in our blog on the *Harvard Business Review* website. We have featured them in the PBS documentary film series *Indique: Big Ideas from Emerging India*.[38] Finally, we have drawn on the principles of jugaad to help organizations around the world implement them in order to innovate better, faster, and cheaper. The response to these efforts from readers, corporations, viewers, and clients around the world has been overwhelming.

Western leaders—inured to a world of relative abundance and used to operating for so long in a relatively predictable environment—have perhaps the most to learn from jugaad. We have consulted with Western companies that have begun to implement the principles of jugaad—companies that enjoy a culture that promotes openness and adaptability and that have harnessed the creativity of employees, customers, and partners alike. These companies have found that jugaad has given them the agility needed to sense and respond to rapid shifts in the highly volatile environments in which they operate—and deliver more value to customers at less cost.

Although it's been a long time since the previous 19th century era of jugaad in the West, we may now be coming full circle, as some firms begin to appreciate and adopt its principles again. In the coming chapters, we will illustrate how Western companies across diverse sectors—such as 3M, Apple, Facebook, Philips, GE, Google, IBM, PepsiCo, Procter & Gamble, Renault-Nissan, Siemens, and Wal-Mart—as well as forward-thinking Indian corporations—such as Future Group, Suzlon, Tata Group, and YES BANK—have already adopted the principles of jugaad, to their great advantage. These vanguard companies are combining the frugal and resilient spirit of jugaad with more structured traditional approaches to innovation to generate breakthrough growth.

However, corporate leaders are not the only ones rediscovering the spirit of jugaad. In Chapter 9, we describe how a groundswell movement—led by creative citizens, forward-thinking entrepreneurs, venture capitalists, and non-profit organizations—is gaining momentum across societies all around the world. Increasingly, governments and universities are supporting such a jugaad ecosystem as well. For instance, the White House Office of Social Innovation and Civic Participation, set up by President Obama in early 2009, is enabling grassroots entrepreneurs across America to devise bottom-up solutions to address pressing socio-economic issues in their local communities. In India, the National Innovation Council—chaired by Sam Pitroda—is attempting to do exactly the same by, for example, setting up a ₹ 5,000 crore 'India Inclusive Innovation Fund' to financially support grassroots jugaad entrepreneurs who have innovative ideas for driving inclusive development. Similarly, Stanford University's Entrepreneurial Design for Extreme Affordability programme is training future engineers and business leaders in how to develop high-quality products at low cost—such as an infant warmer that costs less than 2 percent of the cost of a traditional incubator—for use in both emerging markets and the US. This emerging ecosystem not only creates an environment for jugaad innovators to thrive in, but also helps firms in their own efforts to adopt jugaad. By joining this *external* groundswell movement, firms can accelerate their *internal* adoption of jugaad—and profit handsomely from it. We show how Indian corporate leaders can stimulate and gain from such a jugaad groundswell within India itself.

In the rest of this book, we present a vision of how whole sectors of economies from around the world—from education and healthcare to energy and manufacturing to retail and financial services—can be rejuvenated by embracing jugaad. At the heart of that vision, however, lie those six fundamental principles of jugaad innovation. We turn to an exploration of each of these principles in the following chapters.

Chapter 2

Principle One: Seek Opportunity in Adversity

'It has done me good to be somewhat parched by the heat and drenched by the rain of life.'

—HENRY WADSWORTH LONGFELLOW

In the late 1980s, Tulsi Tanti moved to Surat, in the Indian state of Gujarat, to set up a textile unit. Like other entrepreneurs in India, Tanti found himself faced with infrastructural bottlenecks. The biggest of these was the power supply. Expensive and unpredictable, this proved a major barrier to growth. His profit margins were only around 5 percent, while energy accounted for a staggering 40 to 50 percent of total operating costs.

Instead of giving in to this problem, Tanti focused on finding a solution to it. He began to experiment with various types of boilers. He looked at different kinds of power generators. He tried out different combinations of boilers and generators. And then he realized that all these were, in one way or another, dependent on fuel, gas, or oil. So he thought, 'Why not find a solution that doesn't require fuel?' This launched him on to a search for an alternative source of power that was both reliable and sustainable.

In 1990, he invested in two wind turbines to supply electricity to his textile unit. It soon became clear that this was the solution he had been looking for. Now he had a power supply that was literally harnessed from thin air. After the initial investment in the turbines was recovered, his operating costs would be low and predictable. The 'fuel' came at no cost. And there was plenty of it.

With time, Tanti began to see the wider implications of his solution. Wind had the potential to power more than just Indian textile factories. It could meet the global demand for a steady supply of affordable energy: 44 percent of 120 crore Indians live outside the electricity grid, and worldwide more than 140 crore people lack access to electricity.[1] Tanti saw this huge challenge as a vast untapped opportunity. So he set out to capture this opportunity by creating Suzlon Wind.

'As an entrepreneur,' says Tanti, 'I firmly believe that at the heart of every challenge lies an opportunity. Entrepreneurs are a league of people who are able to turn obstacles into profitable solutions.'[2] This statement pretty much captures the essence of the resilient mindset that drives jugaad innovation.

Today, Suzlon is the world's fifth largest wind energy solution provider. The company employs more than thirteen thousand people and provides a full spectrum of wind power solutions in over thirty countries on six continents. In the space of two decades, Tanti has gone from being dependent on an erratic and expensive supply of energy to creating—through innovation—a plentiful supply of it for crores worldwide.

Reflecting on this astounding growth, Tanti says: 'The journey called Suzlon, embarked upon fifteen years ago, was my solution to an obstacle. The beginnings were humble, and the odds were against me, but my dreams were big. And when dreams are pursued with conviction and fortitude, they not only become a reality, they are a force that guides you and shapes your life and those of the people around you.'

Jugaad innovators like Tulsi Tanti are adept at taking on the arduous challenges that emerging markets pose and reframing them as opportunities to learn, innovate, and grow. These innovators respond to even the most adverse circumstances by demonstrating resilience, ingenuity, and an aptitude for risk. Seeking opportunity in adversity is often the first and most critical of the six principles that jugaad innovators have to apply. After all, jugaad innovators face adversity from the very beginning of their innovation journeys; if they are unable to apply the principle of seeking opportunity in adversity at the outset, they will be unlikely to move on to discover and apply the other five principles of jugaad.

A resilient jugaad mindset can also enable corporate leaders to systematically turn adversity into an opportunity for innovation and growth. In this chapter, we show how large corporations can unlearn practises that worked in a bygone era of relative predictability and find new ways to succeed in a future of adversity and constant change. But first, we explore why and how jugaad entrepreneurs seek opportunity in adversity.

A Harsh Environment Nurtures Resilience

Entrepreneurs and managers in emerging economies face adversity at every turn. For instance, starting a business in India is a daunting task. Doing so takes an average of 165 days (compared to 9 in the US).

Securing the necessary licenses to construct a simple warehouse is complex, time consuming, and costly, involving 34 procedures over 227 days and costing 1631 percent of the country's per-capita income.[3] Running a business is even harder. Property rights are often unclear or hard to ascertain, so acquiring land is fraught with difficulties. Labour laws are restrictive or complex or both, and can be a minefield to navigate. Due to India's federal structure, there are currently 47 national laws and 157 state regulations that directly affect India's labour market.[4] Hiring and firing of workers presents its own challenges. New taxes may be instituted and applied at any time.

On top of all this bureaucracy, political upheavals are a fact of life. A state government with a policy favouring business may fall overnight and be replaced by another that favours agriculture over industry. Land that was granted to a company to set up a factory may be confiscated and returned to the original owners or fall under litigation. Court cases are expensive and drag on for years, often with no clear resolution in sight.

But perhaps there is no greater challenge to starting a business in India than its poor infrastructure. Jugaad entrepreneurs in India—as in other emerging markets like China, Africa, and Brazil—do not have access to many of the basic things that are taken for granted in the West. Roads can be poor, heavily congested, or non-existent (40 percent of India's villages do not have access to all-weather roads).[5] Education and training systems are patchy, so skilled personnel are hard to come by. Healthcare services are scant, and workers who get sick may stay out of work for long periods.[6]

Emerging markets like India also face acute shortages of resources: natural, human, and financial. It can be hard to raise capital. Banks are typically conservative, and venture capital and angel investor networks are underdeveloped. As a result, jugaad innovators cannot afford to invest in capital-intensive equipment. Jugaad innovators also typically serve a market that is economically deprived: 80 percent of Indians live on less than

₹ 100 a day; 26 percent of Brazilians live below the poverty line; 23 crore African households are unbanked—that is, they do not have a bank account; and nearly 40 percent of rural Chinese can't afford basic medical treatment.[7, 8, 9] (The extent of scarcity in emerging markets is so dire that how innovators respond to it constitutes the second principle of jugaad—do more with less—which we discuss in Chapter 3.)

Trying to operate in such a harsh environment could drain the energies of even the toughest business person. Yet jugaad innovators are unfazed by the reality that surrounds them. Indeed, it is this very harshness that gives them their particularly resilient mindset. Extreme *external* circumstances seem to heighten their *internal* resolve to succeed. As with Tulsi Tanti, rather than becoming passive victims of current circumstances, jugaad innovators are driven to take charge of events and steer them in a direction of their own choosing. For them, adversity exists largely in the mind.

Dr Thomas Müller, a psychologist who specializes in crisis management, observes that in a crisis some people simply attempt to go back to how things were before. In the process, they make compromises for the sake of security. Others, however, withstand the pressure and ask themselves, 'If I go one step further, what's the opportunity to be exploited?'[10] Jugaad entrepreneurs belong to this second category. When confronted with adversity, they don't retrench but embrace the difficulties and learn from the experience.

Armed with resilience, perseverance, and a willingness to learn, jugaad innovators strive to respond to the harsh world they face and find opportunities for growth and expansion in it. In doing so, they are able to create a better world, not just for themselves but also for their communities.

Reframing the Half-Empty Glass as Half Full

Jugaad innovators find opportunity in adversity in three ways: reframing challenges as opportunities for growth, making constraints work for them, and constantly adapting to a changing environment by improvising solutions to challenges they face along the way. In this section, we examine each of these strategies and look at specific examples of each.

The first and perhaps most important strategy of jugaad innovators is *reframing or changing the lens through which they perceive the situation they face*. Jugaad innovators perceive and interpret the world differently from the rest of us.[11] Their ability to reframe means they are likely to see the glass half full even when everyone else sees it as half empty. Indeed, one may think of jugaad innovators as modern-day alchemists who *mentally* transform adversity into opportunity.

An example of such an alchemist is O.P. Bhatt, former chairman of the State Bank of India (SBI), India's largest and oldest bank, with more than 2 lakh employees and 20,000 branches across India. O.P. Bhatt was appointed its chairman in 2006. A lifelong banker, he was deeply aware of the immense creative potential of SBI's large employee base and was eager to find ways to unleash it. But he also knew that his hands were tied in many ways. The SBI is partially owned by the Government of India, which in turn is run by risk-averse bureaucrats who vet every hiring and firing decision. (In fact, it's virtually impossible to fire anyone once he or she gets a job in a government-owned Indian enterprise.) As Dr Prasad Kaipa, a CEO coach who has advised Bhatt, points out: 'It was clear to Bhatt from the start that he could neither "get the right people on the bus nor get the wrong people off the bus". It was also obvious to him that he lacked the resources to financially motivate his managers to take risks and drive innovative projects.'[12]

These challenges, though significant, did not faze Bhatt. Instead, he used a jugaad approach to ignite the genius within SBI. First, he drew on his superior communication skills to rekindle his employees' feelings of pride about SBI, a bank with a distinguished 200-year-old history. Then, through an in-house training programme called Parivarthan (Sanskrit for transformation), he instilled a new sense of commitment into SBI staff across all levels and departments. In time, the programme began to bear fruit: SBI employees felt more empowered, demonstrated greater creativity, and took customer service to new heights. Across the country, employees began to devise bold and ingenious solutions to problems they had always faced but had never felt the desire or had the support to address. For example, in the city of Hyderabad, Mr Sivakumar, the local head of SBI operations, launched within five months an SMS-based customer complaint unit of four people to deal with seven thousand complaints—thus building a loyal customer base receptive to the bank's future marketing and promotional initiatives.[13]

By reframing a seemingly adverse situation as an opportunity, Bhatt unleashed the creative genius in his employees. And the payoff was huge. In four years, SBI increased its market share from 16.5 percent to 19 percent, doubling its stock price and boosting customer satisfaction—and all this in a mature and highly competitive market. In this period, SBI also won many international awards for its stellar performance.

As Bhatt's story shows, jugaad innovators don't find opportunity *in spite of* adversity; for them, adversity often *is* the opportunity. They perceive constraints not as a debilitating deterrent but as a creative stimulus. Indeed, their creative juices begin to flow when they are confronted with a seemingly insurmountable challenge.

The second way jugaad innovators find opportunity in adversity is by *making constraints work for them rather than against them*. In Chapter 1 we introduced Kanak Das, a jugaad innovator who hails from Morigaon, a village in Assam. Like many Indians, Das rides a bicycle to work. And, as in many parts of India, the roads he travels on are full of potholes and bumps. These not only gave him back problems but also slowed him down considerably. Das knew there was little or nothing he could do to improve the quality of these roads. So instead he posed a quintessentially jugaad question: 'What if I can actually find a way to make my bike run *faster* on these cratered roads?' That question inspired him to retrofit his bicycle so that every time the front wheel hits a bump, a shock absorber compresses and releases energy to the rear wheel. By converting the energy in the shock absorber into a propulsive force, his bicycle can run faster on bumpy roads.

'Making the bumps work for you' is how Professor Anil Gupta of the Indian Institute of Management, Ahmedabad, refers to Das's ingenious solution. Gupta is a passionate advocate of grassroots innovations in India. He notes, 'You have hybrid cars today that generate energy from brakes, but not from shock absorbers: it is a whole new concept that Kanak Das has pioneered.'[14] The National Innovation Foundation, where Professor Gupta serves as executive vice chairperson, has helped patent Das's invention. Who knows where this might lead? In the not-too-distant future, cyclists all over the world may benefit from Kanak Das's jugaad innovation. Already, engineering students at MIT are using Das's invention as inspiration for how to convert the energy generated by shock absorbers in automobiles into acceleration.[15]

The third way that jugaad innovators seek opportunity in adversity is by *being quick to act in response to the opportunities they see*. Not only did Kanak Das and O.P. Bhatt *think differently* in response to adversity, but they also *acted quickly* to adapt their models and strategies to the challenges in their environments. Jugaad innovators aren't attached to old business models and will let go of past successes if conditions require this. This ability to constantly adapt and reinvent themselves—with a crystal clear focus on the future—is key to jugaad innovators' long-term survival.

An example of such adaptability is Enrique Gómez Junco, a Mexican engineer turned jugaad entrepreneur.[16] In the late 1980s, Junco was driven by a vision to create a sustainable energy business. In 1988, he set up a company called Celsol to sell thermosolar panels to Mexican businesses, especially hotels. But he found it hard to crack this market: it was highly regulated, subsidized, and dominated by monopolies, and he had trouble finding capital to finance Celsol. Rather than give up on his vision, Junco shut down Celsol and launched a new venture—Optima Energía—in 2000. Optima's initial plan was to sell energy technologies to building owners and facility managers to help them use electricity more efficiently and save on energy costs. These energy-saving technologies would also provide an environmental benefit, as commercial buildings account for 7 percent of manmade carbon dioxide emissions worldwide. But again he failed. Optima's value proposition didn't impress facility managers much, because it required them to make a large upfront investment that would not yield significant returns in the short term.

This new setback shifted Junco's perspective once again. He realized that as an engineer he had fallen in love with technology for its own sake, and in the process had forgotten about his customers. His customers, he realized, didn't care how good his technology was: what they wanted was to save money. Immediately he knew that he had to shift his positioning again: from being a high-risk, niche *technology* vendor to being a low-risk, end-to-end *business solution* provider.

Armed with this insight, in 2004, Junco went back to the drawing board and reinvented his company's value proposition. Rather than merely selling a technology, Optima began offering an integrated solution to risk-averse commercial building operators. Specifically, Optima would sign a performance-based contract with a client to implement an energy efficiency project that could potentially save the client up to 50 percent in energy costs. The client would not have to invest a dime, however. Instead, Optima would directly finance the installation of the relevant technology in partnership with leading financial institutions, including the World Bank's International Financial Corporation.[17] The client would then use the initial savings in energy costs generated by the project to pay back Optima's capital investment over a ten-year period. All additional savings would then be split between Optima and the client. Optima has been especially successful in selling this value proposition to major hotels—in particular, the energy-hungry resorts located along the coastline of the Gulf of Mexico.

After reinventing his business model twice, Junco finally realized his vision of saving clients' energy costs while protecting the environment.[18] Since its founding, Optima has consulted with more than 120 different clients and implemented its turnkey solutions in more than 50 facilities. The firm has saved its customers $100 million (₹ 500 crore), 1.6 crore cubic metres of water, 23 crore kilowatts of electricity, 4.1 crore litres of natural gas, and 1.4 crore litres of diesel. Junco is now planning to take his integrated solution into other sectors—especially manufacturing and public services (such as municipalities), where the market for energy saving is an estimated $7 billion (₹ 35,000 crore) in Mexico alone.[19] Optima began its life as a clean technology provider but has evolved into a successful financial services provider that happens to be in the energy sector. Junco's adaptability allowed him to overcome adversity. For his unrelenting efforts to drive greener construction and provide clean energy in Mexico, Junco was selected by the World Economic Forum as one of the 100 Global Leaders for Tomorrow; he also received the Wharton Infosys Business Transformation Award in 2006.[20]

Jugaad entrepreneurs like Junco approach innovation—indeed approach life in general—as a potentially never-ending experiment. Trial and error is an important part of the process; individual failures and successes are merely way stations on a longer journey. As such, jugaad allows innovators like Junco to adapt, evolve, and continuously reinvent their ideas over time.

To sum up: jugaad innovators are experts at reframing challenges as opportunities, making constraints work for them, and adapting to changing circumstances by improvising solutions along the way. Jugaad innovators develop these strategies in response to the sometimes extreme forms of adversity they face in the business environment in emerging markets. But what relevance do these strategies have for large corporations in India, whether they are domestically owned or multinational? We now explore how adversity is increasingly an important factor in the business environment and the implications of this for corporate leaders.

Buckle Up, Large Firms: Major Adversity Ahead

It would be easy to assume that jugaad innovators' reframing of adversity and adaptation to a constantly changing environment is not relevant to managers in large corporations. After all, large firms and their leaders are somewhat insulated from a constantly turbulent political and economic environment and do not typically have to worry about poor infrastructure or scarce resources. It is instructive, therefore, to look at the major sources of adversity that large companies increasingly face:

- *A worsening global economy*: The already anemic US and European economies may soon become comatose as demand fails to pick up inspite of umpteen stimulus packages. The International Monetary Fund (IMF) predicted that the US economy will grow by just 1.8 percent in 2012 and expects the Euro-zone economy to limp along at 1.1 percent.[21] This poor growth will place severe constraints on the capital that Western companies will have access to in the years to come. Meanwhile, in an increasingly interconnected and interdependent global economy, firms in emerging markets like India also face the negative consequences of the continuing global crisis. For them too, capital is relatively scarce and growth has started to slow. Indian firms, for instance, are struggling to repay loans due to high interest rates, escalating commodity prices, and lower demand. As a result, default rates among corporate borrowers in India hit a ten-year high of 3.4 percent in fiscal 2011-12.[22] And high interest rates and global demand slowdown have dragged down the Indian economy, which is now projected to grow at only 6.9 percent or less in 2011-12 (compared to 8.4 percent in 2010-11).[23]

- *An avalanche of new regulations to come*: In addition to healthcare and financial services, other industries—from automotive to food to energy—are likely to face a host of new regulations from legislators in the years to come. For instance, the US carmakers reluctantly agreed to an Obama administration plan to push for stringent federal fuel economy standards that would double efficiency targets to fifty-four miles per gallon by 2025.[24] These stringent regulations will place further constraints on businesses— forcing them, in the coming decade, to radically change their current practises and even their business models to meet new regulatory requirements. In India, whose economy is already over-regulated, companies are facing a whole set of new regulations. For instance, the Reserve

Bank of India is soon planning to introduce comprehensive consumer protection legislation in the financial services sector.

- *Tectonic shifts in demographics*: European firms have to contend with a rapidly ageing workforce. For instance, Germany will lose 50 lakh workers—or 12 percent of its total workforce—over the next fifteen years due to retirement.[25] And US firms have to contend with the growing diversity of their multigenerational, multi-ethnic workers and consumers. In India, firms face a rapid increase in the working age population (India will add 1.1 crore workers to the workforce every year for the next several years) combined with growing mobility (10 crore Indians will move to cities over the next decade) and increasing numbers of middle-class consumers (already 30 crore strong and rising). All these changes will put pressure on employee recruitment and retention and make it hard for firms to meet the diverse needs of a heterogeneous customer base.

- *The social computing revolution*: The explosive growth of social media networks such as Facebook, Orkut, and Twitter—which enable improvised and informal grassroots interactions among hundreds of crores of users worldwide—is challenging the corporate orthodoxy embodied in hierarchal communication, linear planning methods, and insular approaches to innovation. In this regard, it is interesting to note that Facebook's user base in India increased by 132 percent in 2011 compared to only 16 percent in the US during the same year.[26]

- *The accelerating scarcity of natural resources*: Natural resources such as oil and water that have hitherto been relatively cheap and plentiful will become scarcer in the years to come. According to a report by Ceres, sectors such as agriculture, food and beverage, hi-tech, and pharmaceuticals could be severely affected by water shortfalls. For instance, a water-related shutdown at a semiconductor factory operated by Intel or Texas Instruments could cost them $100-$200 million (₹ 500-1,000 crore) in missed revenues during a quarter. This grim outlook led Nestlé chairman Peter Brabeck-Letmathe to comment: 'I am convinced that . . . we will run out of water long before we run out of fuel.' This increasing scarcity will force companies to find sustainable methods to generate more energy or food using less of these increasingly expensive resources.[27]

• *Unforgiving competition from emerging markets*: Large Western firms are facing stiff competition in North American and European markets from low-cost rivals in emerging economies. For example, Chinese consumer product companies HTC and Haier are giving Nokia and Whirlpool a run for their money by introducing feature-rich cellphones and kitchen appliances at low prices—which greatly appeal to cost-conscious Western consumers. Meanwhile, there is stiff competition among emerging markets companies themselves. For instance, Indian pharmaceutical companies face intense competition from Chinese rivals as they scramble to meet their $25 billion (₹ 125,000 crore) annual export target by 2014.[28]

All these challenges are generating constraints within the environment in which large firms operate. These constraints could paralyze corporate leaders and cripple their decision-making processes, but they could also galvanize these leaders into innovating for growth. For the latter to be the case, corporate leaders must learn to reframe the adversity they face as not a debilitating challenge (or 'risk', as management consultants call it), but rather a unique opportunity to innovate and grow—just as Tulsi Tanti, O.P. Bhatt, and other jugaad innovators have done.

But doing so is more challenging than it looks. Faced with harsh challenges like those just mentioned, large firms tend to gravitate toward adopting one of four responses to adverse situations. They fail to notice adversity or simply ignore it, they try to tackle it head-on, they address it with old frames of reference, or they think too small or incrementally in response to adversity. But all of these responses are counterproductive in today's business environment. Here's why:

- *Failing to notice—or ignoring—adversity until it's too late*: CEOs of large firms often fail to read the handwriting on the wall, because of complacence, inertia, or overconfidence. Gary Hamel, author of *The Future of Management*, notes that many executives don't pay sufficient attention to the early warning signs of big shifts in demographics, technology, and regulation—thus missing out a great opportunity to proactively innovate their business models to take advantage of these shifts.[29] Instead, corporate leaders generally react to problems only after things have gotten out of control and their companies are up against the wall. For instance, right after the September 11, 2001 terrorist attacks, when the US economy plunged into the red, US carmakers failed to recognize a structural shift in American consumers' behaviors. Consumers weren't just looking for cheaper cars—which GM and Ford offered with tons of rebates and 0 percent financing—but *better* cars that were fuel-efficient and eco-friendly. Consequently, US automakers failed to invest early in innovation to make energy-efficient cars—losing out to forward-thinking German and Japanese rivals and facing looming competition from nimble Asian rivals like Tata Motors with their ultra-low-cost offerings like the Nano.

- *Tackling adversity head-on, rather than seeking to leverage it*: When faced with the possibility of harsh constraints, CEOs often attempt to neutralize them rather than find a way to use them to their advantage. For instance, when facing regulatory constraints, many CEOs choose to oppose such constraints and lobby to have them repealed or delayed. We see this with large Western pharmaceutical companies that face shrinking drug development pipelines and a patent cliff, competition from emerging markets' generics manufacturers, and a US government keen to reduce healthcare costs. Many of these firms have chosen to lobby to keep their business model intact, extend patents, and keep foreign competition out rather than respond innovatively to these challenges—for instance, by fundamentally rethinking and changing their business models.

- *Addressing new problems with old frames of reference*: Successful executives often resemble generals fighting an earlier war. They fight new battles using strategies that may have achieved victory in the past but are toothless in the present changed conditions. For instance, consumer goods companies continue to rely on traditional mass-marketing strategies like TV advertising, even though it is clear that consumers want to engage brands in a two-way dialogue using social media tools such as Facebook and Twitter.[30]

- *Thinking small when facing big challenges*: According to Adam Richardson, author of *Innovation X* and creative director at frog, a global design and innovation consultancy, most executives play it safe when confronted

43

with extreme conditions.[31] Thus, in response to hyper competition or rapid technological or market change, they are more likely to come up with incremental innovations and 'me too' products, rather than reach for the big, untapped 'white spaces' in the market that are up for grabs. For example, the US bookstore chain Borders recognized the Internet's potential early on, but failed to take adequate advantage of it; its e-commerce initiatives were tepid at best. In fact, when the Borders.com site was launched in 1998, it allowed readers to only check the availability of books but not to actually purchase them. Eventually, Amazon established its dominance, and Borders folded in 2011. Borders' demise has ominous lessons for the Indian book retail industry: within 5 years of its launch in 2007, Flipkart—India's online book retailer—has seen its registered user base skyrocket to a whopping 20 lakh customers in 2012. Today, Flipkart ships 30,000 items a day and clocks ₹ 2.5 crore in daily sales. Sachin Bansal, co-founder and CEO of Flipkart, has a bold plan to boost his firm's revenue to ₹ 5,000 crore within three years, well ahead of the company's 2015 target.[32]

Tempting as it may be to dismiss adversity as a problem that only small firms face, there is increasing evidence that adversity affects large firms too. But even if corporate leaders recognize this fact, they may fail to deal with it effectively, for the reasons just discussed. If corporate leaders want to avoid the pitfalls of these four counterproductive responses to adversity—and wish to truly turn challenges into opportunities—they would be wise to learn a thing or two from the resilient mindset of jugaad innovators such as Tulsi Tanti, O.P. Bhatt, Kanak Das, and Enrique Gómez Junco. We now turn to a discussion of how they might do so.

Learning to Capitalize on Adversity

Corporate leaders can systematically turn adversity into an opportunity to innovate and grow by adopting the resilient mindset of jugaad innovators and their coping strategies.

RECOGNIZE THAT THE GLASS IS ALWAYS HALF FULL

Corporate leaders can learn from jugaad innovators how to turn adversity on its head and get it to work in their favour. The key to doing so is being able to reframe challenges as opportunities and use constraints as a spur to innovate. But one cannot reframe (that is, see that the glass is actually half full) while one operates in a state of fear. Fear only clouds one's perspective and inhibits one's reactions. Rather, when facing crises and challenges, leaders must cultivate a sense of equanimity and demonstrate what Justin Menkes, author of *Better Under Pressure*, calls 'realistic optimism'.[33]

Menkes, who works for the executive search firm Spencer Stuart, studied more than 200 candidates for the CEO position and interviewed over sixty current and retired CEOs in his research. He found that a key attribute that enables leaders to achieve their potential (and that of their organizations) is 'realistic optimism'; that is, the ability to clearly recognize the risks that threaten survival and yet remain confident that the company will prevail. In other words, at the first sight of a dark cloud, successful CEOs don't pull out the umbrella but strive instead to identify the silver lining around the cloud—just as jugaad innovators do.

For instance, many Fortune 500 CEOs feel threatened by the explosive growth of social media (as of this writing, over 25 crore tweets are sent each day and Facebook has more than

80 crore members), especially after witnessing the damage done by Wikileaks. They fret about how social media tools, when placed in the wrong hands, can be used to spread false rumours, damage brands, and ruin corporate and personal reputations within hours. In contrast, as early as the year 2000, well before Twitter and Facebook saw the light of day, Procter & Gamble's top management identified the tremendous potential of social networking tools. They wholeheartedly embraced these tools as a new *social engagement* platform on which to build and sustain a meaningful dialogue with consumers in the digital economy of the 21st century. In the past, when developing new products, Procter & Gamble's R&D teams used to rely on expensive, time-consuming focus groups and physical prototyping to test their new ideas. Now they use social media tools like Affinnova to test dozens of new product ideas with hundreds of customers voting online on their favourite features. Thanks to this real-time collaboration with customers, Procter & Gamble can swiftly weed out unprofitable product ideas early on and dedicate R&D resources to developing product concepts that customers like the most.[34] Likewise, Procter & Gamble has turned the viral marketing power of social networks to its advantage—by converting satisfied customers into 'word of mouth marketers' of the firm's brands in cyberspace. For example, the company has built Vocalpoint—an online community of more than 6 lakh socially engaged mothers it can tap for early feedback on new promotional campaigns before launching them nationally—helping to get each marketing message right the very first time. Vocalpoint members also generate positive buzz on social networks for Procter & Gamble's upcoming products.[35] Thanks to this reframing of social media and their business value, Procter & Gamble has not only boosted customer loyalty but has also established new industry-leading practises in social engagement—well ahead of its rivals. The firm has even packaged its social marketing skills

to create Tremor, a software service sold to other companies such as Kellogg, Sears, and MasterCard seeking to harness the power of word-of-mouth marketing to boost their own brands.[36]

REALIZE EXTREME CONDITIONS ARE FERTILE SOIL FOR EXTREME INNOVATION

Taking a cue from jugaad innovators, corporate leaders should view extreme conditions—such as massive technology shifts, draconian regulations, or competitive threats that come out of the blue—as an opportunity to develop radical innovations that disrupt industries and shape whole new markets. Marc Benioff, Chairman & CEO of salesforce.com, is one such Western innovator. In 1999, Benioff founded salesforce.com in his San Francisco apartment with a bold vision: he wanted to make the business software—which enterprises use to manage their customer interactions—affordable and accessible to more companies. He envisioned using the Internet as a platform to deliver business software to corporations as a service, rather than as a product—as it had been so far. The idea was that firms would subscribe to software applications hosted by salesforce. com on a 'pay as you go' basis and access them using just a web browser rather than having them installed on employees' PCs—thus avoiding the expensive license fees and maintenance costs charged by large software vendors like Oracle, Siebel, and SAP.

Yet in 2001, just as salesforce.com was about to take off, the dotcom bubble burst and the stock market plummeted. Large corporations perceived Benioff as yet another dotcom entrepreneur peddling snake oil and refused to buy into his vision of Software as a Service (SaaS). Benioff and his start-up were ridiculed by large competitors who questioned the security and scalability of the SaaS model. In April 2001, Tom

Siebel, CEO and founder of Siebel, a large business software vendor, predicted that salesforce.com would be out of business by 2002.[37]

Benioff persisted even in the face of all this adversity. He saw a silver lining in the dark economic cloud that engulfed corporate America in the early 2000s. He realized that his cost-conscious potential customers—small to large firms—were confronted with their *own* challenges. In particular: (1) they were struggling to extract more value from their software investments without breaking the bank, and (2) they wanted their existing software solutions to quickly adapt to rapidly evolving business needs. Unfortunately, firms were stuck with software applications that were too expensive to maintain and not flexible enough—and they had trouble conceptualizing what an alternative solution might be.

Sensing an opportunity, Benioff started evangelizing to potential customers the merits of the SaaS model—rather than touting salesforce.com's capabilities. He passionately articulated the value of SaaS, not only to frugal technology buyers but also to flexibility-seeking C-level executives. For instance, he explained to corporate leaders how—with the explosion of mobile devices—the SaaS model could enable their employees to access their business applications anywhere, anytime—something that could not be done with the traditional, centralized software delivery model. Benioff also tirelessly promoted the SaaS model to the press, analyst firms, and other influential tech industry figures. Eventually, large businesses warmed to SaaS and began to buy into Benioff's vision—and into salesforce.com. Thanks to Benioff's persistent evangelizing of SaaS, a groundswell movement was ignited in the tech sector. As more software developers recognized the benefits of the SaaS model, they started building more solutions using the model—spawning a whole new software ecosystem that made the model self-sustainable.[38]

Salesforce.com was comfortably positioned to lead this SaaS movement—and it did. Salesforce.com's subscriber base grew by 1,500 percent in the following seven years, and it currently serves more than 1 lakh customers.[39] Averaging an annual revenue growth of 36 percent in recent years, salesforce.com expects to reach a $3 billion (₹ 15,000 crore) annual revenue run rate during its fiscal year 2013.[40] Benioff has set for salesforce.com a '$10 billion (₹ 50,000 crore) vision', which he believes 'consists of customer success'.[41]

The SaaS movement that Benioff initiated has since evolved and is now known as 'cloud computing' (an appropriate name, considering it was born out of Benioff's ability to see a silver lining in every dark cloud). The cloud computing market, which was worth ₹ 2 lakh crore in 2010, is predicted to balloon to ₹ 12 lakh crore by 2020.[42] All the major software vendors who initially ridiculed salesforce.com's business model have since jumped onto the cloud computing bandwagon—and those who didn't have disappeared (salesforce.com's archrival Siebel was bought by Oracle in 2005).

Benioff believes that extreme conditions can generate groundbreaking innovation: 'salesforce.com is a living example of how resilient entrepreneurs—and corporations—can transcend the extreme difficulties they face and turn them into opportunities for success.'[43]

BUILD PSYCHOLOGICAL CAPITAL TO BOOST CONFIDENT RESILIENCE

Corporate leaders cannot build a resilient organization without a resilient workforce. Fred Luthans, professor of Organizational Behavior at the University of Nebraska—Lincoln, puts it this way: 'The true value of a company is no longer its tangible assets or even its technological processes: it lies in its human capital and underlying psychological capital—neither of which is open to imitation. Anyone can buy technology or obtain money from financial markets; but we cannot buy motivation, engagement, confidence, resiliency, hope, optimism.'[44]

It's not enough for business leaders to be optimistic, resilient, and adaptable. They also need to *empower employees at every level* to think and act like jugaad innovators—by embracing ambiguity, tolerating risks, and being willing to learn from challenges rather than trying to wish them away. Franck Riboud is one such leader, keen to boost his firm's psychological capital. Riboud is the CEO of Danone—a French multinational that is one of the world's largest suppliers of dairy products and bottled waters. (Danone has been selling its dairy products in India since 2010 under the brands Dahi, Cremix, and Danette.) Riboud believes that his 92-year-old company is confronted with two major challenges: (1) consumers worldwide are clamouring for healthy, nutritious food items that are affordable and sustainably produced; and (2) the biggest business opportunities in coming decades will come from emerging markets—such as Mexico, Indonesia, China, Russia, and Brazil—where Danone needs to innovate, and adopt, new business models to effectively capture the exploding growth opportunities. These two challenges are making the business environment in which Danone operates highly complex, simultaneously creating more constraints while opening new opportunities. As Riboud explains: 'Our future hinges on our ability to explore and invent new business models and new types of business corporations.'[45]

To navigate this complex environment, Ribou recognizes that Danone needs a more adaptable workforce with a resilient mindset. To succeed in a 'multipolar' world characterized by multiple centres of growth, Riboud is gradually transforming Danone—a very traditional French firm with most decision-making power and R&D activity concentrated in Europe—into a *polycentric organization* with a decentralized decision-making structure and a globally distributed R&D network.[46] Such a polycentric structure will empower frontline managers worldwide—especially in fast-growing emerging markets like China and Brazil—to address local challenges and opportunities by improvising robust solutions just as jugaad innovators do—all the while sharing innovative ideas and best practises through peer-to-peer knowledge networks.[47, 48] Unlike other multinationals that compel employees worldwide to do things *the right way* (using rigid and highly-standardized processes), Riboud is motivating its global workforce to do *the right thing* (by embodying the company-wide values of openness, enthusiasm, and humanism).[49] By decentralizing decision making and R&D operations—all the while enabling collaboration and knowledge sharing among regional units—Danone has been able to increase its organizational flexibility and successfully expand in emerging economies—which account for 60 percent of Danone's future growth—all the while maintaining its stringent standards for social and environmental sustainability.[50]

This, however, is only half the story. Riboud's real objective in creating a polycentric, multipolar organizational structure is to initiate a veritable *revolution of the mind* within Danone's leadership team. As economies around the world enter an age of scarcity and complexity, Riboud wants to cultivate in his managers a whole new way of thinking and acting under constraints—a resilient mindset that is prevalent in emerging markets like Brazil and China. In particular, Riboud wants Danone's senior managers to innovate frugally and flexibly under severe resource constraints—by learning from jugaad innovators in emerging markets who know how to turn adversity into an opportunity to innovate. Riboud explains: 'Until recently, we assumed that the richest countries would be the main source of innovation. As I see it, it's the countries with strong growth that should inspire us.'[51] For instance, building a micro dairy product factory in Bangladesh requires the same amount of capital that one needs to buy a house in France—a fact that inspired Danone's Western leaders to adopt radically new solutions to reduce operating costs in big traditional plants without compromising quality. Riboud believes that by adopting a flexible mindset, Danone's corporate leaders can not only reduce manufacturing costs but also dramatically improve product design, marketing, and distribution across the company. Riboudalso believes that emerging markets can teach the company how to adapt its products to meet unique local tastes. In March 2012, the company launched Danone Lassi, developed from scratch in the company's R&D lab in India. The product retails for ₹ 15 and comes in three flavors: mango, masala, and sweet lassi. As Jochen Ebert, managing director of Danone India, points out: 'What the (Indian) consumers told us very clearly is that they wanted to have Indian lassi in fantastic quality, available cold and fresh of course. This is where we learn from India to adapt. The masala-flavoured lassi is a very unique product. (But) mango lassi is a product that you can probably also sell in France, Germany, or elsewhere (...)'[52] Ebert also heads Danone's newly set up global Bottom of Pyramid (BOP) division, which will develop frugal business models aimed at making healthy foods affordable and accessible to crores of low-income people in developing nations. Danone's BOP division has, for instance, developed Fundooz, a ₹ 5 milk-based dessert sold primarily in rural areas in Northern India. The company plans to introduce more nutritious products like Fundooz at extremely low prices designed from the ground up, specifically for BOP markets. Interestingly, Danone's BOP initiatives are heavily influenced by earlier work in Bangladesh, where Danone established a joint venture with Muhammed Yunus's Grameen to develop a yogurt fortified with micronutrients to reduce malnutrition among Bangladeshi children, especially in villages. The yogurt is manufactured using solar and biogas energy and is distributed in environmentally friendly packaging. After launching production in their first factory in 2006, the joint venture plans to establish over 50 such plants over ten years, creating hundreds of distribution jobs for women in rural areas while enabling eco-friendly consumption with self-degradable packaging.[53]

In recent years, despite challenging market conditions, Danone has posted financial results that have exceeded targets: with sales up nearly 7 percent in 2010, the firm is among the best performers in the food industry worldwide. Riboud is convinced that Danone has found the right business model to succeed in today's complex global economy. More important, Riboud believes that Danone's unique culture, which emphasizes pragmatism, adaptability, and local decisions—what he calls being 'quick on your feet'—is a huge advantage in adverse circumstances. Interestingly, one of the six big 'emerging markets' that Danone is targeting is the US. Unlike other CEOs who complain about the moribund US economy, Riboud sees huge opportunities for his yogurt products in the US, where per-capita yogurt consumption is still low compared to European markets.[54]

APPROACH BIG CHALLENGES WITH A GROWTH MINDSET

According to Carol Dweck, professor of psychology at Stanford University, most leaders operate with one of two mindsets: a fixed mindset or a growth mindset. Leaders with a fixed mindset believe their qualities—and others'—are carved in stone, compelling them to stick to tried and tested solutions to challenges. In contrast, leaders with a growth mindset believe that their basic qualities can be nurtured and improved through efforts. Jugaad innovators are endowed with a growth mindset:

they confidently focus on building the future, rather than clinging to the safety of the past.

We believe that as the business environment becomes increasingly complex and adversarial, it is vital that corporate leaders cultivate a *growth mindset*. This is critical because, when leaders face adversity with a fixed mindset, their minds are clouded by fear or pride, they tend to innovate incrementally, and their efforts yield limited results. Instead, a growth mindset helps leaders approach even big challenges with optimism and curiosity—enabling them to generate breakthrough innovation that delivers more sustainable results in the long term. Specifically, those with a growth mindset are willing to let go of old business models and embrace new ones to maintain long-term success.

IBM is one company that has been successful in cultivating a growth mindset among its leaders. IBM celebrated its one hundredth anniversary in June 2011. The company has survived two world wars, the Great Depression, the 1970s oil crisis, the dotcom boom and bust, and even the current global economic recession. Over the past century, the firm's leaders have used a growth mindset to proactively disrupt the company many times over, completely reinventing its business model again and again. Thus, IBM has gone from selling tabulators to typewriters to mainframes to networked PCs to software and services—effectively riding one technology wave after another.[55] Compare this with HP, IBM's rival in Silicon Valley, whose leaders seem to have waited too long to reinvent the firm's 70-year-old business model. With stock prices plummeting and a leadership crisis under way, HP's top management seriously considered selling its PC business in late 2011 but finally decided to retain it.[56] The leadership of IBM has been more proactive; in the early 2000s, they recognized that although the company had invented the PC, its PC business was rapidly being commoditized by the emerging Internet-based computing model. In 2004, IBM's former CEO Sam Palmisano made the radical decision to sell its PC business—freeing resources so the company could move up the tech industry value chain.[57] Here is how Palmisano explains his decision: 'In 1981, the PC was an innovation. Twenty years later, it had lost much of its differentiation. It was time to move on—to the future. This enterprise (IBM) has always moved to the future. Continual forward movement is, in fact, inherent in IBM's value proposition, our business model. The frontier of what is truly innovative keeps moving . . . and that compels us not to sit still.'[58]

TAP THE POWER OF NETWORKS TO TACKLE BIG MARKET THREATS

Rather than deal with adversity by relying exclusively on internal resources, corporate leaders can benefit from working with customers, partners, and even competitors to co-create innovative solutions. Take Tata Consultancy Services (TCS): CEO N. Chandrasekaran is breaking out of the Big IT Service Provider mold and trying to think and act like a nimble jugaad innovator. This is particularly interesting as TCS was among the first Indian companies to embrace the structured R&D innovation model. Indeed, in 1981, TCS inaugurated Tata Research Design and Development Centre (TRDDC), India's first dedicated R&D centre. And yet, rather than depending exclusively on internal R&D for innovation, under Chief Technology Officer Ananth Krishnan's leadership, TCS is multiplying innovation alliances with external partners—including nimble jugaad entrepreneurs in India and abroad—under a programme called Co-Innovation Network (COIN).[59] While ensuring that TCS's R&D-driven structured innovation continues to be supported and institutionalized via formal management processes, Krishnan is also exploring ways to 'improvise' innovation by harnessing the jugaad ingenuity of TCS's nearly 240,000 employees—especially the collaboration-minded Gen X and Y employees who account for the majority of TCS's workforce. In some ways, TCS, whose annual revenue has crossed $10 billion (₹ 50,000 crore), has no choice: its clients—both Western and domestic—no longer want TCS to just provide low-cost IT services, they also want innovation. But they want TCS to deliver innovative solutions cost-effectively and quickly. Krishnan's goal is to leverage the creativity of all TCS employees and partners to innovate faster, better, and cheaper for—and with—the customer. To enable such fast-paced, collaborative jugaad innovation, TCS has invested heavily in social networking technologies. As Krishnan explains: 'We are today probably one of the largest users of the social web inside the enterprise, and we have improved our ability to look at the structured and the unstructured opportunity. In the last three years, we have really launched into the exploitation of the social web as a means for ideation, as a means of finding the expert, as a means of learning. We use the Web to form groups to look at specific problems and tapping into a collective intelligence.'[60]

To sum up: large companies and their leaders can find opportunity in adversity in a number of ways, including

- Recognizing that the glass is always half full
- Realizing extreme conditions are fertile soil for extreme innovation
- Building psychological capital to boost resilience
- Approaching big challenges with a growth mindset
- Tapping the power of networks to tackle big market threats

Although many individual leaders and their companies have employed one or more of these coping strategies, few firms and their leaders have employed many—if not all—of these strategies consistently over time. An exception is 3M; under several legendary leaders over 110 years, the company has applied many of these robust strategies to turn adversity to its advantage and continually stimulate growth. We turn to a detailed case study of 3M with a view to understanding how the company and its leaders were able to seek and find opportunity in adversity in a sustained way over a long period of time.

How 3M's Jugaad Spirit Bucked the Recession

Founded in 1902, 3M has come to epitomize American ingenuity. Over the course of a century, its prolific inventors have churned out breakthrough products that have become part of Americana: the Scotch® Tape, Scotchgard™ Protector for Fabric & Upholstery, Thinsulate™ Insulation, and the omnipresent Post-it® Notes. 3M's jugaad innovators like Art Fry—who invented the Post-it® Notes—have produced scores of useful products that have made life easier for crores of consumers across the globe.[61]

What makes 3M so innovative can be summed up in two numbers: 30 percent and 15 percent. Both figures are deemed sacrosanct by 3M's management and employees. Decades ago, recognizing that its consumer products face rapid obsolescence, 3M set itself the goal of generating 30 percent of its total revenues from new products it had introduced in the preceding five years. This bold goal—known within 3M as the New Product Vitality Index (NPVI)—helped create an innovate-or-die culture that sustains a constant sense of urgency among 3M designers and engineers who continually develop hundreds of new products each year (3M currently boasts a portfolio of seventy-five thousand products). Interestingly, some of 3M's most successful products to date were invented by its engineers in their 'spare time'. Indeed, way back in 1948, long before the idea was popularized by Silicon Valley firms like Google, 3M launched the 15-percent programme—a radical initiative that allows 3M employees to use 15 percent of their paid work time to pursue their dream projects—especially left-field jugaad innovations.[62] The 15-percent programme's objective was to loosen up the corporate culture and make it nimble and risk-tolerant—allowing 3M employees to swiftly sense and respond to new market opportunities in a dynamic bottom-up fashion. 3M's management has been totally supportive of many maverick innovations that have come out of this 15-percent programme—whether they succeed commercially (like Post-it® products) or not.

After proving its mettle as an exceptional corporate innovator for nearly a century, 3M experienced declining performance in the late 1990s. The nimble Midwestern manufacturer had become too big, complacent, and risk averse—resting on its laurels rather than creatively shaping the future. Its stock price took a hit, and its sales and profits began to decline. When faced with such adversity, corporate leaders can demonstrate either a fixed mindset—by playing it safe and seeking incremental change—or a growth mindset—by seeking opportunity in adversity and turning it to the company's advantage. In 3M's case, a leader with a growth mindset would have deepened 3M's existing commitment to jugaad thinking and innovation and used it to fashion a more radical response to adversity.

In 2001, 3M hired Jim McNerney as CEO to revive 3M's fortunes. McNerney, who had previously worked at GE (he had been a frontrunner to replace Jack Welch), brought in management discipline and streamlined the bloated firm's cost structure by implementing Six Sigma management techniques. This significantly boosted 3M's profitability: its operating margins shot up from 17 percent in 2001 to 23 percent in 2005. The highly structured Six Sigma processes—which emphasize predictability and sameness—worked wonders in 3M's factories by making production systems more cost-efficient. Initially, it seemed as if this structured approach to reviving 3M's fortune was working. But the same structured approach had the opposite effect when McNerney applied it in 3M's R&D labs to standardize and systematize the *innovation* process and make it faster and cost-effective. Six Sigma arguably choked 3M's free-flowing jugaad creativity. In the process, Six Sigma failed to tap into the psychological capital of 3M's innovators whose ingenuity and resilience to adversity had been built up over several decades. Rather than dreaming big and producing breakthrough products, 3M's engineers became risk averse and played it safe—by generating incremental innovations that met Six Sigma performance goals. 3M's management began to frown on disruptive ideas proposed by its jugaad innovators. As a result, 3M's sales revenues and reputation as a cutting-edge innovator began to flag. By 2005, 3M's share of revenues derived from new products had gone from its traditional 30 percent to only 21 percent. Its ranking in Boston Consulting Group's Most Innovative companies list gradually slipped as well; from number one in 2004 to number seven in 2007.[63] It seemed as if 3M's jugaad spirit had waned.

Faced with the adversity of declining revenue and brand reputation, George Buckley, who had replaced McNerney as CEO in 2005, focused on reviving 3M's risk-tolerant jugaad culture. In particular, Buckley began rolling back Six Sigma initiatives—and reinstituted the 15-percent programme, giving 3M engineers more flexibility and freedom to pursue radical ideas without fear of retribution. Buckley acknowledges: 'Perhaps one of the mistakes that we made as a company—it's one of the dangers of Six Sigma—is that when you value sameness more than you value creativity, I think you potentially undermine the heart and soul of a company like 3M.'[64]

Buckley had to move fast, as several of 3M's products were becoming outmoded or increasingly commoditized. It was facing growing competition from agile competitors in all its major product segments. But 3M was facing an even bigger challenge: rapidly shifting customer preferences. In today's digital environment, consumers value aesthetics as much as function in the products they buy—as demonstrated by the huge success of the well-designed iPhone. This new reality made 3M's leadership realize that while the company was great at *engineering* products, it had to get better at *designing* them in an appealing fashion.

Sensing an opportunity in this situation of adversity, 3M decided to broaden its traditional jugaad mindset to include not only great technical performance but also great design. To drive that transformation, 3M hired Mauro Porcini as head of global strategic design. The flamboyant and passionate 37-year-old Italian, who reports directly to the head of R&D for 3M's Consumer & Office Business, runs a large team that is attempting to make both 3M's existing and new products more visually appealing without sacrificing their technical performance.[65]

We met Mauro at his sleek new office at 3M's headquarters in Saint Paul, Minnesota. The crisp white walls and décor and the curved fuchsia-colored path paving the way to Mauro's office offered a creative oasis that stood in stark contrast to the claustrophobic brown cubicles in the rest of the building. Porcini, whose stylish sartorial esthetic also stood out, explained to us the challenge 3M is now facing and how his team is helping address it:[66]

'Customers are no longer just "buying" products—rather, they are seeking new *experiences* that delight them. They want to establish an emotional bond with the products they buy—even if it's an ordinary household item or office product. This challenge presents an opportunity for 3M to rethink the way we develop products. We are learning to pay more attention to aesthetics—rather than obsessing about functional excellence. We are also changing the way we engage with customers. When you listen to customers, you merely react to needs; when you empathize with customers, you anticipate their needs; but when you truly love your customers, you *surprise* them by introducing them to products they couldn't even fathom'.

Porcini points to Apple as a company in love with its customers: by marrying superior design with excellent engineering, Apple keeps surprising—and thrilling—customers with each new product it launches. 'Companies like Apple and Target have proven that good design can help capture not only bigger market share but also customer mindshare and heartshare. 3M's new challenge is to find ways to increase our customer 'heartshare' by using superior design to differentiate our products in a crowded market.'[67]

Porcini's team of jugaad designers are given carte blanche to rejuvenate 3M's signature office and consumer products by giving them a bold, sexy look. For instance, they gave a facelift to 3M's 50-year-old transparent Scotch® Tape Dispenser by creating a high-heel tape dispenser. Porcini himself redesigned an existing multimedia projector by making it sleeker, and 'something consumers want to touch': it was an instant hit. Some award-winning products that Porcini helped develop at 3M include the MPro150 Pocket Projector, the Scotch® Pop-Up Tape Dispenser with precut strips, and the Scotch® Pet Hair Remover. Porcini's designers are now actively involved in new R&D projects from the very beginning—thus influencing both business and technical decisions associated with new product development. Porcini quips: '3M used to be known as a company of "maverick engineers". Now we also want to be famous for housing "maverick designers".'[68]

Crushed by the Six Sigma juggernaut in the early 2000s, 3M reignited its jugaad spirit by giving its employees more creative freedom and by integrating left-brain functional excellence with a right-brain design sensibility. These efforts have paid off handsomely. They have helped rebuild the psychological capital of 3M's innovators which, in turn, has given 3M resilience in the face of subsequent adversity. Although 3M's sales revenues fell during the recessionary year of 2009, they have bounced back since, increasing 15 percent to $26.7 billion (₹ 133,500 crore) in 2010 (one of the highest growth rates ever achieved in 3M's hundred-plus-year history). In 2010, 3M posted a record operating profit of $5.9 billion (₹ 29,500), with margins of 22.2 percent. By 2010, 3M was once again generating 30 percent of its revenues from new products—and that percentage may even reach the mid 30s in 2012. Ajay Nanavati, Managing Director, 3M India, wants to boost that percentage within India to even 40 percent in the next five years by launching a slew of low-cost but high-quality products designed from scratch in India and targeted at India's second-tier cities and rural markets.[69] Globally, 3M now launches about 1,200 new products a year. George Buckley notes with satisfaction: 'Even in the worst economic times in memory, we released over one thousand new products.'[70] 3M seems to have found a sticky growth formula fit for the post-industrial economy—as evidenced by a 2011 survey conducted by Booz & Company with global executives, who ranked 3M as the third most innovative firm in the world—right after Apple and Google.[71]

Conclusion

In an increasingly complex business environment that throws all kinds of challenges at companies, demonstrating resilience in the face of adversity and turning it to one's advantage is a new competence that business leaders must urgently develop.

Although it is difficult to adopt as many different strategies designed to turn adversity into opportunity as 3M did, it is certainly not impossible. As 3M and the various other companies featured here prove, strong leadership is key to getting these resilient strategies to work.

But seeking opportunity in adversity is only the first of the many jugaad principles that corporate leaders—and their organizations—can apply to succeed in a unpredictable and fast-moving global economy. Of all the forms of adversity that emerging economies and firms face, none is as severe or threatening to survival and growth as scarcity. How jugaad innovators respond to scarcity by 'doing more with less'—and what corporate leaders can learn from this frugal principle—is the subject of our next chapter.

Chapter 3

Principle Two: Do More with Less

'If I had one dollar to spend, I would invest in solving the biggest problem today—the economics of scarcity.'

—Jeffrey Immelt, chairman and CEO, General Electric[1]

Gustavo Grobocopatel is a fourth-generation Argentinian farmer of Russian-Jewish extraction. For three generations, his family pursued a small-scale, subsistence model of farming in Argentina. Grobocopatel's dream was to break out of this mold and do something more ambitious. But his vision was hindered by scarcity from the very start.[2]

First, Grobocapatel had difficulty accessing large tracts of land. Although Argentina is a vast country, endowed with rich soil and a favourable climate, farmland is actually hard to come by. Only 10 percent of the land is arable—and much of the arable land is controlled by a few owners who are reluctant to part with it.[3]

Next, Grobocopatel faced a shortage of the skilled labour needed to scale up his business. Farming is labour intensive, as people are needed to fertilize, sow, tend, and harvest crops. In Argentina, such labour is in limited supply, is not formally organized, is spread out across the country, and can be costly to hire, especially during peak harvest seasons.[4]

Third, Grobocopatel didn't have the capital to buy the farm equipment he needed to achieve scale without using labour. Funding opportunities to bootstrap new businesses are very limited for entrepreneurs in Argentina.[5]

Instead of giving in to these challenges, Grobocopatel conceived and then implemented an ingenious business model. He overcame the scarcity of land by *leasing* it rather than acquiring it. He dealt with the scarcity of labour by *subcontracting* every aspect of farm work to a network of specialized service providers, giving him access to 'freelance' labourers he hires only when they are needed. And he overcame the cost of owning equipment and the lack of access to capital by *renting* the equipment needed from networks of small local companies.

By cleverly leveraging a grassroots network of 3,800 small and medium-size agricultural suppliers, Grobocopatel's company Los Grobo operates as an *asset-light* company, and in this way, is able to *do more with less*. Overcoming the skepticism of his peers, this jugaad entrepreneur has proven the value of his 'more with less' model. In 2010, Los Grobo became the second largest grain producer in Latin America, farming over 3 lakh hectares, trading 30 lakh tonnes of grain per year, and generating ₹ 3,750 crore in revenue—all without owning land or a single tractor or harvester. Having succeeded in Argentina, Los Grobo is now exporting its 'frugal farming' model to Brazil, Uruguay, and Paraguay, and helping farmers there produce more with less in their local contexts.

Emerging markets are teeming with innovators like Grobocopatel. Faced with scarcity across the board, these jugaad innovators have mastered the art of doing more with less. In this chapter, we get inside the minds of jugaad innovators and the enterprises they run to better understand how they create more value with fewer resources. Although many factors hinder large companies from adopting a 'more with less' approach, doing so is increasingly imperative. Indeed large firms that succeed in adopting frugal innovation methods to create affordable offerings are very likely to gain a significant competitive advantage over their peers in the age of scarcity that lies ahead.

Scarcity is the Mother of Invention

To even a casual observer, the most striking thing about jugaad innovators in emerging markets is their frugal mindset. These entrepreneurs and managers—whether they come from Argentina, Brazil, China, India, Kenya, Mexico, or the Philippines—are constantly looking for new ways to do more with less and deliver greater value to customers at a lower cost. What makes this mindset so fundamental to jugaad innovators, and why are they so good at getting 'more for less'? We believe that such a mindset is a rational response to the pervasive scarcity in their environment. For jugaad entrepreneurs, being frugal is not a luxury—it's the key to survival.

While Silicon Valley entrepreneurs typically operate in a resource-rich environment, jugaad entrepreneurs face scarcity of every possible kind. First, they must contend with the scarcity of capital. Quite simply, the availability of financial resources in emerging markets is limited. Banks are conservative, and venture capital and angel investor networks underdeveloped. For instance, 80 percent of South African entrepreneurs report difficulties in accessing funding.[6] Thus, jugaad innovators cannot afford to invest in capital-intensive R&D equipment. This partly explains why a country like India spends only

0.8 percent of its GDP on R&D (compared with 3 percent in developed countries), and why the private sector's share of this spending is only 20 percent.[7]

Second, jugaad innovators must deal with the scarcity of natural resources. Raw materials in emerging markets—from water to electricity—are expensive and hard to obtain reliably. This makes setting up and running new businesses—especially in the manufacturing sector—costly and difficult.

Third, jugaad entrepreneurs face a scarcity of qualified talent. Emerging markets like India, Brazil, and China have huge populations. But only a small percentage of these populations are qualified professionals who can use or deploy the offerings of emerging market entrepreneurs. According to a survey conducted by Manpower Group, 67 percent of enterprises in India and 57 percent of those in Brazil have difficulty finding qualified technicians, sales representatives, engineers, and IT staff. As a result, it is hard to sell complex medical devices in rural areas with few qualified doctors. Or to sell PCs to village schools where teachers lack computer literacy.[8]

Finally, jugaad innovators face a scarcity of quality infrastructure. The poor roads and limited transportation options in emerging markets make it difficult to get goods and services to far-flung places in a timely fashion. Moreover, the cost of doing so becomes a huge challenge, limiting the reach of markets in emerging economies.

In addition to pervasive scarcity, jugaad innovators also have to contend with a frugal and demanding consumer base. This consumer base has low disposable income. For instance, 30 crore Indians earn less than ₹ 50 a day. Many of these people either go without or are very careful about what they buy. This forces jugaad innovators to radically rethink price points. Their offerings have to be extremely affordable, not just barely so.

These consumers are also very value conscious. They may be low earners, but they also are high 'yearners'. Given their high aspirations, these consumers reject new offerings that do not deliver significantly higher value than existing offerings do. This puts a lot of pressure on jugaad innovators to develop higher value offerings at a lower price.

Finally, the consumer base in emerging markets is huge and diverse. Markets like China, Brazil, and India have crores of consumers. But these consumers are not homogeneous. To deliver higher value to a large and diverse base, jugaad innovators have to find clever ways of deriving both economies of scale *and* scope in whatever they do.

The pervasive scarcity and the demanding nature of the consumer base make jugaad innovators masters of frugality. Let's consider some of the ways in which they manage to do more with less.

Being Resourceful in a Resource-Scarce Environment

Jugaad innovators are able to get more from less by applying frugality in every activity they perform at every step along the value chain. They are frugal in how they design products, how they build them, how they deliver them, and how they perform after-sales maintenance. Their frugality shows up not only in their parsimonious use of capital and natural resources, but also in how they maximize their limited time and energy: rather that doing everything themselves, they extensively rely on partners to perform various operations, thus saving time and energy. The following are some frugal approaches employed by jugaad innovators to gain more from less.

They Reuse and Recombine

Rather than creating something entirely new, from scratch, jugaad innovators are more likely to reuse or seek new combinations of existing technologies or resources—both to come up with new solutions and to commercialize them in markets. For instance, Zhongxing Medical, a Chinese medical device maker, borrowed Digital Direct X-ray (DDX) equipment technology from its parent company (Beijing Aerospace), which wasn't using it effectively, and reengineered DDX for use in everyday applications like chest X-rays. As a result, its X-ray machines cost just $20,000 (₹ 10 lakh) to build, compared to $150,000 (₹ 75 lakh) for the equivalent GE and Philips models (which use DDX only for high-end applications). By creating low-cost, mass-market applications out of an underused technology, Zhongxing cornered 50 percent of the Chinese X-ray machine market—forcing rival GE to cut its prices by 50 percent while Philips, unable to compete, withdrew from this segment altogether.[9]

Similarly, jugaad innovators in African countries are leveraging existing cellphone networks to devise frugal business models that make services like healthcare and banking affordable to more people. In Kenya, for instance, only 10 percent of the population has access to banking services. Yet mobile penetration is over 50 percent. Sensing an opportunity, Safaricom, a local telecoms service provider, 40 percent owned by UK-based Vodafone, launched a service called M-PESA in 2007. M-PESA is an SMS-based (text message) system that enables people to send, save, and transfer money using their cellphones at a fraction of the cost of money transfer services like Western Union—and *without* having a bank account. Users of M-PESA can convert cash into electronic money that is stored on their cellphone at any one of hundreds of M-PESA outlets, including village mom-and-pop shops that act as M-PESA agents. On receiving an M-PESA user's cash, the agent texts the equivalent amount in electronic money (e-money) to the user's phone. The user can then text a part or all of this e-money to either an M-PESA agent or to another M-PESA user. All the e-money in circulation is backed up by real money in a bank account owned and managed by Safaricom. This safeguards the system against fraud while obviating the need for users to have their own bank accounts. As of this writing, over 1.4 crore Kenyans—or 68 percent of the country's adult population—have subscribed to M-PESA. This is much more than the number of people who have bank accounts![10] Migrant workers in Kenyan cities now routinely use M-PESA to safely and cost-effectively transfer earnings to their families who live in remote villages. (M-PESA was the inspiration for YES BANK's YES MONEY, a mobile payment and remittance service, which we describe in Chapter 5.[11])

THEY REMAIN ASSET-LIGHT

A second strategy that jugaad innovators use to get more from less is to leverage the capital assets of others to scale up their business model. This is precisely what Gustavo Grobocopatel did in Argentina. But Grobocopatel is hardly an exception. Many jugaad entrepreneurs in emerging markets choose to operate an 'asset-light' business model with as few fixed assets as possible on their balance sheet. Thus, instead of owning physical assets, they rent or share them. This approach not only makes their cost structures lean, but also allows them to quickly scale operations up or down to meet shifts in demand without investing in additional assets.

For instance, Indian cellphone companies like Bharti Airtel used this frugal strategy not only to get started, but also to turn their industry into one of the largest and most competitive in the world. In the early 2000s, when mobile revolution was taking off in India, Airtel was short on both the capital and the technology it needed to scale up its business. Undeterred, Airtel's Chairman Sunil Mittal used a jugaad approach to getting more with less: he boldly decided to outsource all but key marketing and branding activities to partner companies that had capital, technology, or both.[12] Today, IBM manages Airtel's IT infrastructure while Ericsson and Nokia Siemens Network (NSN) manage its network infrastructure. (This might just be one of the first examples of Indian companies outsourcing to Western ones, with both benefiting hugely from the process.) Today Airtel—which boasts of over 17 crore subscribers—is the world's largest 'asset-free' telecom service provider. It is also the first mobile carrier that dared to outsource all its core network infrastructure; most telecom operators prefer to own and manage this in-house, given its strategic nature. Its frugal operating model enables it to deliver better value to its customers at less cost. By transforming fixed technology costs into variable costs, Airtel not only succeeded in getting more for less, it also did so at breakneck speed—at times signing up as many as 1 crore subscribers per month.

THEY LEVERAGE EXISTING NETWORKS FOR DISTRIBUTION

A third 'more with less' strategy that jugaad innovators use is focused on solving the 'last mile' problem—that is, the difficulty of reaching far-flung customers in an economical way. Rather than investing in expensive logistics networks, jugaad entrepreneurs leverage existing networks to cost-effectively deliver their products and services to people in hard-to-reach markets. In particular, they rely on grassroots partners in local communities to reach more customers and personalize their offerings for them. These grassroots distribution partners are often micro entrepreneurs themselves. By building on already developed and trusted social networks in emerging markets, jugaad innovators can compensate for the poor state of the physical infrastructure there. More importantly, by enrolling grassroots entrepreneurs as their channel partners, jugaad innovators drive their own financial sustainability while also creating new economic opportunities in local communities.

For instance, toothpaste maker Colgate Palmolive scaled up its logistics network to serve remote villages in India by creating a mobile network of young people. Mounted on bicycles with a few oral-care products, these sales people go from village to village with their 'micro-stores on wheels'—thus solving the last mile problem. This solution costs less to Colgate than setting up physical distribution in these villages would. Plus it delivers more value to local communities—improving their health and providing jobs for local youth.[13]

Similarly, MicroVentures in the Philippines—co-founded in 2006 by Bam Aquino, nephew of former President Corazon Aquino—is making a wide range of consumer products and services accessible to consumers at the *base of* the (socio-economic) *pyramid* (BOP).[14] Rather than setting up its own distribution network—a costly and nearly impossible task, given the fragmentation of the BOP market spread across hundreds of villages—MicroVentures leveraged an existing ad-hoc logistics network made up of 8 lakh *sari-sari* (mom-and-pop) stores. These tiny stores—found across the entire seven-thousand-island Philippine archipelago—are operated by entrepreneurial women who set them up as an extension of their homes.[15] MicroVentures applied what is known as the *conversion franchising* model which consists in converting already existing, independently-owned stores into members of a standardized and branded network known as the Hapinoy Programme.[16] By converting and upgrading some of the existing sari-sari stores into branded Hapinoy Community Stores, MicroVentures rapidly scaled up its distribution network: ten thousand sari-sari stores have joined the Hapinoy Programme since 2007—a figure that Aquino predicts could go up to 1 lakh in the coming years. It's worth noting that a number of sari-sari stores that have joined the Hapinoy Programme are also members of CARD MRI, the largest microfinance institution in the Philippines, with whom MicroVentures had established a synergistic partnership.

The women who own sari-sari stores enjoy many benefits by joining the Hapinoy Programme:

1. They pay less for their supply of goods, because MicroVentures can—by aggregating demand from multiple Hapinoy stores—negotiate bulk prices from consumer goods manufacturers.

2. They can generate more income by selling a broader variety of goods and value-added services—such as mobile payments—sourced from MicroVentures' partners.

3. They learn how to professionally run their businesses—and scale them up—by receiving personalized training from MicroVentures in areas such as inventory management, marketing, leadership, and personal development.

Aquino explains: 'Rather than building a new logistics network from scratch, our business model leverages the *human network* of micro entrepreneurs—the women who own sari-sari stores. By building on an existing grassroots distribution infrastructure, we have created a sustainable solution that benefits all members of BOP communities. First, BOP consumers gain access to a greater variety of affordable goods and services. Second, sari-sari store owners in villages increase their income levels by joining the Hapinoy Programme—and learn how to improve their own lives and meaningfully contribute to their communities. And third, more micro-producers in villages can now extend their market reach by joining our distribution network. Our vision is to turn the Hapinoy Programme into the social equivalent of an iPad: a platform that gives our network members [the women micro-entrepreneurs] access to hundreds of 'social apps'—i.e., products and services offered by our partners. Our network members can pick and choose specific apps [products/services] that deliver the most value to their local communities'.[17]

Helping Customers Get More Value

By relying on a frugal operating model, jugaad innovators strive not just to reduce their own costs, but also to pass value on to consumers. Thus, unlike their counterparts in the West, they do not typically focus on wowing customers with products that have cool features or the latest technologies. Instead, they pursue functionally minimalist solutions that offer superior value to customers—often transforming their lives in the process. Simply put, they help their customers get more value for less cost by offering them quality products and services at highly affordable prices.

For instance, in 2010, KPIT Cummins Infosystems, an Indian engineering and IT services provider, unveiled Revolo, a low-cost plug-in parallel hybrid solution for cars. (Revolo is the brainchild of Tejas Kshatriya, an engineer who works for KPIT Cummins. Kshatriya came up with the idea while stuck in a traffic jam in Mumbai in 2008.) By installing the Revolo kit in their cars, owners of cars that run on petrol can cost-effectively convert their existing vehicles into fuel-efficient, high-performance hybrids. The conversion kit—which includes a rechargeable battery pack, an electric motor, and a pulley—can be retrofitted into most cars in just six hours by a KPIT Cummins–certified mechanic.

Revolo works best in stop-and-go city traffic, as it captures the kinetic energy generated every time the brakes are applied and stores it in its batteries for later use. Tests show that the Revolo technology boosts fuel efficiency by over 35 percent and reduces greenhouse gas emissions by at least 30 percent. Most important, at a price between ₹ 65,000 and ₹ 1.62 lakh for the Indian market—and around ₹ 2.5 lakh when sold in Western markets—the Revolo system costs 80 percent less than other hybrid car options.[18] Revolo can be plugged into any car, whatever its brand or age, without interfering with the carmaker's transmission configuration. KPIT estimates that, when used at an average daily run of 49.8 kilometres, the Revolo conversion kit pays for itself in less than two years. Hence Revolo is a win-win for both car owners and auto manufacturers. Ravi Pandit, CEO of KPIT Cummins, notes: 'With Revolo, we found an affordable and retrofittable solution to transform a gas-guzzling car into an environmentally mindful, fuel-efficient, high-performance hybrid. With Revolo, car owners get more value at less cost.'[19]

KPIT Cummins is negotiating licensing deals with several US and European carmakers that are eager to initially offer Revolo as a branded aftermarket service to their existing car users—while exploring the long-term possibility of incorporating Revolo as a standard feature in their future cars. Large-scale commercial production of Revolo is expected to begin in 2013.[20] It is worth noting that it cost KPIT less than $2 million (₹ 10 crore) to develop the Revolo technology—much less than the $1 billion (₹ 5,000 crore) it costs, on average, to develop a new car.[21]

How do jugaad innovators know what is of value to their customers and how much customers will be willing to pay to get that additional value? Rather than considering these questions in the abstract in an R&D lab, jugaad innovators spend time in the field observing and interacting with potential customers to identify their latent needs and requirements. Only then do they zero in on the essential features of a solution that are most relevant to their unique customers. In other words, they first seek to identify the *appropriateness* of a solution. Armed with these insights into what customers need rather than want, jugaad innovators design, from the ground up, an appropriate product or service—as well as a business model—that can best fulfil these needs. Very often they don't get it right the first time. But by trial and error and rapid experimentation, they eventually settle on the set of features—and the business model—that is likely to deliver the highest value at the lowest price for their market.

To understand this better, let's consider another jugaad example, one that can make a life-or-death difference to many people around the world. Two crore babies are born prematurely or with a low birth weight each year worldwide, and 40 lakh of them die, most in developing nations. Those who survive often suffer from low IQ, diabetes, and heart disease when they reach adulthood. Many of these deaths and ailments can be averted by simply keeping these premature babies warm. Unfortunately, current options for warming babies in developing nations are either expensive or unsafe. The incubators sold in Western countries cost up to $20,000 (₹ 10 lakh) and require electricity—which is unreliable in developing nations. And ad-hoc solutions like positioning babies under bare light bulbs are simply risky.

Jane Chen, Linus Liang, Naganand Murty, and Rahul Panicker co-founded Embrace to come up with an affordable infant warmer for use in developing countries, one that costs far less than incubators available in the West. The founders came up with the idea for Embrace's frugal business model while they were all attending Stanford University's Entrepreneurial

Design for Extreme Affordability programme. After producing an initial prototype—a stripped-down version of traditional incubators powered by electricity—they traveled to Nepal to test it in an urban hospital. But they soon found that 80 percent of babies that die prematurely in developing nations like Nepal are born at home in villages, far from well-equipped hospitals and without access to regular electricity.[22]

That insight led them to fundamentally rethink who their *users* really were. Realizing that their customers were doctors and parents in villages, they set out to identify what product features would bring the most value to these rural users. That inquiry led them to design a *portable* infant warmer that looks like a tiny sleeping bag and gives mothers greater mobility and more intimate contact with their babies. The bag in turn contains a pouch of phase-change material (PCM)—a wax-like material—that keeps babies warm for up to six hours at regular body temperatures. Not only is this infant warmer intuitive to use, but it requires only 30 minutes of electricity to heat up the PCM pouch—using a portable electric heater that comes with the product. Further, this design dovetails well with the recommended practise of 'kangaroo care', whereby a mother holds her baby against her skin (hence the company name 'Embrace').[23] Most importantly, the Embrace portable infant warmer costs about ₹ 10,000—nerely 1 percent of the cost of incubators available in Western markets.

In 2011, Embrace piloted this product in India, where 12 lakh premature babies die each year. Early results have been very encouraging. A preliminary study validated Embrace's safety and efficacy with twenty infants. Embrace then undertook a more extensive clinical study of 160 premature babies. In one instance, a two-pound baby born to parents from a village near Bangalore, in Southern India, was kept in the Embrace infant warmer for twenty days and began to gain weight—bringing great joy to its parents who had lost two babies previously.

Embrace uses rapid prototyping techniques to get customer feedback on new product features fast and zero in on the product attributes that are of highest relevance and value to rural customers. For instance, after noticing that mothers in Indian villages don't trust numerical displays that indicate whether the temperature is right, Embrace replaced the numerical scale with symbols indicating 'OK' or 'Not OK'. Similarly, Embrace is planning to release a future version of its product targeted at mothers who live in far-flung villages with no electricity at all: in this version, the PCM pouch will be heated—and thus 'recharged'—using a heating device that runs on *hot water* (instead of electricity).

Embrace is also experimenting with different pricing models—such as a rental option—to make its product affordable in countries like India where tens of crores in villages live on less than ₹ 100 a day. 'Entrepreneurs often fall in love with their original product idea or business model and fail to listen to customers,' Chen explains. 'We, on the other hand, have no qualms about modifying our product features and pricing again and again till we find a solution that delivers the highest value to our customers at the lowest cost for them. For us, innovation is a dynamic process that never ends.'[24]

Embrace is currently negotiating partnerships with multinational pharmaceutical and medical device companies such as GE as well as local NGOs to piggyback on their extensive distribution networks to make the Embrace infant warmer accessible to as many hospitals and clinics as possible in countries like India. Finally, Embrace is testing its infant warmer at the Lucile Packard Children's Hospital at Stanford University—as it believes there is a big market for Embrace's product in the US where infant mortality rates are among the highest in the developed world. Embrace has set itself a bold target of saving the lives of over 1 lakh babies over the next three years, as well as preventing illness in over 7 lakh babies.

In sum, jugaad innovators are able to find abundance in scarcity—and to share that abundance with customers and other stakeholders who also face scarcity. Jugaad innovators may lack financial, natural, and technological resources, but they compensate by finding ingenious ways to leverage social networks and their intimate knowledge of customers to create and deliver more value at less cost. In many ways, jugaad innovators embody these words of Theodore Roosevelt: 'All the resources we need are in the mind'.

Welcome to the Age of Frugality

Prestigious organizations such as GE and Lucile Packard Children's Hospital at Stanford are adopting Embrace's low-cost incubators, even though they clearly have access to many high-performing incubators in the West. These forward-thinking organizations recognize that a frugal approach is increasingly critical to survival in the age of scarcity that is increasingly upon us. The warning signs are all around. Indeed, these signs are not very different from the more general indicators, discussed in Chapter 2, of increased adversity in the global economic environment. Nevertheless, it's worth examining the specific factors that are creating a new era of austerity in many parts of the world. These include:

- *Increasing numbers of frugal customers:* The recession has made Western middle-class consumers far more cost-conscious than they were in the boom years of the housing bubble. Similarly, in business-to-business markets, power is shifting from buyers who value features and functionality to those who prefer value pricing. For instance, in hospitals, the technology buyers are no longer doctors (who typically favour technically superior but overpriced medical devices), but instead cost-conscious purchasing managers.[25] In India, 70 crore people earn ₹ 100 or less a day. These people may be low earners, but they are high *yearners*—they want to gain access to the same products and services enjoyed by India's 30 crore strong middle-class consumers. For example, ASSOCHAM projects that the market for consumer durables in rural India will grow 40 percent in 2012 due to higher disposable income among rural consumers.[26] These rural consumers at the bottom-of-the-pyramid are not only extremely frugal but they also expect *a lot more* value for every paisa they are willing to spend—which explains why Indian companies—both domestic and multinationals' subsidiaries—have trouble meeting their needs.

- *Dwindling natural resources:* Because the oil and water needed to produce energy and food are in short supply, largecompanies are motivated to identify more efficient ways of using these scarce resources. Also, consumers around the world are becoming environmentally conscious and voting with their wallets for eco-friendly brands that use less of those natural resources. More than 75 percent of consumers surveyed by Burson-Marsteller, a public relations firms, mentioned that social responsibility is an important factor in their purchase decisions, and 70 percent said they would willingly pay a premium for products from a socially responsible company that, among other things, strives to protect the environment.[27]

- *Government regulations:* More policies are being put into place to deal with financial and environmental pressures. For instance, to deal with its huge budget deficit, the US government is asking Big Pharma to make more drugs available to more Americans at a lower cost. Similarly, increasingly stringent environmental regulations are forcing US carmakers to develop cars that deliver more miles with less fuel and greenhouse emission. In India, the auto industry accounts for nearly 18 percent of the total CO2 emissions in the country.[28] With the domestic car sales expected to increase from 27 lakh units in 2010 to 1.1 crore in 2020 (India will be the world's third largest car market by then), the Indian government plans to introduce more stringent emission standards that local car manufacturers will need to comply with when designing and building new vehicles.[29]

- *Competition from low-cost rivals from emerging markets.* Across industries, Western companies are facing competition from low-cost emerging market companies. For example, Western pharmaceutical companies are threatened by generic drug makers from Brazil and South Africa who produce and sell cheaper medicine; Western automakers are being challenged by low-cost car manufacturers from India and China who are producing affordable electric vehicles and ultra-compact cars. But this rivalry is being played out within India itself: well-entrenched cellphone companies such as Nokia and Samsung are being taken on by low-cost domestic and Chinese cellphone makers such as Spice, HTC, and Huawei.

- *Rivalry from agile start-ups.* Around the world, start-ups with high-value offerings for cost-conscious consumers are popping up across industries, from hospitality to consumer goods to fashion. In the process, these start-ups are stealing customers from larger players. For example, Warby Parker, founded by four Wharton MBA graduates while still at the B-School, is trying to break the oligopoly—steeped in the old 'more for more' business model—that controls the global eyewear industry. The start-up offers fashionable high-quality prescription eyewear for just $95 (₹ 4,750), a fraction of what high-end eyewear manufacturers charge.[30] It provides more value to consumers by allowing for home try-ons of different frames and contributes to a larger cause by donating one pair of glasses for each pair it sells. In India, nimble e-commerce start-ups are disrupting traditional brick-and-mortar business models across industries. Take Flipkart, the online book retailer that is giving well-established brick-and-mortar retail chains a run for their money. Here is a telling statistic: In September 2009, the day Dan Brown's *The Lost Symbol* was released, Flipkart sold more than 2,000 copies of the book—as much as any brick-and-mortar retail chain in India did.[31] Flipkart's secret is its customer-centric business model which consists of cash/card payment on delivery, 30-day replacement policy, monthly installment plans, and 24/7 customer support. Not surprisingly, Flipkart is expected to close the 2011-12 financial year with ₹ 500 to ₹ 600 crore in sales—a ten-fold year-on-year increase in revenue.

Around the world, frugal consumers and competitors are rewriting the rules of engagement for manufacturers and retailers alike—pressuring them to develop goods and services that are affordable and eco-friendly. As a result, businesses are being forced to rethink how they address the aspirations and needs of their value-conscious customers. But doing so will not be easy.

For Most Large Companies, Bigger is Still Better

In the new era of scarcity, large companies must learn how to produce higher value with fewer resources. Despite the benefits of doing more with less, large companies face significant obstacles in adopting this approach.

For a start, the top management in many large companies is wedded to a previously successful 'more for more' strategy. To differentiate their products from competition, large companies are used to spending huge sums on R&D to develop expensive, often over-engineered products for which they charge customers a hefty premium. In the past, this strategy worked because customers were able to afford such premiums, and these premiums in turn enabled companies to recoup their large R&D investments. However, this 'bigger is better' approach is no longer sustainable as large companies face an increasing resource crunch and a growing number of aspirational but relatively low-income consumers seeking value-for-money offerings.

Not only is top management wedded to a 'more for more' strategy, but senior managers in large companies also lack the incentive to pursue opportunities in low-income segments. They perceive these segments as too small, unprofitable, or both—and the margins that companies can charge in value segments are typically low. So, even though the numbers of potential consumers in low-income segments may be large, these markets need up-front investment and require time to develop and grow. Therefore, senior managers who are under pressure from shareholders to deliver quarterly results are not motivated to make these long-term investments in growing value markets.

On the R&D side, engineers in large companies tend to equate complexity with progress. These engineers come to work every morning with a desire to push the boundaries of technology. For many of them, 'doing less' would seem a step back rather than forward. As a result, they tend to design products that cost more and that are overloaded with features that customers don't necessarily want. For example, the most effective way of making cars fuel efficient and inexpensive is to make them lighter. But the pursuit of technology for its own sake—and the need to differentiate cars from each other—has resulted in their getting heavier with time. Specifically, designers add more electronics to cars to deliver ever more bells and whistles. This increases their weight, drag, and hence fuel inefficiency, which in turn makes them more, not less, expensive.

Arguing against this trend, John Maeda, President of the Rhode Island School of Design, says: 'It's not necessarily beneficial to add more technology features just because we can. R&D engineers must make frugal simplicity the core tenet of their design philosophy. They must design for the "real world" by practising what I call "radical incrementalism"—which is doing more with less. Wouldn't it be nice if rather than complimenting their R&D teams with "Wow! You worked so hard to come with this new product with all the bells and whistles: it is amazing!" CEOs told R&D engineers "Wow! You did almost nothing—and yet produced a 'good enough' product that gets the job done: Congratulations!"' (In Chapter 5, we discuss the importance of simplicity when designing new products and services.)[32]

Engineers may be the ones who create more expensive products by piling on complex functionality and features that customers don't want. But sales managers have a role to play too: more often than not, they love to sell these expensive products. In fact, they typically lack the motivation to sell affordable products, fearing that these products might draw consumers away from their more expensive offerings. After all, selling cheaper products doesn't help them earn larger commissions. Further, a common misconception among sales managers is that the market for low-cost products is 'too niche' and therefore doesn't deserve time and effort to build. But they fail to recognize that even mainstream customers are now turning away from premium products and seeking affordable solutions that deliver better value at a lower cost. Seventy-eight percent of US online consumers say that they are willing to switch from their current brand to a private label for personal goods primarily because the price is lower.[33] And 22 percent of the customers shopping at dollar stores earn $70,000 (₹ 35 lakh) or more annually. When even Middle America begins patronizing thrift stores, the trend is undeniable, (In Chapter 6, we explore the impact of the shrinking American middle class on businesses.)

Despite these changes in consumer behavior, however, marketing executives in large companies still equate 'low-cost' with 'poor quality' and are concerned that promoting low-cost offerings will damage their company's brand. But marketing executives must recognize that, in this new age of austerity, with a rapidly dwindling middle class, the notion of 'premium' is being redefined as 'more value for money', even in middle to high-end markets.

Large companies face a conundrum: they are confronted with a growing number of frugal consumers clamouring for affordable solutions, yet their existing corporate culture and incentive systems are not designed to deliver more with less. As scarcity deepens across global markets, corporate leaders will have no choice, really: they will have to bite the bullet and infuse their organizations with a frugal mindset. A jugaad approach could be just the way to undertake such a transformation.

How Large Companies Can Find Abundance in Scarcity

To compete and win in the dawning Age of Scarcity, corporate leaders must boldly revamp their companies' R&D approaches, business models, and incentive systems for sales and marketing—all of which were designed for success in the Age of Abundance. Rather than caving in to shareholders' demands for short-term gains, CEOs of large companies must restructure their organizations to boost their long-term ability to continually design and deliver affordable and sustainable solutions to value-conscious consumers. Here are some valuable suggestions for undertaking such systemic changes.

TIE SENIOR MANAGEMENT'S COMPENSATION TO FRUGAL PERFORMANCE

It's not enough for CEOs to adopt a frugal mindset and strive to do more with less. They must also encourage their senior managers to follow suit. One way to do that is by linking senior executives' compensation to performance metrics aimed at driving frugality. Take the case of Ramón Mendiola Sánchez, CEO of Florida Ice & Farm Co., a large food and beverage producer and distributor in Costa Rica that is deeply committed to sustainability. In 2008, Mendiola set up a balanced scorecard with a set of key performance indicators (KPIs) to track how well his company was reducing its consumption of natural resources such as water while simultaneously delivering more value to customers and other stakeholders. He linked these KPIs to his senior executives' compensation so they have some skin in the game: 50 percent or more of their compensation is tied to their meeting—or exceeding—these KPIs. Mendiola is leading by example—he has linked 65 percent of his own pay to the balanced scorecard that combines financial, social, and environmental KPIs to compute a 'triple bottom line' of people, planet, and profit.

This strategy has been successful: since its implementation, Florida Ice & Farm's senior executives have found creative ways to do more with less by motivating their employees to improve manufacturing and distribution processes and help local communities better conserve natural resources. Under Mendiola's leadership, Florida Ice & Farm has reduced the amount of water it requires to produce a litre of beverage—from 12 litres to 4.9—and aims to further reduce it to 3.5 litres soon. It has also eliminated solid waste from all its operations, and is well on its way to meeting its target of becoming 'water neutral' in 2012 and 'carbon neutral' by 2017.[34] Meanwhile, the company achieved a compound annual growth rate of 25 percent between 2006 and 2010—twice the industry average. Mendiola notes: 'By using incentives, we motivate our employees at every level to get creative and invent frugal and sustainable ways to deliver significantly more value to all our stakeholders by using far fewer natural resources—while saving substantial money for our company.'[35]

SENIOR MANAGEMENT MUST CHALLENGE R&D TO DO MORE WITH LESS

A worsening global economy and growing resource constraints are forcing many CEOs to cut their R&D spending with the hope of increasing their innovation performance at lower cost. But this will happen only when engineers and scientists are offered challenging projects that give them the incentive to do more with less. For instance, in the late 1990s, Louis Schweitzer—former CEO of Renault, the French carmaker—visited Russia, where he found that low-cost domestic cars like the Lada—that cost merely €6,000 (₹ 3.9 lakh)—were outselling his company's €12,000 (₹ 7.8 lakh) cars. Following this visit, Schweitzer challenged his R&D team to come up with a modern, reliable, and affordable car for less than €6,000. As Schweitzer recalls: 'Seeing those antiquated cars, I found it unacceptable that technical progress should stop you from making a good car for €6,000. I drew up a list of specifications in three words—modern, reliable, and affordable—and added that everything else was negotiable.'[36] The result was the

Logan, a no-frills car priced at €5,000 (₹ 3.25 lakh), which, since its launch in 2004, has become Renault's cash cow all across recession-wary European markets as well as in many developing economies. Interestingly, Schweitzer's successor Carlos Ghosn—who coined the term 'frugal engineering' in 2006—is now pushing Renault's R&D team in France to do *even more with less* to compete effectively with low-cost carmakers from emerging market such as Tata Motors (which developed the ₹ 1 lakh Nano).[37]

MARKETING EXECUTIVES SHOULD CREATE SEPARATE BRANDS FOR THEIR AFFORDABLE OFFERINGS

To avoid brand dilution, large companies need to create distinct brands for distinct segments. Given that they might already have well-established brands for higher-priced segments, they should develop distinctive *new* brands for their affordable segments. Doing so will reduce the problems of brand dilution while ensuring greater market coverage. For instance, the Starwood Group—which owns the Sheraton and Le Méridien brands—opened two affordable but chic hotel chains—Aloft and Element—to cater to value-conscious consumers.[38] Similarly, in an attempt to reach mainstream consumers, high-end designer Vera Wang has recently adopted a three-tiered branding approach: the top-tier includes her pricey luxury bridal wear, the mid-tier is made up of her eponymous line sold at accessible prices, and the bottom-tier includes casual budget-priced brands—such as Simply Vera—that are selling like hotcakes through mass-market US retailers like Kohl's.[39] Finally, high-end restaurateurs and star chefs have now adopted a low-cost venue—the food truck, traditionally used by hot dog vendors—to dish out gourmet items at affordable prices.

In New York City you now find food trucks that sell lobster rolls and Van Leeuwen's artisanal ice cream.

CREATE INCENTIVE SYSTEMS FOR SALESPEOPLE TO SELL AFFORDABLE PRODUCTS

Large companies must recognize that jugaad innovation isn't just about *designing* affordable products. It is also about successfully *selling* these products in the marketplace. But successful selling won't happen as long as salespeople have the incentive to sell only big-ticket items. Instead, companies will have to align their sales force's incentive systems with the corporate strategy of doing more with less. Companies can address this issue by reorganizing their sales force along brand lines, with different salespeople responsible for the low-end and high-end segments. This will also help reduce any internal resistance based on the fear of cannibalization. Even better, healthy internal competition between divisions could drive sales and marketing personnel responsible for different brands to be more innovative in how their reach and keep their respective customers. For example, Procter & Gamble for decades maintained a homogeneous sales structure selling premium products to mainstream middle-class. But as the purchasing power of middle-class Americans declines, P&G has restructured its sales force into two distinct groups that separately target high-income and low-incomesegments.[40] In India, Godrej is setting up a separate business unit to sell its new 'Chotu' line of low-cost products aimed at rural markets. The line includes ChotuKool, an affordable fridge priced at ₹ 3,790 (50 percent less than Godrej's traditional refrigerator) and ChotuWash, a low-cost washing machine.[41] The dedicated 'Chotu' business unit is experimenting with innovative sales and distribution models never tried before by Godrej. These include tie-ups with grassroots self-help groups, panchayats, NGOs, and India Post to make the 'Chotu' family of products accessible even to consumers in very remote villages. The unit has also partnered with micro-financing institutions to make micro-loans available to potential rural buyers, thus making the 'Chotu' family of products still more affordable for the masses.

DESIGN AFFORDABLE SOLUTIONS FROM THE GROUND UP

R&D teams should move away from pursuing over-engineered 'perfect products' and focus instead on developing 'good enough' solutions. By 'good enough' solutions we don't mean stripped-down versions of existing high-end products. Such solutions could leave customers feeling shortchanged and less than satisfied. Although such an approach could help reduce costs in the short term, companies will pay the price later, as designers will have to return to the drawing board down the road and undo the problems caused by such quick-fix solutions. Rather, engineers of large firms need to create affordable solutions from the *ground up*. And emerging markets can help with this: they offer engineers a great training ground to practise such frugal innovation. Indeed, a few forward-thinking Western companies across sectors are increasingly using their R&D teams in emerging markets like India and China to develop minimalist solutions from the ground up that deliver higher value to customers. For example, when GE Healthcare's R&D engineers in India had to come up with low-cost alternatives to the company's high-end ECG machines to serve local needs with limited means, they didn't attempt to strip down GE's existing product to meet local price points. Instead, they went back to the drawing board and, based on deep observation of customers, they developed the MAC i, a radically affordable, portable ECG machine with basic features and a long battery life that is priced at around $500 (₹ 25,000)—one-twentieth of the cost of ECG devices available in the West.[42] Similarly, Nokia's 1100 model, an ultra-low-cost cellphone with a simple interface and a flashlight to help users see their way in the dark, was designed from the ground up for emerging markets. This product has been a huge seller in India and Africa, where crores of people who live beyond the reach of the electricity grid find a simple feature like a flashlight invaluable.

ENGAGE ECO-AWARE CONSUMERS IN THE SUSTAINABILITY DIALOGUE

An explosion of social media tools, such as Facebook and Twitter, has given rise to well-informed and powerful consumer communities around the world. Often, the consumers who participate in these communities congregate on product fan pages or websites created by other consumers, far beyond the reach of the company that offers these products. Frequently, participants in these user communities are young, frugal, and environmentally conscious. They aren't just looking for a deal; they're searching for—and willing to champion—products that fit into their personal value system. These consumer communities can help build brands they favour, or cause the demise of brands they disapprove of. Companies should proactively engage with such communities on issues like sustainability and resource scarcity—and use such engagement to identify ways to do more using fewer natural resources. Doing so will not only help companies shape their own strategies but also bolster their brand and help them differentiate themselves from competitors. Because most companies have been slow to understand how to work with user communities online, those companies that succeed in doing so can stand out from the competition and garner long-term brand loyalty.

PARTNER EXTENSIVELY

Partnering with key external players offers a powerful way for companies to get more out of their limited R&D dollars. Partners can cost-effectively bring companies better ideas than they already have, help companies develop existing ideas more efficiently, or enable them to commercialize these ideas more extensively and at lower cost. An outstanding example of a company that has used partners to improve its R&D efficiency is Procter & Gamble (P&G). In 2000, AG Lafley, then P&G's CEO, noted that 'for every P&G researcher there are 200 scientists or engineers elsewhere in the world who are just as good—a total of 15 lakh people whose talents we could use'.[43] Lafley wanted to tap into this global brainpower so P&G could innovate more widely, radically, and rapidly than before—without investing more in internal R&D. To do so, he set a challenge for his until-then internally focused R&D organization. Within ten years P&G was to move from being a research and develop (R&D) company to being a connect and develop (C&D) organization, one that sources as much as 50 percent of its new product ideas from *outside* the company. To achieve this ambitious goal, Lafley opened up P&G's old R&D model to the creative input of a wide array of external stakeholders—customers, suppliers, universities, venture capitalists, and think tanks. In one instance, P&G found a cost-effective and speedy external solution to the problem of printing trivia questions in edible ink on Pringles chips. Rather than solving the problem internally (as they would have done in the past, thereby costing the firm a fortune), P&G used its links with universities around the world to identify a professor in Bologna, Italy, who had already developed a means of printing on pizza and bread. P&G then worked with this professor to adapt his solution to printing on Pringles chips.

This collaboration yielded a commercially successful P&G product without incurring huge in-house R&D expenditure. Similarly, Xerox has tightly integrated its R&D activities in India with local partner networks from the outset. For instance, Xerox has partnered with the Indian Institute of Technology Madras (IIT Madras) to use cloud computing to improve the efficiency of document services delivery. It is also working with IIT Madras's Rural Technology Business Incubator (RTBI) to co-create affordable solutions to improve workflow at small rural businesses in India. Such smart partnerships enable Xerox to generate locally-relevant solutions faster, better, and cheaper.[44]

Our research shows that the strategies just outlined are among the more common ones adopted by large companies who are embracing the jugaad approach to innovation. These frugal strategies are also the ones that we are increasingly called on to share with corporate leaders who seek our advice on incorporating a 'more with less' approach in their organizations. Of all the invitations we've received to consult on this jugaad principle, one stands out as particularly memorable.

PepsiCo: A Refreshing Approach to Doing More with Less

In January 2010, we had lunch with Indra Nooyi, Chairman and CEO of PepsiCo Inc. and, according to *Fortune* magazine, one of the world's most powerful women.[45] Nooyi had read an article in *Bloomberg Businessweek* that profiled our research on jugaad, and she was eager to discuss how PepsiCo had infused the efficient and innovative mindset that is jugaad's trademark into its operations.[46]

Jugaad innovation is definitely on top of Nooyi's mind—and for a strategic reason. PepsiCo's products are made, manufactured, or sold in more than 200 countries. They cover consumer preferences and needs that evolve on an ongoing basis. Given that the macroeconomic environment in a constant state of change, PepsiCo must be ready to refresh and diversify its products to meet the needs of a dynamic marketplace—especially in light of the growing consumer demand for healthy and nutritious food.

Understanding the demonstrated potential of the global packaged-nutrition market—valued at $500 billion (₹ 25 lakh crore) and growing—PepsiCo, the second largest food and beverage business in the world, has expanded its vast product portfolio to include foods and beverages that deliver positive nutrition.[47] Today, PepsiCo provides foods and beverages that are 'good-for-you' (featuring brands such as Quaker and Tropicana), complementing its 'fun-for-you' (with brands such as Pepsi and Lay's) and 'better-for-you' (including brands such as zero-calorie Pepsi Max and Propel Zero) portfolios. This expansion into products that deliver positive nutrition is in line with Performance with Purpose, PepsiCo's guiding principle.

For PepsiCo, Performance with Purpose means delivering sustainable growth by investing in a healthier future for people and the planet. Specifically, there are four planks that make up Performance with Purpose: financial performance, human sustainability, environmental sustainability, and talent sustainability.[48] It is this push for sustainability, both financial and societal, that stimulates jugaad innovation at PepsiCo.

Nooyi has brought in the right talent to enable PepsiCo's expansion into the nutrition area. To hone PepsiCo's focus on nutrition, Nooyi appointed Dr Mehmood Khan—an MD whose experience includes serving at the Mayo Clinic as the Director of the Diabetes, Endocrinology, and Nutrition Clinical Trial Unit and as Consultant Physician in Endocrinology—as PepsiCo's Chief Scientific Officer as well as CEO of its Global Nutrition Group (GNG).[49] Khan's crossover role, which is unique in the global food and beverage industry, enables him to translate the science of nutrition—in which he is an expert—into commercially viable products. Khan's goal as head of GNG is to grow PepsiCo's portfolio of good-for-you products to $30 billion (₹ 150,000 crore) in net revenue by 2020 by increasing the amount of whole grains, fruits, vegetables, nuts, seeds, and low-fat dairy in its global product portfolio. For instance, Khan's GNG team is researching ready-to-eat—and even drinkable—breakfast products that combine fruit, dairy, and grains like oats.

With the goal of identifying *frugal business practises*, PepsiCo also set up the Global Value Innovation Centre in India in late 2010. Here is how Tanmaya Vats, who heads the Centre, explains his mandate: 'We want to discover disruptive business practises that can significantly lower the cost of operations in our supply chain—in manufacturing and distribution. We look for radical ways to reduce the *capital intensity* in our business model—by, for instance, developing cost-effective and eco-friendly capital equipment that delivers significantly more value and yet costs drastically less than currently available solutions.'[50] Rather than reinventing the wheel, Vats' unit is partnering extensively with jugaad innovators worldwide—such as academic institutions, researchers, entrepreneurs, and domain experts—who have already invented—or helped in inventing—jugaad solutions for making manufacturing and distribution processes more efficient. Once a promising jugaad innovation is identified for reducing capital intensity, Vats's unit then works with various business units at PepsiCo to help adopt and roll it out globally.

Nooyi is also using a 'bottom-up' approach to dealing with scarcity. She is empowering her employees in different regions to experiment with out-of-the-box solutions that address scarcity in their local supply chains.

One of the critical resources fundamental to PepsiCo's business is water. There is a clear need for PepsiCo to achieve water use efficiency to both improve product outputs and provide access to safe water for those in water-distressed areas. In India, an environment of severe water scarcity prompted members of the PepsiCo India team to investigate ways to reduce water use throughout the supply chain. One technique they developed is an eco-friendly agronomic technique called 'direct seeding' of rice paddies. Here is how direct seeding works. In India, rice is traditionally cultivated by sowing seeds in a small nursery where they germinate into seedlings. The seedlings are then manually transferred into the main field and grown with four to five inches of water at the base of the crop for the first six to eight weeks, mainly to prevent weed growth. Direct seeding, in contrast, avoids three basic water-intensive operations—puddling (compacting the soil to reduce water leakage), transplanting, and growing in standing water—thereby saving on average about 30 percent of the usual water requirement in paddy cultivation, or approximately 900 kilolitres (238,000 gallons) of water per acre. In addition, direct seeding also cuts greenhouse gas emissions by 70 percent.[51] In essence, direct seeding helps farmers increase their yields while reducing their water input and saving time. While experimenting with direct seeding, the PepsiCo India team members relied heavily on jugaad. For instance, rather than designing their direct sowing machine from scratch, they repurposed an imported peanut planter powered by a normal tractor—and had their repurposed machine prototyped and built by a small local manufacturer.

Impressed by the success of the direct seeding experiment, PepsiCo's management picked up this grassroots innovation and piloted it on a larger scale across a few Indian states over a three-year period. The pilot was a huge success—farmers were raving about the results, which generated cost savings of more than

₹ 1500 ($33) per acre, thus raising net revenue/return per acre. In 2010 alone, through direct seeding, PepsiCo India saved more than 700 crore litres of water, which helped make it *water positive* in India—meaning that the company was saving more water through frugal initiatives such as direct seeding than it was consuming in the rest of its business.[52]

Nooyi is also fostering some healthy competition among its regional business units to encourage them to embrace the 'do more with less' principle.[53] For instance, PepsiCo's beverage plants in India generate about two-fifths of their energy input from renewable sources such as biomass and wind turbines. The jugaad example set by the PepsiCo India team is serving as inspiration for—and is being replicated in—other regions, including in the US, where PepsiCo Frito-Lay's Casa Grande, Arizona facility has achieved 'near net zero' status, running primarily on renewable energy sources and recycled water while producing nearly zero landfill waste.[54]

In the end, PepsiCo's pursuit of efficient and responsible use of resources is what allows the company to deliver on its Performance with Purpose promise, using jugaad principles. As Nooyi told us: 'We need to bring a frugal mindset to the US, which is going to face scarcity of all sorts in coming decades. PepsiCo and other US companies need some jugaad thinking to come up with economical and healthy solutions that deliver better value to our customers—and do so in a responsible way.'

By reframing scarcity as an opportunity to drive disruptive innovation—a key attribute of jugaad thinking—Nooyi is positioning PepsiCo for sustainable success in a global economy characterized by eco-aware, frugal, and health-conscious consumers. Indeed, if Nooyi's experiment with 'doing more with less' succeeds, PepsiCo's efficient business model will revolutionize the global food and beverage sector for many years to come.

Conclusion

As we've seen, because emerging markets face scarcity on a grand scale and across the board, jugaad innovators who operate within them are masters of frugality and the art of doing more with less. But large companies are facing such scarcity too—as they confront dwindling natural resources and value conscious and demanding consumers. To survive in this dawning age of austerity and scarcity, corporate leaders need to learn from jugaad innovators like Gustavo Grobocopatel of Los Grobo (Argentina) and Sunil Mittal of Bharti Airtel (India) how to get more from less by applying frugality in every link of the value chain. Corporate leaders can also learn from Jane Chen (Embrace) and Ravi Pandit (KPIT Cummins) how to help their customers get more value for less cost by offering them quality products and services at very affordable prices.

Practising frugality, however, requires a fundamental shift in how leaders of large companies think and operate. Corporate leaders need to eschew their traditional 'bigger is better' R&D approach. They need to radically overhaul their R&D structure and incentives systems to create and sustain a frugal *culture* in their organization that espouses 'doing more with less' as its core value—just as Indra Nooyi is doing at PepsiCo.

Jugaad innovators aren't only focused on frugality, however, and on responding to adversity. To do more with less and turn adversity into opportunity, they also draw on another key principle of the jugaad approach: thinking and acting flexibly.

Chapter 4

Principle Three: Think and Act Flexibly

'One cannot alter a condition with the same mindset that created it in the first place.'

—ALBERT EINSTEIN

With an estimated 6.2 crore diabetics—a statistic expected to increase to 10 crore by 2030—India now has the second largest number of people with diabetes in the world after China.[1] The disease is being diagnosed particularly frequently in Indian villages, where 70 percent of Indians live. One person who has successfully responded to this alarming trend is Dr V. Mohan, a globally renowned diabetes expert and Chairman of Dr Mohan's Diabetes Specialities Centre based in Chennai, the capital of the South Indian state of Tamil Nadu. Dr Mohan is also Director of the Madras Diabetes Research Foundation, also based in Chennai.

Dr Mohan operates a mobile tele-medicine clinic in some of the remotest villages of Tamil Nadu. Care for rural patients is provided by a network of primarily urban doctors who are supported by rural technicians and grassroots community healthcare workers. These technicians travel in a van equipped with tele-medicine technologies that permit transmission of diagnostic tests via satellite uplink even in areas too remote for internet connectivity. Dr Mohan and other doctors sitting in their offices in Chennai can see and communicate remotely in real time with patients through video monitors, while tests conducted in the van, such as retinal scans, are transmitted within seconds for immediate evaluation.

'Why should patients come to the doctor when it could be the other way around?' Dr Mohan explains. 'I asked myself: What if I can come up with a service that allows physicians to *remotely* consult patients without either group having to travel?'[2]

Turning this vision into reality required Dr Mohan to improvise new solutions to the various obstacles he faced along the way. For instance, he decided *not* to use regular doctors and nurses to run most of the operations in his mobile clinic. Doctors and city technicians are expensive; employing many of them in his van would have strained his frugal business model. Even if he could bring in healthcare providers from the city, retaining them would be hard. So Dr Mohan recruited young people from small towns with only a high school education (or less) and gave them highly focused training so they could carry out specific functions, such as using the equipment in his van. Meanwhile, Dr Mohan also trained local people in villages to provide simple follow-up care for his diabetes patients. They could, for example, go from home to home enquiring whether a patient is reducing daily sugar intake or has visited the van for follow-up care. Because Dr Mohan could not afford to pay these young people for their work, he instead convinced them to volunteer by appealing to their sense of goodwill for the community and their pride in being able to help. To that end, he gave them crisp white uniforms as well as formal recognition, including the title 'Dr Mohan's Diabetes Ambassador'. All these actions enhanced their status in their communities and boosted their employability. Finally, unlike other health organizations that have access to expensive communications technology from vendors like Nokia and Cisco, Dr Mohan had to improvise a way to equip his van with cost-effective communication capability. To do so, he partnered with the Indian Space Research Organization (ISRO) which has produced and launched dozens of communication satellites for socially relevant applications—to get free satellite communications for his ingenious tele-medicine service in remote areas where neither mobile nor wireless services are available.

Jugaad innovators like Dr Mohan constantly employ flexible thinking and action in response to the seemingly insurmountable problems they face in their economies: they are constantly experimenting and improvising solutions to the obstacles they frequently face, and adapting their strategies to new contingencies as they arise. In this chapter, we delve into the minds of jugaad innovators to understand why and how they think and act flexibly. We then examine what constrains large companies from thinking and acting flexibly—despite the growing pressure to do so—and what they stand to gain by overcoming such constraints. We end the chapter with a discussion of how large companies can adopt such flexibility in their own innovation initiatives.

Jugaad Innovators Adapt to Survive

Anyone who has attempted to negotiate street traffic in India (or in any other emerging market, for that matter) knows instinctively the importance of thinking and acting flexibly. The sheer unpredictability and diversity of life on the road demands such flexibility. Vehicles come in all shapes and sizes and travel at a range of speeds. Animals and pedestrians compete with buses, trucks, cars, scooters, and cycles. The terrain can be of varying quality and topography: roads, such as they are, may be dug up or undergoing repairs. Vehicles are likely to veer in and out of lanes (if there are any), and all this with the liberal aid of horns (though not necessarily with any other type of signalling). Paradoxically, a linear and orderly approach to driving in such an environment would lead to an accident. The only way to survive is, ironically, to accept the unpredictability of everyone else on the road and to respond by being similarly adaptable—in both thoughts and actions.

As with the roads, so too with the economic environment in emerging markets. The sheer diversity, volatility, and unpredictability of economic life in emerging markets demands flexibility on the part of jugaad innovators. It demands that they think out of the box, experiment, and improvise: they must either adapt or die. In many ways, this diversity, volatility, and unpredictability also *enables* flexible thinking and action on the part of jugaad innovators.

Through our interactions with jugaad innovators, we have identified four crucial ways in which they think and act flexibly in response to the environment they face. We explore each of these in detail.

JUGAAD INNOVATORS THINK THE UNTHINKABLE

There is mind-boggling diversity in emerging economies. The heterogeneity of populations in these markets demands unconventional, nonlinear thinking. Traditional approaches and cookie-cutter solutions to complex challenges are unlikely to work. Jugaad innovators therefore dare to challenge many ingrained beliefs and turn conventional wisdom on its head. Dr Mohan, for instance, questioned a convention of the medical industry. Why should patients come to visit the doctor, when it can be the other way around? That radical question then led him to consider an original solution that allows physicians to remotely consult patients without *either* party having to travel.

Harish Hande is another jugaad entrepreneur who dared to think the unthinkable, and succeeded. Hande, who founded India's Solar Electric Light Company (SELCO) in 1995, set out to provide solar energy to the rural poor of India with the intention of debunking three popular myths: (1) poor people cannot afford sustainable technologies, (2) poor people cannot maintain sustainable technologies, and (3) social ventures cannot be run as commercial entities.[3] Having installed his solar energy solution in more than 125,000 rural households in India, Hande has successfully busted these three myths by demonstrating his flexible thinking in three particular areas: (1) financing his business, (2) pricing his services, and (3) distributing and maintaining his solution.

Take financing: Hande started his business in 1995 with very little seed money, as conservative banks and cautious venture capitalists deemed his unproven business model in an unproven industry (solar energy) too risky. Undeterred, Hande bootstrapped SELCO with his own money—₹ 1,500, to be precise. With it he produced his first solar home lighting system, which he then sold. With the revenues, he then made additional systems, which he also sold, and so on.

Hande, however, soon hit a wall. As he penetrated deeper into rural areas of India, he learned that his potential consumers—many of whom earn less than ₹ 50 a day—could not afford the up-front costs of buying and installing his solar lighting systems. Even if these systems somehow got installed, there was no economical way for him to maintain them for rural consumers scattered across multiple villages. To overcome these twin problems, Hande applied flexible thinking to improvise a truly creative solution that involved a network of small-scale entrepreneurs in rural communities. These grassroots entrepreneurs would own and maintain the solar panels as well as the batteries they could charge in their stores. The entrepreneurs would then rent out the batteries to end consumers daily on a pay-per-use basis—and collect payment every day. This ingenious 'just-in-time' energy distribution model made SELCO's solution affordable and accessible to scores of rural customers who couldn't make an up-front investment in SELCO's solution. These customers included mom and pop store owners, small-scale farmers, and women who worked from home. SELCO's approach also created an incentive for local entrepreneurs to distribute and maintain the equipment over time. Using this approach, SELCO was able to scale up the distribution of its solar lighting system to over 125,000 households within a few years. It now aims to serve 2 lakh households by 2013.[4] For thinking the unthinkable—that is, that poor people can indeed afford and maintain renewable energy solutions—Hande was awarded the World Economic Forum's Social Entrepreneur Award in 2007 and, in 2011, the Ramon Magsaysay Award, considered by many to be Asia's Nobel Prize.

Jugaad Innovators Don't Plan—They Improvise

Emerging markets are characterized by high volatility. Economic circumstances are constantly changing. Growth rates are often in double digits, and the competitive landscape is often shifting. New laws and regulations are constantly being put into place, and policy is constantly evolving. So jugaad innovators need to experiment as they go along and be willing to try multiple options, rather than adopting one approach at the start and sticking to it thereafter. Unlike their counterparts in Silicon Valley, jugaad innovators do not attempt to work everything out in advance or rely on a business plan to determine the mid- to long-term roadmap for their new ventures. Instead, they improvise their next course of action as circumstances change, and they do so from within a framework of deep knowledge and passion. Their approach is in fact more akin to a jazz band than to an orchestra: everything is improvised, fluid, and dynamic. As such, their strategies are organic and emergent rather than predetermined. Jugaad innovators' flexible thinking—their ability to improvise—serves them especially well when confronted with adversity.

Given their propensity for improvisation, jugaad innovators don't rely on forecasting tools like scenario planning, as many companies do, to assess future risks. They believe in Murphy's Law—anything that can go wrong will go wrong—so what's the point of anticipating every single obstacle that might appear down the road? Jugaad innovators don't have a Plan B, let alone a Plan C. Rather, when confronted with an unexpected hindrance, they rely on their innate ability to improvise an effective solution to overcome it, given the circumstances at that time.

A good example is that of Tata Motors, the maker of the ₹ 1 lakh Nano car. The Nano was the brainchild of Ratan Tata, chairman of the Tata Group (Tata Motors' parent company), who conceived it as an affordable, comfortable, and safe alternative to the perilous two wheelers that often carry entire families on Indian roads. In 2006, Tata Motors announced that the Nano would be manufactured in Singur, West Bengal, an east-Indian state. The factory was to be built on land acquired from farmers by the state government in a bid to boost local industry. Tata Motors intended to roll out its first Nanos from the Singur plant in late October 2008.

In 2007, however, local farmers began protesting against the acquisition of land for the factory. The dispute rapidly escalated into a political issue—and caught Tata Motors off guard. As the protests intensified through 2008, Ravi Kant, then Managing Director of Tata Motors (and later its Non-Executive Vice Chairman) made a bold decision. He set aside his firm's prior manufacturing plans and swiftly shifted the production of the Nano to Sanand, in the investor-friendly state of Gujarat, on the other side of the country. He didn't hire a management consultant to advise him on the move; he just trusted his instinct that this was the right thing to do, given the circumstances.[5] In just fourteen months (compared to the expected twenty-eight months for the Singur plant), Tata Motors built a new factory in Sanand, Gujarat. The new factory began production of Nanos in June 2010.[6]

One year later, Ravi Kant and his team had to demonstrate the ability to adapt to rapidly changing circumstances yet again: the Nanos weren't selling as well as expected. Monthly sales had fallen well below the optimistic forecast of twenty thousand units. Rather than being disappointed by the Nano's lacklustre performance, Tata Motors' leadership used this early market feedback to improvise a plan to shore up sales. Ratan Tata originally envisioned a distributed supply chain model whereby Tata Motors would dispatch flat packs to local entrepreneurs across the country, who would do the final assembly of Nanos close to customers—thus creating gainful employment in local communities. With flagging sales, however, this original vision had to be revised: Tata Motors' executives went back to the drawing board and quickly revamped Nano's logistics network to a more straightforward one, which involved manufacture and assembly at one site in Gujarat, and distribution through a traditional dealer network throughout the country. But again Tata Motors hit a snag: rural customers—such as farmers— were not venturing into Tata Motors' showrooms in small towns. Among other things, they felt intimidated by dealers dressed in suits and ties.

This setback led Tata Motors' management to redesign their rural showrooms to make them more informal—for example by staffing them with casually attired salesmen who could pitch the Nano to Indian farmers over a cup of *chai*. Tata Motors also launched a nationwide TV campaign and began offering consumer financing at highly attractive rates to lure frugal Indian consumers. By constantly adapting and refining its business model—and implementing changes within weeks, not months—Tata Motors invigorated sales of the Nano, which, although still lower than expected, are gradually beginning to pick up.[7] Indeed, it is very likely that the future success of the car will depend on more such quick adaptation and flexible thinking by the managers of Tata Motors.

JUGAAD INNOVATORS EXPERIMENT WITH MULTIPLE WAYS TO REACH A GOAL

Unpredictability is the norm in emerging markets. Because of diversity and rapid change, it is hard to predict how consumers will respond to new products and services—and how new business strategies will perform in, say, rural markets. Jugaad innovators may have a single-minded vision of where they want to get to, but they must be willing to try different paths to get there. Specifically, they must be willing to keep experimenting in order to attain their goals—and they must be flexible enough to quickly switch from one path to another along the way.

Dr Mohan, for instance, experimented with a number of different ways to frugally yet effectively engage rural communities both as consumers (patients) and employees. When he first sent his expensive technicians from his city hospital to work in remote villages, he found that these technicians—although highly competent—would soon leave, wanting to return to city life. Learning this, he developed a training curriculum in his city hospital to impart to young men and women from villages the basic skills they need as healthcare workers. After about three months, these newly trained healthcare professionals would return to their rural homes, where they were more likely to want to remain. This in turn helped reduce costs and turnover in Dr Mohan's model. Dr Mohan had a similar experience with his attempts to work with non-traditional partners to develop a cost-effective tele-medicine platform. Although he initially contemplated partnering with more typical—and expensive—technology providers, Dr Mohan eventually linked up with ISRO, which provides his roaming tele-medicine van with a free satellite uplink to his clinic in the city of Chennai.

JUGAAD INNOVATORS ACT WITH SPEED AND AGILITY

In emerging markets, new threats and opportunities can emerge from out of the blue. This forces jugaad innovators to not only think but also *act* flexibly. By demonstrating agility, jugaad innovators can deal with unanticipated challenges faster and seize unexpected opportunities—such as changing customer needs—more swiftly than their competitors. Zhang Ruimin is one such jugaad innovator who thinks *and* acts quickly.

Zhang, introduced in Chapter 1, is the CEO of Haier, a Chinese consumer goods company that is making appliance makers like GE and Whirlpool nervous. Under Zhang's leadership, Haier has, in the space of a decade, made huge inroads into North American and European markets by selling quality appliances at lower prices than those of Western suppliers like Whirlpool and GE. Armed with its 'value for money' strategy, Haier is disrupting the consumer goods market not only in mainstream segments like air-conditioners and washing machines, but also in niche segments like wine coolers. For instance, Haier launched a $704 (₹ 35,200) wine cooler that is less than half the cost of industry leader La Sommelière's product. Within two years of this launch, Haier has grown the market by a whopping 10,000 percent and now controls 60 percent of the US market by value.[8] By leveraging its value for money strategy, Haier has also rapidly established a strong presence in the Indian home appliances market, where it commands 8 percent of market share. In coming years, Haier aims to grow its Indian market share to at least 10 percent and achieve ₹ 4,500 crore in revenue and become one of the top five brands in India by 2014.[9]

What makes Haier so innovative is not just its cool products, but also its flexible organizational structure. Zhang believes that in the internet era, appliance makers like Haier need to shift from mass production to mass customization—and start thinking and acting nimbly, as Facebook and Google do. As Zhang explains: 'The focus on promoting your cost or price advantage has shifted to a focus on service differentiation, mostly centring on customer experience.'[10]

To sense and respond to his retail customers' needs faster than rivals can, Zhang came up with a jugaad innovation: he radically redesigned Haier's organization, which currently employs over fifty thousand people worldwide. Specifically, he replaced Haier's organizational pyramid with a loosely coupled network of more than four thousand self-managed, cross-functional units (including R&D, supply chain, sales, and marketing) that interact directly with customers and autonomously make decisions. Each unit operates as an independent profit centre and is evaluated as such. Zhang refers to this organizational innovation—which empowers autonomous units of frontline workers to sense and respond to consumer demand—as 'making a big company small'— that is, allowing a big company like Haier to maintain the unique flexibility of a small start-up.[11] To make this bottom-up, customer-centric organizational structure work, Zhang shifted the role of managers from being commanders and supervisors into being supporters and providers who ensure that the independent units have the resources they need to meet customer demand as promptly as possible. He doesn't want managers to be in charge, as they aren't directly in touch with customers.

Haier's organizational agility enables it to react swiftly to rapidly changing—or unexpected—customer needs, and to innovate faster, better, and cheaper than its rivals. For instance, in China, any call placed to Haier's national customer service centre is answered within three rings and a technician is dispatched to your house within three hours—even on Sundays. A few years back, one such call came from a farmer in a remote village in Sichuan province who complained about the constantly clogged drainpipe in his washing machine. The Haier technician who went to investigate found that that the farmer was using the machine to wash the mud off his freshly harvested potatoes; it was this mud that was causing the clogging. 'Most companies would react by saying "This machine is not designed for this purpose",' explains Philip Carmichael, Haier's president, Asia-Pacific, 'but Haier's approach was to say, "This guy (farmer) isn't the only one who's tried to wash potatoes. Is there a way to adapt this product to this requirement? Maybe we can make a machine that actually washes potatoes and clothes"'.[12]

Haier's flexible thinking was spot on: it turns out that crores of farmers across China routinely use their washing machines to clean their vegetables. Sensing a big market opportunity, Haier's cross-functional teams quickly acted on their intuition by developing a washing machine with larger pipes that could also handle vegetables. The product was a big hit among farmers. But Haier's creative teams didn't stop there. They also invented a washing machine that can *peel* potatoes and even designed a model for herders in Inner Mongolia and the Tibetan Plateau to help churn yak milk into butter! These inventions eventually inspired Haier to introduce, in 2009, a washing machine able to wash clothes *without* detergent. That groundbreaking innovation helped propel Haier to the number one position in the laundry equipment market not only in China, but also around the world.[13]

Jugaad innovators—such as Haier's employees—are highly adaptable. They are capable of thinking on their feet and acting with great agility. Being nimble-minded and nimble-footed serves them well in the context of emerging markets which are characterized by extreme unpredictability. Corporate leaders confronted with increasing volatility and uncertainty in their own business environment must also learn to think and act flexibly—but, as we discuss next, that's easier said than done.

What Makes Large Firms So Inflexible?

Being flexible and coming up with new business models—as Dr Mohan, Harish Hande, Ratan Tata, and Zhang Ruimin have done—is increasingly critical for firms. However, many companies continue to operate their businesses as usual, paying little attention to the impending upheaval in their home environments. We believe that large firms' inability to think and act flexibly in response to change has five chief causes: complacency; binary logic; an aversion to risk; disengaged employees; and rigid, time-consuming product development processes. Let's look at each in detail.

COMPLACENCY

As we discussed in Chapter 2, according to Carol Dweck, a professor of psychology at Stanford University, individuals typically have one of two mindsets:[14]

- A fixed mindset—that is, they believe their qualities and others' are carved in stone
- A growth mindset—that is, they believe that their basic qualities can be nurtured and improved through effort[15]

Every corporation too has one of these mindsets, and many large corporations tend to suffer from the fixed type. Such a rigid mindset often comes from structured innovation processes and, ironically, past successes, which can breed complacency and sow the seeds of failure. Specifically, the complacency that comes from past successes blinds companies to the fact that every challenge is unique and requires a different approach for success. Consequently, when faced with new challenges, companies tend to reapply 'tried and true' solutions rather than develop radically new ones. As Prasad Kaipa, a CEO coach and leadership expert explains, in doing so, 'The same core competence that made Western companies so successful in the early stages of their life cycle eventually also becomes their Achilles' heel—or their "core incompetence" that eventually brings them down'.[16]

Shashank Samant, President of GlobalLogic, a company that provides R&D services to large technology vendors, observes that:

'Many large tech firms have become victims of their own success: they first rose to success by riding the wave of one major technology cycle—which typically lasts seven to eight years—but they don't know how to ride the next wave. They fail to understand that the innovation born out of the previous cycle isn't relevant in the new emerging cycle: they are as reluctant to go back to the drawing board and invent next-generation solutions as they are unwilling to unlearn their past generation best practises. The bad news is that technology cycles are now getting shorter and shorter—forcing incumbents to unlearn and relearn even faster.'[17]

GlobalLogic recently partnered with a US tech company to overhaul its 15-year-old product, which was invented before the web era. This technically superior product was very successful in its early years but eventually lost its edge when younger users, who prefer the cleaner interface of Facebook and Google, deemed its user interface clunky. The company hired GlobalLogic to give its product a facelift so that it would appeal to a new generation of users. GlobalLogic's developer team—made up of twenty- and thirty-something software programmers from India and Ukraine—designed a user interface that was as easy to use as Facebook's. Their demo impressed top managers of the US tech firm. However, one middle manager anxiously raised his hand and said: 'This new user interface looks great. But it doesn't comply with our 15-year-old software development standard back in the US.' He didn't realize that the very purpose of partnering with the IT outsourcer *was to get rid of that clunky old standard* and introduce a new one fit for the 21 century. In the end, the tech company stuck to its old user interface—forgoing an opportunity to reinvent its product for adoption by Generation Y and Z users. Complacency often leads to an inability to get rid of old thinking patterns and entrenched behaviors. This often sounds the death knell for individuals and organizations, especially when they are confronted with complexity.

BINARY LOGIC

Large companies and their leaders often operate in a black-and-white world that confers a sense of predictability on things. Competitors are 'bad' and partners are 'good'. Regulations are typically 'bad for business', whereas protectionist policies are 'good'. And although some companies may like 'doing good' as part of their corporate social responsibility (CSR) initiatives, they worry primarily about 'doing well' in their core for-profit businesses. Such binary thinking—anchored in deep-seated assumptions—prevents companies from reconciling polarities, a process that could, ironically, yield disruptive innovation. Doreen Lorenzo, President of frog, a global design and innovation consultancy, points out: 'We are entering a 'gray world' where things are no longer black or white—as yesterday's competitors can become tomorrow's partners—but exist in multiple shades of gray. So many shades can be disconcerting at first, but then you realize they represent as many opportunities for disruptive innovation.'[18]

An instance in which shades of gray were at first disconcerting but were later recognized as an opportunity is the case of big pharmaceutical companies. Many Western pharmaceutical companies have traditionally ignored the low-income segments in emerging markets because these consumers were too poor to afford their drugs. But these companies failed to adapt to changing circumstances and recognize a truth we pointed out in Chapter 3: although the poor are low earners, they are also high *yearners*—a counter-intuitive fact of life in emerging economies.[19] Unlike Harish Hande of SELCO, in the past Big Pharma didn't take the time to experiment with for-profit business models that would allow them to cost-effectively manufacture and deliver drugs to the 400 crore low-income consumers worldwide.[20] Only now, as Western markets have become saturated and increasingly regulated, is Big Pharma scrambling to find innovative ways to reap the 'fortune at the bottom of the economic pyramid'—a fortune that continues to elude them.[21]

RISK AVERSION

Many large companies do not attempt to develop radically new products, as they are afraid that these products will cannibalize the market for their existing offerings. Even if they do develop such products, many companies fail to commercialize them, even as nimble competitors encroach on their core markets. This is such a common phenomenon that Clayton Christensen of Harvard Business School has dubbed it the 'innovator's dilemma'.[22] This problem is compounded by the fact that the tenure of CEOs is shrinking, forcing them to deliver short-term results rather than drive long-term transformational changes. For instance, the average tenure of the CEO of a hospital is less than six years—not enough time to invest in bold innovations like Dr Mohan's initiative, which may take several years to show results.[23]

Perhaps the most obvious example of the 'innovator's dilemma' is Kodak. Over a ninety-year period, the company succeeded by selling cheap analog cameras and making most of its revenues from selling and processing photographic film. Even though Kodak actually invented the digital camera, it failed to adapt its old business model, suited for the analog world, to the world of digital cameras, a world in which users could easily print their photographs at home or store and distribute them digitally, online. Similar rigidities in thinking and action—shaped by risk aversion—are responsible for the failure, if not the actual demise, of brick-and-mortar book retailers like Borders in the face of the breakthrough business models of online retailers like Amazon.com.

DISENGAGED EMPLOYEES

Some large companies dabble in 'intrapreneurship' (also known as 'skunkworks') and 'jamming'—initiatives that encourage employees to think flexibly and come up with unconventional ideas for new products or processes. Unfortunately, the bright ideas that come from these initiatives are rarely implemented, because of either management's lack of commitment to them or their fear of cannibalization. Worse, employees may even be punished when their ideas fail commercially. As a result, employees grow cynical or fearful: they begin to feel that their flexible thinking is underappreciated, and they start playing it safe. All this further encourages groupthink, and nobody dares to question or change the status quo. Over time, everyone is content with incrementally innovating existing offerings, rather than investing time and effort in truly disruptive innovation. Employee disengagement grows and cripples the firm's innovation engine.

In support of this view, a Gallup survey in late 2011 found that only 29 percent of American workers feel engaged in their jobs, meaning only 29 percent work with passion, feel their input is appreciated, and have a deep connection to their company. A full 52 percent say they don't feel engaged in their jobs. Most worrisome of all, the remaining 19 percent say they are actively disengaged.[24] In India, only 37 percent of employees in large corporations feel engaged at work. This widespread employee disaffection is both the symptom and the cause of the rigid, inflexible approach to innovation in many large firms.

RIGID, TIME-CONSUMING PRODUCT DEVELOPMENT PROCESSES

Of course, several large companies do think flexibly—and come up with truly innovative ideas. But even these companies struggle to commercialize their trailblazing ideas fast enough, for two reasons. First, they take a long time to conduct market research to validate their idea and an equally long time planning and developing a product to get it 'right'. Second, they are paralyzed by rigid go-to-market processes like Six Sigma and the fact that departments such as R&D and marketing, whose cooperation is needed for innovation, tend to work independently of each other in corporate silos. Eric Schmidt, Google's executive chairman, points out that employees who work too long at any company get inculcated in a repeatable development process that eventually becomes too rigid and stifles their creativity and innovation. Schmidt says: 'Real innovation is hard to do when you have a process culture with Six Sigma (i.e., extremely low defect manufacturing). Risk management is around the process, keeping it the same.'[25]

In a fast-moving business environment that is ripe with ambiguity, where customer needs shift overnight and product life cycles get truncated by aggressive competitors, it's not enough to think flexibly—companies must also *act* flexibly. Tim Harford notes in his book *Adapt*: 'The world has become far too unpredictable and profoundly complex... We must adapt—improvise rather than plan, work from the bottom up rather than the top down, and take baby steps rather than great leaps forward.'[26] For instance, it could take Western cellphone makers like Motorola many months to plan, develop, and launch what often is an 'over-engineered' cellphone. In contrast, agile Chinese and Indian rivals like HTC, Huawei, and Spice rely on rapid experimentation: they crank out 'good-enough' models within *weeks* and keep improving their design with each subsequent model using real-time market feedback.[27] The secret weapon of these Asian innovators is their organizational flexibility. HTC, Huawei, and Spice routinely employ cross-functional development teams that eliminate communication gaps among the key players responsible for product development and launch—much like Haier, as discussed earlier. Similarly, Google has organized itself as a flexible and dynamic network of small teams that can quickly react to market needs—by building and launching new products in rapid-fire fashion. '[At Google] we don't have a two-year plan. We have a next week and a next quarter plan', explains Eric Schmidt.[28]

Learn to Improvise

To break free from the constraints that keep companies inflexible—complacency, binary thinking, risk aversion, disengaged employees, and rigid processes—these companies must learn to improvise, experiment, and adapt their business models to changing circumstances. But breaking free is not easy: pressures to deliver strong short-term quarterly results often deter management from thinking radically. Still, there are many strategies that large companies—knee deep in traditional, structured processes and approaches to innovation—can employ to cultivate and sustain flexible thinking and action.

BREAK RULES AND SHIFT VALUES WHEN NECESSARY

Even conventional beliefs and values have a shelf life: there is nothing eternally wise about them. Breakthrough innovation occurs when commonly held beliefs and values are challenged, not reinforced. For instance, in many companies, flexible thinking is sacrificed at the altar of 'corporate values'. These companies often fail to realize that their corporate values *have lost their value* as the times have changed—and need to be overhauled to reflect new market realities and major societal shifts. In July 2003, to prevent such ossification from setting in, IBM's then CEO Sam Palmisano organized 'Values Jam'—a three-day long online brainstorming session in which all employees were invited to renew and update IBM's century-old value system.[29] This collaborative exercise re-contextualized the very notion of innovation—IBM's core value—as something measured not by the number of patents filed or products shipped but by the impact that IBM makes on society. This ability to reassess where the company stands and this willingness to change its direction led IBM to embark on its Smart Planet initiative, which uses technology to build sustainable communities worldwide.[30]

DON'T LET INFLEXIBLE INVESTORS AND CUSTOMERS DICTATE YOUR INNOVATION AGENDA

Since external stakeholders often tend to be conservative or lack the perspective to appreciate vision or foresight, it is probably best not to seek their validation for bold new products and services. Recall what Henry Ford famously said: 'If I had asked customers what they wanted, they would have said "faster horses"'. More recently, Apple didn't do extensive market surveys to come up with the iPad. This may have been just as well, given that many consumers, analysts, and media experts were convinced that there was no market for the product. Yet the iPad turned out to be a breakthrough innovation now eagerly copied by Apple's rivals.[31]

CREATE TIME AND SPACE FOR EMPLOYEES TO IMPROVISE AND EXPERIMENT

Companies can hardly expect employees to think flexibly while they maintain their regular routine and operate in their usual work environment. To be able to think and act flexibly, employees need dedicated time and an inspiring space to experiment with new ideas. Google is a good example of a company that allows employees ample time for improvisation. It employs a 70/20/10 model for organizing work: its employees spend 70 percent of their time on core business tasks, 20 percent on related projects, and 10 percent on projects totally unrelated to their core work. Many of Google's commercially successful innovations such as Google Maps and Google Mail were developed by employees during the 20 percent of the time spent outside their day-to-day activities—when they were able to unleash their outside-the-box thinking.[32]

Recognizing the company could do still more to encourage such creative thinking, Google launched a new experimental incubator in January 2011 dedicated to building mobile, social, and location-based applications. The incubator is located in San Francisco—an hour away from Google Headquarters in Mountain View—and operates with a small team of twenty people empowered to think flexibly and to 'hatch new start-ups' in Google. Heading the team is John Hanke, who ran Google Maps for six years. 'Our goal will be to pump out prototypes quickly and see what sticks', says Hanke. Of course, many of the ventures conceived at this incubator will fail, but some will succeed and evolve into billion-dollar businesses for Google. By giving its employees a safe place to experiment—and fail—Google can sustain the flexible thinking that leads to truly breakthrough innovation.[33]

V. R. Ferose, the young and dynamic Managing Director of SAP Labs India, is also creating space and time for his 4,000 employees—whose average age is a mere 29 years—to experiment and improvise. Since he took over in April 2010, Ferose has turned SAP Labs India's hierarchical, 'top-heavy' corporate culture upside down by enabling bottom-up creativity and innovation to flourish. He has empowered all his employees to experiment with bold new ideas *during their work time*, a move that not only directly and positively impacts SAP's core business but also improves their working conditions and morale. Ferose is an unconventional thinker: he believes that it is *not* the CEO's job to find ways to make his or her employees happier; the employees *already* know what will make them happy; the CEO's job is to give employees the freedom to test and deploy their own solutions that will make them happier at work.[34] Motivated by Ferose's participative leadership style, many self-organized teams at SAP Labs India have tested and implemented dozens of innovative solutions to boost productivity. For instance, one small team piloted and rolled out a system to expedite expense reimbursement: today, if an employee at SAP Labs India files an expense claim in the morning, he or she is reimbursed on the afternoon of the same day. Another team of employees designed and deployed a crèche for working mothers. Impressively, most of these projects were completed within one week by reusing existing resources—thus requiring no additional budget. Ferose has reaped big rewards by encouraging frugal and flexible grassroots experimentation of novel ideas at SAP Labs India: within two years of taking over, attrition has plummeted from 15.3 percent to 10.1 percent and the India lab now ranks #1 in employee satisfaction within SAP's global network of 15 R&D labs. Not surprisingly, in Dataquest-CMR's Best Employers Survey ranking, SAP Labs India has catapulted itself to #4 in a very short time.

GET OUTSIDE YOUR COMFORT ZONE TO GAIN NEW PERSPECTIVES

To truly think flexibly, managers need to be taken out of their comfort zones and exposed to new situations that challenge them to think differently. DuPont sent its senior executives to rural India, where they received a somewhat humbling revelation. None of their expensive technological solutions, designed for Western urban markets, seemed relevant to low-income Indian villagers. This experience forced these DuPont executives to go back to the drawing board and co-create with local communities a whole new set of affordable and sustainable solutions designed for fast-growing emerging markets like India.[35]

Similarly, V. R. Ferose is encouraging the 4,000 employees of SAP Labs India—primarily technical engineers—to expose themselves to new environments and situations that will challenge their existing perspectives, unleash their innate ingenuity, and accelerate their learning. Ferose believes that the most disruptive innovation don't occur inside a single domain but at the *intersection* of multiple diverse domains (such as the arts and the sciences). Hence, Ferose is encouraging his employees—especially engineers—to cultivate a *cross-disciplinary* outlook and look for inspiration beyond their individual domain of expertise. In one instance, when some employees expressed interest in brushing up on their communication skills, Ferose didn't enroll them in structured training programmes delivered in a classroom setting. Rather he sent these employees to a theater located near the campus of SAP Labs India where they learned to extemporize and become better communicators by performing in live shows that they put on.

PARTNER WITH FLEXIBLE THINKERS

Sometimes the best way to develop a new mindset is to seek inspiration from outside your company. Thus one way to nurture flexibility is to partner with other companies that are already flexible and agile. For instance, the US electronics retail giant Best Buy has deep ties with Silicon Valley start-ups that tend to innovate faster and better than the large electronics vendors that supply Best Buy. As a result, Best Buy is able to bring groundbreaking technologies to market much faster than even its large electronics suppliers can. For instance, after getting an early look at Sling Media's Slingbox (a technology that lets consumers pipe TV programming from their homes to their mobile devices wherever they are), Best Buy brought this innovation to market months ahead of its competition.[36]

IBM is another company that partners with nimble thinkers. Although it employs three thousand in-house research scientists and engineers and files more patents annually than any other company, IBM has nevertheless opened 'collaboratories' in leading universities worldwide—including a collaboratory for 'service science' at the Indian School of Business (ISB). In these collaboratories, IBM technologists work closely with agile-minded university researchers to co-create cutting-edge technologies. These technologies include smart electricity grids, resilient transportation networks, and cost-effective healthcare delivery solutions with the potential to have a big social and economic impact globally.[37]

EXPERIMENT WITH MULTIPLE BUSINESS MODELS

Often companies become too attached to a successful business model and find it nearly impossible to let go of it, let alone to explore alternative options. But competition can spring from unexpected corners and disrupt your business model overnight. Flexible thinkers keep all options open—and experiment with multiple business models simultaneously. For example, Amazon.com, aware of the potential for its own online model to be disrupted by digital e-readers, has been flexible in developing and promoting a new business model around its own e-reader, the Kindle, while maintaining its dominance in online retailing.[38] Similarly, while rapidly expanding its network of brick-and-mortar branches across India, YES BANK is also experimenting with 'virtual' banking models using mobile technologies (see Chapter 5 for a detailed case study of YES BANK). Similarly, to effectively promote its low-cost products like ChotuKool aimed at the BOP market, Godrej has eschewed its traditional top-down distribution model—that relies on large retailers—and is experimenting with 'bottom up' sales and distribution models anchored by grassroots partnerships with microfinance organizations and rural entrepreneurs.

FAIL CHEAP, FAIL FAST, FAIL OFTEN

A corollary of the willingness of jugaad innovators to continually experiment is their willingness to fail cheap, fail fast, and fail often. Fernando Fabre, president of Endeavor, a global non-profit that supports high-impact entrepreneurs from emerging markets, highlights the fact that jugaad entrepreneurs typically do not take *large* risks. Based on a detailed study it conducted on 55 high-impact entrepreneurs across 11 countries, Endeavor found that, unlike Silicon Valley entrepreneurs—who, backed with venture capital, go for broke (it's either the next Facebook or it's not worth doing)—emerging market entrepreneurs start with what they have (not much) and who they know (friends and family). They rarely do something as rash as mortgaging their houses. Consequently, they have small initial budgets to work with—which, rather than cramping their style, forces them to experiment in a frugal manner that does not result in large losses (that is, they fail cheap). Their initial budgets also force them to change tack as soon as one means to achieving their goal shows any signs of not working (that is, they fail fast). Finally, given their willingness to try out different means to reach their goals, they are willing to do so several times over in an iterative fashion (that is, they fail often).[39]

Innovators in large firms have much to gain from adopting these practises of jugaad entrepreneurs. They can look to Google and Best Buy for inspiration. At Google, failure is widely celebrated—especially if you fail fast and cheap. For instance, in June 2011 Google pulled the plug on two high-profile projects—Google Health and Google PowerMeter—which were launched, respectively, in May 2008 and February 2009. The company mentioned its 'inability to scale' as the main reason to shut down these two projects.[40] Similarly, in early 2011, Best Buy shut down its big-box stores in China a mere five years after entering the country—citing stronger-than-expected local competition and the fact that its Westernized store format failed to appeal to Chinese consumers. 'We experimented with a new approach in China,' explains Kal Patel, former president of Best Buy's business in Asia. 'It was worth trying—given the sheer size of the Chinese consumer market. But it didn't work—so we pulled the plug before we incurred too much loss. We tried to be flexible in both entering and exiting China. It's vital that you fail early and cheap in unpredictable markets like China'.[41] In contrast to Best Buy, other Western manufacturers and retailers continue to pump billions of dollars into expanding their presence in China even though they are steadily losing their market share to local rivals.

Break Down Organizational Silos to Gain Speed

Flexible thinking must go hand in hand with flexible action. In today's fast-paced environment, with product life cycles growing ever shorter, companies need to break down organizational silos so they can convert breakthrough ideas into breakthrough products faster. Facebook understands this: although its subscriber base has grown to more than 80 crore users, the company still employs only about thirty-five designers, using a flat organizational structure.[42] These designers work closely with marketing executives, engineers, writers, and researchers in multi-disciplinary teams that can convert bright design ideas into new user experiences within hours. Soleio Cuervo, the second designer that Facebook CEO Mark Zuckerberg hired in 2005, says 'When I started, it was only a handful of product designers. Now, engineers work with us directly. We don't throw documents at them with specs. We all focus on the site's user experience versus the code.'[43] Likewise, V. R. Ferose, Managing Director, SAP Labs India, has set up 'AppHaus'—an open space within the campus where designers, engineers, and marketers work collaboratively and intensively on new products—compressing the whole concept-to-market cycle to 90 days (versus the 2 years it would typically take SAP to develop a new product using the linear and structured software development processes). By leveraging rapid prototyping and continuous customer feedback, the cross-functional teams that operate in the 'AppHaus' are able to innovate faster, better, and cheaper—managing each project as if they were running a startup. Recently, a small 10-member team worked around the clock in the AppHaus using limited resources to develop a social networking site called *Charitra* (short for Charity Transformation). The web site connects people with needs (NGO or volunteers driving a social cause) to people who can give (NGOs/volunteers who can donate their time, skill, or resources). Charitra, a first of a kind portal for driving positive social impact, won the IAMAI—India Digital Awards 2012 in the category of 'Best use of internet for economic and social development' and the National Award in IT Excellence in 2012 in the category of 'Use of IT for a social cause'.

Breaking down internal silos is even more critical when you are trying to quickly bring to market brilliant ideas from external sources. For example, Procter & Gamble has established a mechanism called Connect & Develop to fast-track the sourcing and commercialization of bright ideas from creative external partners. Now P&G can launch promising products within months rather than years. One such product is the Pulsonic toothbrush, which P&G co-developed with a leading Japanese firm. P&G brought this product to market twice as fast as it would have if it had tried to build the product on its own. In October 2010, Bob McDonald, CEO of P&G, set a bolder target for his company: to triple the impact of Connect & Develop so it can potentially contribute $3 billion (₹ 15,000 crore) to the company's annual sales growth. 'We want the best minds in the world to work with us to create big ideas that can touch and improve the lives of more consumers, in more parts of the world, more completely,' explains McDonald.[44]

All the News that's Fit to Digitize

The New York Times Company (NYTC) has successfully demonstrated its ability to think and act flexibly by providing dedicated space and time for its creative employees to experiment with radical new ideas. From 2007 to 2009, US newspapers saw an estimated 30 percent drop in revenues from online and offline circulation and advertising. With the Internet slowly killing print media and sucking away advertising revenues, NYTC decided to reinvent itself.[45] In January 2006, it set up an R&D department—the first ever in the media industry—staffed with thirteen members whose primary focus is to anticipate the future—and imagine the unthinkable.

The department identifies emerging consumer and technology trends, such as social media, e-readers, and mobile devices, and formulates strategies for NYTC to proactively embrace them, rather than being disrupted by them. 'It is not a product development group', clarifies Michael Zimbalist, Vice President of Research and Development Operations at NYTC, describing his team's vocation. 'It is much more focused on monitoring trends and identifying opportunities.'[46]

Foreseeing the potential of Facebook, in 2007, the R&D team launched an application to push content (including a daily quiz as bonus material) onto the social networking site. Today, the *Times* boasts far more followers than any other newspaper on Facebook and Twitter. NYTC's jugaad innovators also linked *Times* content to Google Earth maps to show locations mentioned in stories. Recently, they created Cascade—a data visualization tool that provides a time-based view of how *Times* stories and op-eds virally spread in Twitter's social universe as soon as they go live. Cascade helps NYTC identify critical information such as influential Tweeters and determine the best times of the day to publish a story online.[47]

Zimbalist strongly believes that newspapers need to go beyond the print and even basic web and use platforms such as social networks, smartphones, TV, and even smart cars of the future to reach all users. His team seeks to gain insight into how people consume media content on different platforms and helps NYTC make forays into new platforms.

Predicting an imminent future when all devices will be connected via the Internet, Zimbalist's team of jugaad innovators is working to enable readers to access the newspaper's content across multiple interconnected platforms. Here is one possible scenario that NYTC's jugaad innovators are trying to enable: In the future, a reader may start an article on the *Times* website on her desktop at office in the late afternoon, continue reading it on her iPhone as she leaves works, listen to an embedded podcast in her car on her way back home, watch an accompanying video on the HDTV in her living room, and finally forward the article to friends via her personal laptop. '[We are] investigating the ideas at the edges of today and thinking about how they're going to impact business decisions tomorrow', notes Zimbalist.

In addition to its adaptable and creative R&D team, NYTC has found other ways to encourage flexible thinking among all its four thousand employees. It now hosts internal technology and innovation challenges to encourage employees to think flexibly and come up with a jugaad way to use technology to address a vexing business issue. Recently, NYTC launched beta620.newyorktimes.com, a public website described as 'a springboard for the creativity of our software developers, journalists and product managers, who will use it as a platform to showcase new and exciting ideas for the *Times*'.[48] Its readers are strongly encouraged to provide feedback on the jugaad inventions showcased on this site.

By harnessing the ingenuity of all its employees, NYTC is building an army of jugaad innovators who can conquer the increasingly complex and unpredictable publishing world—by improvising cutting-edge solutions that can sustain the firm's growth in the highly connected web economy. In the process, NYTC is reinventing itself as a nimble, social-media savvy, multiplatform digital content provider.

Conclusion

A baffling number of uncontrollable and unknowable forces determine the future of our increasingly complex business world. In the midst of this uncertainty, long-term plans become toothless—even dangerous—and rigidly structured processes prevent us from coming up with the next big thing and responding quickly to competitive threats. To thrive in this volatile world, the ability to think and act flexibly is crucial.

In emerging markets, jugaad entrepreneurs facing daily uncertainties have become masters of flexibility: frequently challenging conventional thinking, coming up with entirely new value propositions, experimenting with various ways to achieve their goals, quickly responding to changing circumstances, improvising new solutions, and modifying their plans as they go. Large companies and their leaders have much to gain by adopting such flexibility and using it as a foil to their own more structured approach to innovation.

Jugaad innovators like Dr Mohan and Harish Hande aren't just flexible thinkers and doers, however. They are also masters of simplicity. Facing mindboggling complexity in their daily lives, they are driven to *simplify* their products and services to make them more affordable and accessible to their customers, and to simplify their customer interactions to deliver a superior user experience. Yet, jugaad innovators' simple solutions are not simplistic. Quite the contrary: adhering to Leonard da Vinci's credo that 'simplicity is the ultimate sophistication', jugaad innovators pursue what mathematicians call 'elegance' in their solutions. Keeping it simple is the subject of the next chapter.

Chapter 5

Principle Four: Keep it Simple

'I would not give a fig for the simplicity on this side of complexity, but I would give my life for the simplicity on the other side of complexity.'

—OLIVER WENDELL HOLMES

Dr Sathya Jeganathan is a pediatrician in Chengalpattu Government Medical College, a rural hospital in South India. Infant mortality used to run high at her hospital: on average, 39 out of every 1,000 infants died at birth. This statistic, unfortunately, did not differ greatly from overall neonatal mortality rates in India where, of the roughly 2.6 crore children born each year, 12 lakh die during their first four weeks of life.[1]

Wishing to decrease the infant mortality rate in her hospital, Dr Jeganathan first tried to import incubators made in the West. But she soon found the set-up cost of these incubators prohibitively high, and the staff and maintenance needed to operate the equipment unsuited to rural India. Undeterred, she applied some jugaad thinking. She decided to design her own incubator, one that was simple, inexpensive, and easy to use. Teaming up with neonatal nurses and local electricians, Dr Jeganathan developed a minimalist incubator from a wooden table made of locally harvested wood, a Plexiglas top, and standard 100-watt light bulbs (rather than radiant coils) to maintain the baby's temperature. Thanks to its simple design, the incubator cost only ₹ 5,000 to build and was easy to maintain.

Once Dr Jeganathan had the first working prototype of the incubator constructed and implemented in her hospital, infant mortality was cut by half. Now she is working closely with the Lemelson Foundation, a US–based organization that supports entrepreneurs in emerging markets, to fine-tune and rescale her invention so it can be distributed across other rural hospitals in India.[2]

US lawmakers seeking to address America's healthcare crisis might find Dr Jeganathan's incubator story interesting. US medical device makers spend billions of R&D dollars trying to push the frontiers of science and technology—only to come up with highly expensive and complex equipment that requires highly trained technicians to operate. In the process, these device makers often forget the basic needs of end users. After all, why make things simple when they can use their R&D dollars to make them more complicated? High-end incubators sold in the West, like those Jeganathan originally sought to buy, have many high-tech features and can cost up to ₹ 10 lakh. Yet they meet the same fundamental need as Dr Jeganathan's ingeniously simple ₹ 5,000 machine: they keep babies warm.

In this chapter, we look at how jugaad innovators like Dr Jeganathan are at the forefront of a *low-tech* revolution devoted to finding 'good enough' solutions. Rather than offering over-engineered products, jugaad innovators in emerging markets offer products that are easy to use and maintain and address customers' fundamental needs. By designing for the most basic universal needs, jugaad innovators appeal to a wider spectrum of consumers and thus dominate the sectors they operate in.

In contrast, large corporations have long embraced a 'bigger is better' approach to innovation. However, consumers are increasingly put off by the complexity of technology, especially in products like consumer electronics and automobiles that they encounter daily. More importantly, many consumers around the world are 'downshifting'—opting for a simpler, more meaningful life. Companies that respond now to these consumer and societal changes are likely to benefit in the long run. In this chapter, we discuss how some forward-thinking companies like Google, Facebook, GE, Siemens, and Philips are leading this response by building simplicity into their products and services—as well as into their organizational design—and, in the process, creating deep and lasting relationships with consumers.

The Practical Benefits of Simplicity

Jugaad innovators find success in emerging markets by pursuing simplicity in the products and services they offer. They are motivated to do so because this allows them to develop quick yet effective solutions for consumers grappling with complexity in their daily lives.

Simple products offer three advantages to jugaad innovators:

- *They are cheaper to make—and therefore, more affordable*: Resources in emerging markets are scarce and expensive. Simple products—with fewer features—require fewer resources and are therefore easier and cheaper to produce and deliver. Jugaad innovators can pass on these savings to customers in the form of lower prices, making simpler products more affordable and thus more successful in the marketplace.

- *They are easier to install and maintain*: Emerging markets face a lack of skilled workers to install and maintain complex products. For example, in India, 26 percent of adults are illiterate and therefore cannot read basic instruction manuals, let alone complicated ones. The limited availability of skilled workers means that companies cannot create highly engineered products that require skilled staff to set up and maintain.

- *They can satisfy a wider audience*: Emerging market customers are diverse in their needs and in their ability to use and maintain products. To reach as wide an audience as possible, jugaad innovators are compelled to design products that take into account the buying power, literacy, and technical aptitude of the least able members of the population. Designing simple products is the key to achieving universal appeal across diverse groups.

The Art of Simplicity

Jugaad innovators in emerging markets rely on several strategies to design products that are simple to use and maintain. To begin with, they focus more on customers' *needs* than their *desires*. They employ a functional approach to product and service design, and try to develop practical solutions that address well-defined customer needs. They are not in the business of coming up with cool features that appeal to customers' wants. Instead, jugaad innovators aim to make and deliver a good enough solution with limited functionality rather than one with a dazzling array of features.

For instance, to address the high cost of electricity in Filipino slums, Illac Diaz invented an ingeniously simple solution:

IsangLitrongLiwanag (A Litre of Light), a scheme that brings an eco-friendly solar bottle bulb to underprivileged communities across the Philippines. The solar bottle bulb (SLB) is simply a recycled plastic bottle filled with bleach-treated water (to prevent formation of mold) that is fitted snugly into a hole in the corrugated roof of makeshift homes in shanty towns. The water in the bottle refracts the sun's rays, producing the equivalent of a 55-watt light bulb. An SLB produces more light than a conventional window might let in. And, unlike windows, the bulb doesn't break or leak during the typhoon season. The SLB is made from recyclable materials; is very easy to assemble, install, and maintain; and helps create new jobs in underdeveloped communities, as slum dwellers can now work in their normally dark homes during the day. Importantly, an SLB can be installed for just $1 (₹ 50).[3] Diaz's vision is to deploy SLBs in 10 lakh homes across the Philippines by the end of 2012.[4]

Jugaad innovators like Diaz don't try to guess what would make their products simple by sitting in an R&D lab. Rather, they spend a great deal of time with customers in their natural setting to observe and identify what would make a product or service easier for them to use. Nokia, for example, employs ethnographers who spend long periods of time living with customers in emerging markets to understand their latent needs. In one case, Nokia's ethnographers studied migrant workers in Indian slums, the shanty towns of Ghana, and the *favelas* of Brazil to figure out how technology could make their lives easier. They were humbled to discover that regular cellphones were too expensive, flashy, and complex for slum, dwellers to buy and use and that the devices couldn't withstand the dusty, no-electricity environment where these people worked and lived. Armed with this insight, Nokia's researchers set out to develop a simple solution that would blend into the lives of these target users. The result was the Nokia 1100, a rugged cellphone with a minimalist design that allows calling and texting, withstands dust, and can be charged within a few minutes. When Nokia's researchers noticed that many of these customers use their cellphone's bright screen as a light source, they included a flashlight in the 1100 design—making it very popular among, for example, truck drivers in Asia and Africa who use it to repair their vehicles at night. The Nokia 1100 was launched in 2003 and became an immediate hit: it appealed to not only low-income consumers but even middle-class users looking for an uncomplicated cellphone. The Nokia 1100 has sold 25 crore units around the world, making it the best-selling cellphone ever.[5] *Foreign Policy* magazine calls the Nokia 1100 'the most important cellphone on the planet'.[6]

When creating simple products that meet the immediate needs of their customers, jugaad innovators typically design them *from the ground up*. They avoid 'defeaturing'—a practise often pursued by Western multinationals, which involves taking products designed for affluent Western consumers, stripping them of non-essential features, and then selling them at somewhat lower prices to consumers in emerging markets. These defeatured products typically fail in emerging markets because they are not fundamentally designed to take into account the inherent constraints of the local markets' socio-economic context.

For instance, many Western tech giants like Intel, Microsoft, and HP, as well as academic institutions like MIT, have tried to build a low-cost PC for emerging nations.[7] But none of these projects has succeeded because these PCs were either too complex to use or too expensive to buy, or they failed to meet specific local requirements. On October 5, 2011, however, Kapil Sibal, the Indian minister of communications and information technology, launched a ₹ 3,000 tablet (promoted as 'the world's cheapest tablet') that was ideally designed to meet local requirements.[8] Called the Aakash ('sky' in Sanskrit), it was developed by DataWind, a UK-based tech start-up, in partnership with several leading Indian technical universities, with local needs and constraints in mind.[9] The initial market for the Aakash will be students—from primary schools all the way to universities—who will receive the first ten thousand units at the subsidized price of ₹ 1,750 per unit. The Aakash boasts of a simplified user interface and is preloaded with educational software developed in local languages.

The Aakash clearly cannot match the computing power or the features of Apple's iPad (which costs ₹ 25,000) or Amazon's Kindle Fire (priced at ₹ 10,000). However, it was designed with a different set of users in mind—Indian students, who needed a simple and practical computing device. The Aakash meets those needs very well. First, it provides basic capabilities students need, like web browsing, video, Wi-Fi, and word processing software. Second, the Aakash runs on Google Android and other open-source technologies, which are cheaper and easier to maintain than proprietary technologies. Third, the Aakash comes with a solar charging option, a huge advantage in many parts of India where the electricity supply is either non existent or unreliable. Fourth, the Aakash touch screen makes it easier for students to navigate educational content and makes learning more intuitive and fun. In sum, the Aakash is *simple*. It is part of the Indian government's broader initiative to extend broadband access to 25,000 colleges and 400 universities across India. Given its simplicity and affordability, the Aakash has the potential to become a runaway success, not only in Indian schools but also in academic institutions abroad. Even US–based experts who tested the Aakash in their labs gave it rave reviews.[10] For instance, after thoroughly testing the first version of Aakash, Chikodi Chima, a well-respected American tech reporter, wrote a highly positive review in *VentureBeat*, saying: 'Jugaad is an Indian word which means 'to make-do'. The Aakash tablet is a jugaad in a very high tech way. The components inside the Aakash tablet are cheap, and easily sourced. What makes the Aakash tablet different is that its creators didn't strive for perfection. Instead, the emphasis was on getting the product into the market quickly so it could be adopted, tinkered with, and improved over time. The unmistakable impression we all got from using the Aakash tablet was that it is built for performance.'[10]

It is worth pointing out that jugaad innovators infuse simplicity into not only how they design products, but also how they interact with customers, from the sale of their products and services to their delivery and after-sales support. Such *service innovation*—that is, innovation in the way jugaad innovators interact with customers, deliver services to them, or use technology to support them—is crucial to simplifying and enriching the user experience throughout the solution's lifecycle. In particular, many jugaad entrepreneurs who sell products to the base of the economic pyramid in emerging markets rely on a grassroots network of distributors and technicians who make it easier for customers in villages to learn more about a product, get it installed quickly, and have it maintained without hassle. For example, SELCO, introduced earlier as a company that provides solar lighting to over 125,000 Indian village homes, relies on a vast network of grassroots entrepreneurs who install and repair SELCO's solar lanterns at very short notice—even in the most far-flung villages.

Finally, jugaad innovators ensure that their solutions are simple but not *simplistic*. There is an important distinction between the two. Jugaad innovators follow Albert Einstein's exhortation to 'make everything as simple as possible, but not simpler'. In other words, jugaad innovators don't necessarily try to simplify the nature of the problem the customer is facing. Doing so runs the risk of producing simplistic solutions, ones that may appear simple in the short term but prove ineffective in the long run. Instead, jugaad innovators often embrace complexity but mask it from customers by giving them a simple user interface. In other words, rather than simplifying the problem the customer is facing, jugaad innovators often simplify the *use* of the solution. As a result, they produce robust and resilient solutions that address users' complex needs, comprehensively and sustainably.

For instance, Ushahidi, which originated in Kenya, is a simple solution that relies on mobile SMS (text messaging) to coordinate grassroots responses to cataclysmic events like hurricanes, earthquakes, or epidemic outbreaks. According to the company website, the Ushahidi platform enables 'the gathering [of] crisis information from the general public [and] provides new insights into events happening in near real-time'—in the aftermath of, say, an earthquake.[11] Via text messages, the general public can learn—and inform others— where food and medical supplies are located, and receive SMS alerts when missing persons have been found. Within hours of a cataclysmic event, Ushahidi can help coordinate relief efforts in a highly targeted fashion: medical supplies and food can be dispatched precisely to those locations that need them the most, based on real-time information gathered by thousands of people at the scene. Contrast this with the traditional hit-or-miss relief management approach that is onerous and time consuming: as relief workers lack precise information on which specific locations need help the most, they plan their relief efforts in a top-down fashion and take a scattershot approach to distributing food and supplies. Ushahidi has been used successfully to rapidly and optimally coordinate relief efforts in the aftermath of the 2010 earthquakes in Haiti and Chile. It was also used by the *Washington Post* to map out blocked roads and other information in the wake of the winter storms that hit Washington, DC in 2010.[12]

The problems Ushahidi is trying to solve are overwhelmingly complex, such as helping people affected by an earthquake or tsunami rapidly locate the food and medical supplies they need. Traditional crisis management tools tend to tackle such huge problems only superficially or partially because the tools are *too* simplistic, as explained earlier. But Ushahidi is able to address complex issues like disaster management *in their full depth and breadth* with relative ease—thanks to an elegantly simple, user-friendly, yet comprehensive bottom-up solution that leverages the power of crowd sourcing.

The Backlash Against Complexity

The trend toward simplicity is also growing in many parts of the world. As such, there are many reasons why large corporations may benefit from keeping things simple:

- *Customers are clamouring for simplicity*: At the dawn of the 21st century, customers around the world are increasingly overwhelmed by technology-driven complexity. For instance, 65 percent of Americans complain that they 'have lost interest in purchasing a technology product because it seemed too complex to set up or operate'.[13] Similarly, having overindulged in technology in the past two decades, Fortune 500 companies now want simpler IT systems that are affordable and easy to deploy and maintain. These technology-jaded users now increasingly equate simplicity with sanity. According to a survey conducted by Siegel+Gale, Indian consumers are willing to pay between 6 and 8 percent more for technology and banking industry brands that offer elegantly simple experiences and interactions.[14]

- *Generations Y and Z and baby boomers are rebuffing advanced technologies*: The members of generations Y and Z, who make up more than half of the current Indian population, are willing to trade high pay for flexibility and work/life balance. Members of these younger generations also eschew complex offerings in favour of simplicity. For instance, a study at Stanford University found that a majority of graduate students actually prefer the average-quality MP3 version of a song played on their iPods to the high-quality CD version, even though the latter is technically superior.[15] Similarly, large numbers of retiring baby boomers—confronted with health issues such as deteriorating eyesight and arthritis—are put off by complex consumer electronic devices that have too many features and are too complicated to use.

- *More consumers around the world are downshifting their lifestyles*: A grassroots cultural movement known as *voluntary simplicity* is growing in the US and other parts of the world.[16] The movement calls for voluntary practises such as reducing one's material possessions or increasing self-sufficiency in order to achieve a simpler, richer, and more meaningful quality of life. For instance, studies show that 15 to 28 percent of Americans have already voluntarily adopted simplified lifestyles.[17]

- *Over-engineered products cost a lot of R&D money and time*: In a time of scarcity, companies can no longer afford to invest lavishly in R&D to come up with complex products bloated with features that require lengthy development cycles. As a result, several Fortune 500 firmshave slashed their R&D budgets (which amounted to a whopping $550 billion (₹ 27.5 lakh crore) in 2010), reducing their products to a more rational number, and simplifying their product development processes to gain efficiency and speed.[18]

- *Nimble rivals are stealing market share using simplicity*: Visionary companies such as Google and Facebook are democratizing technology by making it simple and accessible—and thereby stealing market share from technology rivals who produce over-engineered, counter-intuitive products. Similarly, business software companies like SAP and Oracle face competition from cloud computing vendors like salesforce.com, which simplify the lives of tech buyers by reducing all the headaches associated with expensive software upgrades.

'Why Make it Simple When We Can Make it Complex?'

Despite growing evidence that consumers want simplicity in the products and services they buy—and despite the fact that overengineering products is no longer sustainable, as R&D budgets are increasingly being slashed—many corporations nevertheless find it hard to make simplicity the key tenet of their product development and commercialization processes. There are several reasons for this.

First, large corporations often believe that customers aren't willing to pay a premium for products unless these products are loaded with features and functions. Specifically, the fear of losing the power to charge high prices and earn high margins makes companies shy away from simplicity.

A second, related reason is that complexity has been lucrative in the past. 'New, improved' versions of products and services have allowed large companies to differentiate their new offerings from their own (and other companies') existing ones. That has helped companies convince customers to keep upgrading—or replacing—existing products with ever more complex ones. This in turn has helped large companies secure growth and a steady stream of revenues as well.

Third, large companies are often stuck in an endless innovation war with each other: a perpetual battle of one-upmanship, with each company forced to out-innovate others in order to convince shareholders and customers that they are still 'in the game'.

Fourth, large companies don't always design products with end users in mind. In his book *The Laws of Simplicity*, John Maeda, president of the Rhode Island School of Design, declares that it's high time we 'humanize technology'.[19] Currently technology development is anything but human-centric. Many of the features in new products are determined not by deep customer observation but by the guesswork of R&D and marketing teams, driven by their desire to create a better version than the last one, often regardless of whether it adds value for the consumer or not.[20]

Finally, innovation metrics in large companies—such as the number of patents filed each year and the percentage of revenues dedicated to R&D—currently measure and reward cleverness, not customer value. The value of a product should not be measured by the number of patents associated with it.[21] Rather, it should be measured by the experiential value it delivers to end users. For many users, the best experience is a simple, seamless one. Yet most large companies continue to use the number of patents they file as a key yardstick to measure how innovative they are.

Shifting the emphasis from R&D-driven complexity to customer-valued simplicity, however, will require companies to make some fundamental changes in the way they develop products.

How to Simplify Your Products—and Your Organization

Pursuing complexity for its own sake is increasingly self defeating. Not only are customers moving away from complexity and toward simplicity in products and lifestyle, but R&D costs are high and rising, so pursuing complexity is an increasingly expensive proposition for companies. In such a context, it would be wise for business leaders to go back to the drawing board and find ways to enshrine simplicity into their value propositions and business models. The following strategies may help companies respond to the new economic reality by placing simplicity at the heart of what they do.

REDESIGN THE ENTIRE ORGANIZATION AROUND SIMPLICITY

Large companies cannot design simple products while keeping their business operations complex. For instance, a customer may love the ease of use of a firm's products but hate the convoluted sales process she has to go through to buy the product. Companies must therefore simplify *every* interaction with their customers throughout the product lifecycle—from the initial purchase to the actual use and even to the product's disposal—by streamlining not only their R&D and manufacturing but also their sales and customer service processes.

One company that has done just that is the electronics giant Philips, headquartered in Amsterdam, the Netherlands. In fact, the company redesigned its entire organization—from R&D to manufacturing to customer support—to serve customers better, using the simplicity principle. This process began in the early 2000s when Philips received a big shock following the results of a piece of market research it had commissioned. For more than a 100 years, the company had built a reputation for exceptional technical performance, one that has yielded market-shaping inventions such as the compact tape cassette and compact disc. Yet the two thousand consumers it surveyed globally were now telling Philips that technical superiority wasn't what drove them to buy an electronics product. If anything, consumers felt intimidated by the growing complexity of technology: 30 percent of home-networking products were returned, as users didn't know how to set them up; and nearly 50 percent of people postponed their decision to buy a digital camera, deterred by its complexity.[22] As Stefano Marzano, CEO and Chief Creative Director of Philips Design, observes: 'People are ready for unobtrusive technology'.[23]

Sensing an opportunity, Philips' management team decided to reinvent its entire organization around simplicity—from the inside out. The conglomerate pruned its portfolio of businesses from five hundred to seventy and reduced the number of divisions from seventy to five. It simplified customer service so end users got the same experience, irrespective of the Philips business they were dealing with. Philips even extended simplicity to its corporate communications: no PowerPoint presentation was allowed to exceed ten slides, and all its annual reports since 2009 have been made available only online. In a way, Philips embraced voluntary simplicity as a new organizational principle.[24]

In India, Philips enjoys immense brand reputation: in March 2012, it was ranked as India's Most Admired Company in the consumer durables segment by Fortune India. This ranking recognizes Philips' efforts in India to simplify all its products and services and make them more affordable and accessible for local customers in a socially and environmentally sustainable manner. The 2,500-people strong Philips Innovation Campus in Bangalore, headed by Dr Wido Menhardt, is Philips' largest R&D lab outside the Netherlands. 80 percent of the staff in this India lab are focused on building cost-effective and user-friendly healthcare solutions for the domestic market. For instance, Philips' Indian R&D team has developed a software solution to automate all processes in a radiology department—from patient registration to scanning to billing—making life easier for both hospital staff and the patient. Such an end-to-end solution, given its sheer scale and technology sophistication, would have cost a fortune to build in a Western country and would very likely have been very complex to use. But Philips' Indian centre developed the same solution cost-effectively by *simplifying* its design—by reusing existing technology components and developing software locally. Philips is now rolling out this easy-to-use, affordable, yet comprehensive solution in hospitals across India. Dr Wido Menhardt notes: 'I believe India will soon see what I call Jugaad 2.0. On the one end, you have this ingenuity, these amazing solutions, but these are bandage solutions, they are going to break again. On the other hand, in Bangalore's R&D ecosystem, people have set up a very strong process infrastructure. Marry the ingenuity and the process focus, and you have the best of both worlds.'[25] (In Chapter 8, we explore how large corporations can effectively integrate the jugaad approach to innovation with their traditional structured innovation approach).

By first internalizing simplicity and then actively living it, Philips was able to authentically engage customers in a discussion about simplicity. The company launched a rebranding campaign themed 'Sense and Simplicity'—which has since become its corporate motto.[26] It even set up a Simplicity Advisory Board made up of five leading global experts in healthcare, lifestyle, and technology to help the company deliver on its 'Sense and Simplicity' promise.[27] It began to proactively infuse the end user's perspective into every aspect of new product development, from ideation to prototyping and even packaging. For instance, Philips' R&D team quickly redesigned the packaging for a new flat-screen TV so the TV could be removed from a carton lying horizontally—a decision made after pilot users struggled to pull the heavy set out of an upright box.[28] In recent years, Philips has launched a steady stream of user-friendly products that have won rave reviews from customers and industry experts for their ability to marry simplicity and performance. In 2011, Philips bagged a record twenty-eight iF product design awards for its new products that seamlessly marry advanced technologies, sustainability, and a consumer-friendly design. These products included the Daily Duo vacuum cleaner and the Econova LED TV.[29]

In India too, Philips has won several awards for introducing user-friendly products that are both affordable and sustainable— such as the 'Empower Award 2009' for manufacturing the most energy efficient fluorescent tubelights. Having mastered simplicity, Philips is now encouraging grassroots entrepreneurs in India to embrace 'Keep It Simple' as a key innovation principle. In 2007, Philips India sponsored the Philips Simplicity Challenge in India, a reality show on CNBC TV. The goal of the show was to demonstrate how a simple idea could have immense societal impact. The three finalists—shortlisted from an impressive 8,000 entries—presented simple but innovative solutions with major potential business and social impact. The winner of the ₹ 15 lakh trophy was Samarth Mungali, a graduate of the National Institute of Design, who designed Acceptor—a child-friendly colorful syringe that makes injections less intimidating for kids and easier to administer.[30]

DISTILL CUSTOMER NEEDS TO THEIR BARE ESSENCE—AND DESIGN SIMPLE PRODUCTS AROUND THEM

Simplicity advocates insist that 'user-centric design' boosts the ease of use of products and services. Although this is true, it is important to remember that the urgency of customer needs varies widely. Companies should zero in on consumers' most acute need (or pain point) and build a solution around *that* need before all others. A master of this approach was Steve Jobs, the founder of Apple. Jobs elevated simplicity to an iconic status in computing. In many ways, Jobs was the Michelangelo of the digital age: he could take a piece of hardware, chip away the nonessential pieces, and design wonderfully simple-looking products like the iPod, the iPhone, and the iPad. In a rare interview, Jobs once told *Business Week*: 'Innovation emerges when saying no to thousands of things to ensure that we do not take the wrong path or try to do too much.'[31]

DESIGN SIMPLE OFFERINGS FROM THE GROUND UP

Rather than stripping down existing high-end products—that is, de-featuring them—companies need to design and build products from the ground up so they truly embody the spirit of simplicity. This not only appeals to customers but also helps reduce costs and helps companies come up with more long-lasting breakthroughs in their innovation process.

One company that has learned the ineffectiveness of de-featuring the hard way is Siemens AG. Headquartered in Germany, Siemens is a global powerhouse in electronics and electrical engineering, operating in the industry, energy, and healthcare sectors. Founded by an engineer in 1847, Siemens employs around 30,100 researchers who come up with about forty inventions each working day. It holds a total of 57,900 patents, and filed 4,300 patents in 2010 alone.[32] Siemens sells highly engineered products—ranging from power generators to high-speed trains to MRI machines to wind turbines—to business users ranging from small to large enterprises as well as local and national governments. Siemens competes head-to-head with GE worldwide across all its businesses.

Seeking to escape the recessionary economic climate in the West, Siemens has been aggressively expanding in the booming emerging markets, and especially in Brazil, Russia, India, and China. Over the last five years, Siemens has more than doubled its sales in emerging markets; these markets now account for 30 percent of the company's global sales revenues.[33] Siemens' initial go-to-market strategy in emerging countries consisted of stripping down its existing Western products—such as its expensive and over-engineered MRI machines and power turbines—and adapting them to local requirements. But this 'product localization' strategy didn't sit too well with clients in emerging markets who complained that these localized products were still too costly and complicated to use and maintain. As Dr Armin Bruck, Managing Director of Siemens' Indian subsidiary acknowledges: 'Entry-level users want simple user interfaces. They do not need or appreciate bells and whistles.'[34] This market reality led Mr Peter Löscher, Siemens' global CEO, to recognize that his company's products required a different kind of innovation in emerging markets. 'What counts here [in emerging markets] is simplicity, not sophistication', he notes.[35]

In 2005, the financial and labour constraints of emerging markets led Siemens to come up with a bold new product strategy called SMART, which stands for Simple, Maintenance-friendly, Affordable, Reliance, and Timely-to-Market. Siemens defines SMART as finding new ways to use old technologies and developing solutions that are 'good enough' for an initial market segment, while allowing them to be improved. Besides cost-effectiveness, the SMART philosophy emphasizes ease of setup, operation, and maintenance.[36] As Dr Armin Bruck points out: 'Our new [SMART] product initiative has been set up to design simple products to meet the entry-level requirements [of emerging markets].'[37]

SMART products are being designed cost-effectively from the ground up in emerging economies such as India and China, using entirely local R&D talent that owns end-to-end responsibility for developing these products. The Chinese R&D team, for instance, has produced low-cost medical equipment like X-ray machines that can easily be deployed and operated by hospitals in small Chinese towns where skilled technicians are hard to find. Similarly, Siemens' R&D engineers in India are developing small local power grids that can use multiple sources of energy—from solar to coconut shells—to supply electricity to a typical Indian village of fifty to one hundred households. These micro power plants can be set up easily and require limited maintenance.[38] Siemens estimates the market potential for SMART products in India alone to be about 12 billion éuros (₹ 78,000 crore).[39]

Siemens currently employs 15,500 R&D engineers across emerging markets, many of whom are involved in SMART product development projects. Over 150 products have already been generated in the SMART category since its launch in 2005. In India alone, Siemens has over 60 SMART products in the pipeline and plans to launch half of them in 2012.[40] The company finds that by designing SMART products from the ground up in emerging markets it can save 20 to 40 percent in development costs, compared to adapting or locally producing products designed in the West. Although SMART products are positioned as entry-level products in Siemens' global product portfolio, they are highly profitable. Thanks in part to SMART products, Siemens generated 22 billion euros (₹ 1,43,500 crore) in revenues from entry-level markets in fiscal 2010, *double* the amount it earned in fiscal 2005. Entry-level markets now account for 30 percent of Siemens' total global revenues—up from 20 percent in 2005.[41] Even better, Siemens intends to sell these entry-level SMART products to recession-weary customers in the US and Europe who are looking for simple and affordable solutions. For instance, Siemens' Indian engineers—in partnership with German engineers—have developed Fetal Heart Monitor, a device that monitors the heartbeat of fetuses in the womb. This device uses simple but ingenious microphone technology instead of expensive ultrasound. As such, the device holds great market potential in both emerging and developed economies.[42]

EMBRACE THE UNIVERSAL DESIGN PHILOSOPHY TO BOOST THE USABILITY OF OFFERINGS

Universal design is a philosophy that celebrates humanity's diversity and exhorts companies to design products that are usable by as many people as possible.[43] Examples of universal design include buildings with access for all instead of a separate entrance for those with disabilities, unisex facilities where both men and women have a place to attend to a child's needs, and graphics on signs that can be recognized and understood by anyone regardless of language.

OXO, the consumer product company, is one of America's most ardent corporate advocates of universal design. Over time, OXO has built a well-deserved reputation for simplicity, and the company offers products that are both technically superior and easy to use. How does OXO pull it off? It zeroes in on the essence of the problem shared by a large number of customers across demographic segments and then designs user-friendly products that precisely meet customers' latent needs. This approach has helped OXO produce many best-selling products whose simplicity appeals to a wider audience—including kitchenware such as a salad spinner that can be used with one hand, liquid measuring cups that can be read from above without bending over, and kettles with whistle lids that open automatically when tipped to pour.[44] OXO even applied its universal design thinking to develop an easy-to-use syringe for patients of all ages with rheumatoid arthritis who struggle to administer self injections.[45]

GET ENGINEERS AND INDUSTRIAL DESIGNERS TO WORK TOGETHER

Bringing down the Berlin Wall may have been easier than dismantling the mental wall that keeps technology-enamored engineers and user-centreed designers separate. Yet that mental wall must be torn down in order to achieve a proper balance between complex function and simple design. Companies must recognize that incorporating simplicity up front during the product conceptualization phase is *several* times more cost-effective than doing it as an afterthought in the later stages of the development process. Recognizing this fact, forward-thinking companies such as Google and Facebook encourage engineers and designers to work in cross-functional teams from the very start to ensure that performance is not sacrificed for the sake of simplicity—and vice-versa. At Facebook, for instance, communication and product designers, engineers, writers, and researchers, all work together in multi-disciplinary teams that create new product features with a shared goal: keep improving the user experience without sacrificing simplicity (see the detailed case study on Facebook later in this chapter).

SIMPLIFY PRODUCT ARCHITECTURES AND REUSE PLATFORMS ACROSS PRODUCTS

R&D engineers are like craftsmen: they often like to create their own technologies or components from scratch, even if comparable technologies or components are readily available in the market. But this 'reinvent the wheel' approach often leads to long product development cycles and results in expensive, over-engineered products. In a resource-constrained economy, however, it is vital to reuse readily available components to make 'good enough' products that get the job done. One way to do that is to simplify product architectures and reuse similar parts across multiple products in a portfolio.

Mary Barra is attempting to do exactly that at General Motors (GM). Barra, the highest-ranking female executive in GM's history, is in charge of design and engineering for all GM cars worldwide. Her boss, Dan Akerson, GM's CEO, has given her a tough assignment: shave several months off GM's three- to four-year-long product development cycle, reduce development and production costs by 25 percent, and make every GM car look cool and appealing. Barra is tackling this herculean task with bravery (and gusto even), weeding out complexity from GM's notoriously complex R&D processes by enshrining simplicity as a core tenet of GM's new product development approach.[46]

Two factors have historically plagued GM's R&D processes. First, given its decentralized culture, different brands across multiple geographies were all running independent, often redundant R&D projects. This led to a proliferation of product platforms and higher costs. Second, GM's engineers had a predilection for creating every new car from scratch. This made the whole product development process lengthier and costlier. The result was a disorganized, under-optimized global R&D organization as complex as a jigsaw puzzle.

Barra is striving to streamline and simplify this chaotic structure by creating *global platforms*. These will allow every GM brand to be built off the same core architecture, whether it is produced in the US, Europe, China, India, or Brazil. Such global platforms will allow engines and sub-systems to also be shared across brands—gaining huge cost savings and faster time-to-market for all new GM models worldwide. Currently, only 30 percent of GM's products share global core architectures. By 2018, however, Barra wants 90 percent of GM's models to be built on global platforms.[47]

Platform sharing is only one facet of Barra's great simplification strategy. The other facet is called *lightweighting*(aka *mass reduction*). The goal is to simplify the core architecture itself in order to make cars that are significantly lighter. Lightweighting happens when you make hundreds of small reductions of mass in the entire product architecture; for instance, by replacing heavy steel and aluminum with lighter carbon fibre. The net result will be far better fuel efficiency, an obsession for carmakers like GM since US legislators passed a new law in July 2011 imposing stringent mileage requirements. US automakers, including GM, are engaged in a race to improve their cars' current average 27.5 miles per gallon performance to 54.5 mpg by 2025—as required by the new law.

At the outset, Barra's efforts to simplify GM's development processes may appear to stifle the creative freedom of its R&D engineers. However, these constraints could provide the spur for developing a jugaad mindset at GM by fostering healthy 'competition'. Indeed, one can imagine GM's R&D teams across the US, Europe, and Asia collaborating to simplify the core product architecture—while simultaneously competing with each other as jugaad innovators to show which region can develop the hippest and most affordable, user-friendly, and sustainable cars, all using the same simplified core product architecture.[48]

MAKE IT SIMPLE, NOT SIMPLISTIC

Simplicity is often the most powerful antidote to complexity. But simple does not necessarily mean simplistic—realistically, complexity cannot either be ignored or avoided. Rather, innovators must embrace the complexity of a problem and then find a simple way through or around it. Consider the Google search engine. The technology behind it is the stuff of rocket science: the search software can solve, in less than a second, an equation of more than 50 crore variables to rank 800 crore web pages by relevance. But the 30 crore users who do 200 crore searches every day on Google are totally oblivious to the complex algorithms executed behind the scenes every time they choose Search. Google's minimalist and intuitive home page cleverly hides the highly complex functionality of its search engine.[49]

According to Marissa Mayer, Google's vice president of location and local services who previously was in charge of the search site's look and feel and acted as Google's 'simplicity cop', 'Google has the functionality of a really complicated Swiss Army knife, but the homepage is our way of approaching it closed. It's simple, it's elegant, you can slip it in your pocket, but it's got the great doodad when you need it.' Building on this metaphor, Mayer compares Google's competitors' products to 'an open Swiss Army knife'—which can intimidate users and even potentially harm them. It's this obsessive attention to simplicity that helps explain why Google controls a nearly 60 percent (and growing) share of the search market.[50]

In sum, Western companies can gain in simplicity by focusing on customer needs, rationalizing their product architectures, streamlining their R&D processes, and boosting collaboration between designers and engineers—just as Siemens, GM, and Google have done. Ultimately, to make simplicity part of their DNA, Western leaders must redesign their entire organizations around simplicity—a bold move undertaken by large corporations such as Philips and digital-age start-ups like Facebook.

How Facebook is Leading the Low-Tech Revolution

Facebook, the social networking site, understands the importance of creating an interface of simplicity for the rich social media content it provides to its hugely diverse user base. By making simplicity the lynchpin of its product design strategy, Facebook has developed an easy-to-use social networking site that has rapidly conquered the hearts of more than 80 crore users worldwide.

Nearly half the US population has a Facebook account. *Entertainment Weekly*, in placing Facebook on its end-of-the-decade 'best-of' list, wondered: 'How on earth did we stalk our exes, remember our co-workers' birthdays, bug our friends, and play a rousing game of Scrabulous before Facebook?'[51]

Facebook's huge popularity and global appeal stem largely from its hyper-simplified user interface. Compared to some other flashy sites, Facebook may even feel anachronistic. The website has a clean look: easy-to-navigate content, few menu options, and no glitzy graphics. Creating new content on Facebook is a breeze; you don't need to be an expert web developer to do so. This may explain why, as of this writing, the average Facebook user creates over ninety pieces of content per month, adding up to more than 3,000 crore pieces of shared content across the network. In sum, Facebook's interface is so simple that even kids can use it, and so they do! According to ConsumerReports.org, there are 75 lakh children under thirteen with Facebook accounts.

Facebook's minimalist interface is not an act of randomness: it was intentionally designed using a frugal and inclusive principle called 'social design'. Unlike traditional software design that produces abstract technology algorithms, social design develops new features based on how real people interact in the real world. The proponents of social design seek to improve the way people build human-to-human—rather than human-to-interface—connections on the Web. As Kate Aronowitz, Facebook's Director of Design, explains:

'Simplicity is key in creating "social design", which is really just about designing products around people. So when we talk about design, we're not just talking about colour schemes and shapes—we're also talking about product design that puts people at its centre. For instance, a lot of people look at Facebook's muted blue and white color scheme and wonder where design plays a role. The real art here is that the product falls into the background so that people remember their interactions with their friends, not the site itself. Ultimately, the challenge of social design is in creating a product that seamlessly enhances both online and offline interactions.'[52]

To deliver such authentic experiences to users, Facebook designers use everyday English words, rather than jargon or buzzwords, for features on the site. As Christopher Cox, vice president of product, explains: 'In 2005, we decided to create a photo product that we called Photos. Other people at the time were using names like Flickr, Picasa, Photobucket, right? Very niche-y. Instead, we use common words. We recede into the background. We design a place where there aren't new objects to trip over. Photos are photos. Chat is chat. Groups are groups. Everything just is.'[53]

'Receding into the background' doesn't come easy to Silicon Valley start-ups, which generally like to impress users with their technological prowess. But on Facebook, the user is king. And this user can be logging in from New York, Cape Town, Mumbai, or Ulan Bator. In an effort to accommodate the mind boggling diversity of its soon-to-be 100-crore-user base, Facebook prefers to opt for the most universal basics when introducing new features—so that any user in any continent can intuitively understand and use them regardless of age, cultural background, and technical ability. Take, for example, the Like, Comment, and Share features that let you share your opinion of a photo, link, or status update. These inconspicuous and easy-to-use features have been a huge hit with users worldwide, irrespective of the language they speak. In many ways, the Facebook vocabulary is providing the building blocks for a long-elusive universal language that strives to unite humanity while simultaneously celebrating its diversity. Reena Jana, a former editor at *Business Week* who has extensively studied Facebook's design culture, notes that the 'plainness' of Facebook's site may appear unsophisticated to the cognoscenti of the design world—museum curators and creative directors—who view the interface as 'cold' and 'unengaging'. But Jana believes these design experts are evaluating Facebook using traditional frames of reference, whereas Facebook is creating a whole new design paradigm—one that seeks to replicate offline human connections online by keeping them straightforward and genuine.[54]

By favouring simplicity over sophistication, Facebook is initiating a veritable revolution in the global technology sector—one that could be called the 'low-tech revolution'.

Conclusion

Jugaad innovators accommodate the tremendous diversity of customer needs in emerging markets by integrating simplicity into their culture and their solution design—much as some large companies like Philips, Siemens, Google, GM, and Facebook are doing. This simplicity makes their solutions affordable and accessible not only to mainstream customers but also to those who live on the margins of society. Indeed, driven by empathy and a sense of social equity, jugaad innovators often use their creativity to devise inclusive business models that profitably meet the needs of the underserved consumer segments that are ignored by traditional enterprises. In the next chapter, we explore how by 'including the margin', jugaad innovators can extend the reach of their offerings to a much larger audience in a socially equitable *and* economically viable fashion.

Chapter 6

Principle Five: Include the Margin

'We need a system of inclusive capitalism that would have a twin mission: making profits and also improving lives for those who don't fully benefit from market forces.'

—BILL GATES, CHAIRMAN, MICROSOFT CORPORATION

In 2004, Dr Rana Kapoor quit his job with a multinational company to start an inclusive bank: one that would sustainably serve the financial needs of the broadest possible swath of consumers. Dr Kapoor felt strongly that banks should be servants of a country's economy rather than its arrogant masters. His vision of serving the needs of the Indian economy extended to the 60 crore Indians who had no access to a bank. To turn his vision into reality, he staffed his new venture—a 'responsible bank' he named YES BANK—with some of the industry's most brilliant minds. He invited these recruits to apply their creativity to meeting the financial needs of average Indian families and businesses.[1]

Over the years, YES BANK has pioneered many initiatives to make financial services accessible to the masses—either directly or through intermediaries. It uses sophisticated financial tools—so far only available to big businesses—to develop offerings for small and medium enterprises and non-profit organizations. Specifically, it borrows cutting-edge products used in high-end investment banking and adapts them for development banking—by, for example, securitizing the micro loans of micro-finance institutions (MFIs) and selling them to institutional investors as convertible debentures. In doing so, these MFIs gain access to additional capital which allows them to lend money to even more people.[2]

YES BANK—founded by a jugaad entrepreneur—is particularly keen to support the development of micro-entrepreneurs who have so far been excluded from the traditional banking system. To that end, the bank has developed several simple but effective financial inclusion tools to streamline access to capital for micro-entrepreneurs. For instance, YES BANK noticed that there was no viable solution in the market for credit appraisal of micro-entrepreneurs who neither maintain formal business records nor file business details with authorities. To address this shortcoming, the bank developed the Credit Appraisal Toolkit (CAT)—an Excel-based data analysis tool that compares details orally provided by a micro-entrepreneur applying for a loan against those collected earlier from his or her peers for a better and quicker credit approval decision.[3]

Importantly, YES BANK's inclusive model—fueled by jugaad innovation—is profitable. Even though 46 percent of the bank's loans are extended to underserved segments of the Indian economy, it still earns 2 percent over its cost of lending, whereas most banks earn 1 to 1.5 percent less than lending costs them. Riding on the back of his successful banking model, Dr Rana Kapoor intends to grow YES BANK's balance sheet from ₹ 36,000 crore in the 2009-10 fiscal to ₹ 1.5 lakh crore by 2015. As Dr Kapoor points out: 'At YES BANK, our primary focus is enabling social sustainability, which, in turn, helps drive our business sustainability. We serve the marginal segments of our society not as part of a CSR initiative, but as a core component of our inclusive business model. I don't see any contradiction between doing good for my society and doing well for my shareholders.'

Emerging markets are full of jugaad innovators who, like Dr Rana Kapoor, are successfully including marginal segments of their society, both as consumers and as employees. These innovators are showing how including the margin not only enables greater social good but also makes great business sense: it is profitable and drives innovation. In this chapter, we look at how and why jugaad innovators include the margin.

Many large companies, in contrast, often ignore marginal consumers and employees. They view these groups as unprofitable, too complex to serve, or not sufficiently valuable to include in their innovation processes. And this is despite growing diversity and large numbers of marginalized consumers in many parts of the world. In this chapter, we also explore how large companies can learn from jugaad innovators like Dr Rana Kapoor to profitably include marginal groups.

Inclusion: A Moral Imperative that Makes Business Sense

To understand what drives jugaad innovators like Dr Rana Kapoor to include marginal consumer segments in their for-profit business models we need to first understand the environment in which jugaad innovators operate. As we've discussed in previous chapters, emerging markets possess three features—scarcity, diversity, and interconnectivity—that together constitute an imperative to include the margin.

First, as we pointed out in Chapter 3, emerging markets are characterized by pervasive *scarcity* on many fronts. Because of underdeveloped infrastructure, ineffective governments, and accelerated population growth, crores of people in Africa, India, and Latin America lack access to basic services like healthcare, education, and energy. In India alone, over 60 crore, mostly rural citizens, are excluded from the banking sector, and a nearly equal number live outside the reach of the electricity grid. There is an upside, however, to this widespread scarcity: crores of excluded citizens equals crores of potential customers. For entrepreneurs willing to rise to the challenge, the choice to include the margin promises many potentially lucrative opportunities to build entirely new businesses.

Second, many emerging economies are also characterized by mindboggling *diversity*. India, for instance, has over 20 official languages and 2,500 dialects, adherents of all the world's major religions, citizens who belong to different ethnic groups, and so on. The sheer social, economic, and cultural heterogeneity of such populations exacerbates the challenges posed by scarcity. Thus, exclusion cannot be addressed with a one-size-fits-all approach—wherein, for example, a single product or service serves the majority of the population—an approach that is often favoured by large corporations. Instead, inclusivity requires an approach to innovation that is sensitive to individual differences and local circumstances. The intellectual and creative challenge of serving the diverse needs of a large number of people in an economical way is a great spur to jugaad innovators.

Third, deepening *interconnectivity* in emerging markets both amplifies the sense of exclusion and offers interesting ways to reduce it. Even poor people in remote villages in Africa or India now have access to cable TV and can see what they are missing out on. This ability to see what the world has to offer drives them to aspire for better and more things. Pervasive cellphone ownership—India alone adds 1 crore cellphone subscribers a month, a majority of whom are in rural areas—creates many new opportunities for inclusion. For instance, even small entrepreneurs can now leverage mobile computing as a cost-effective platform to deliver education, healthcare, and financial services to the masses.

In sum, scarcity, diversity, and inclusivity are together driving jugaad innovators like Dr Rana Kapoor to build their businesses around the needs and aspirations of marginal consumers and employees. But *how* do these innovators successfully and profitably include such marginal groups and what underpins their ability to do so?

Cocreating Value with the Margin

Jugaad innovators like Dr Rana Kapoor are uniquely attuned to respond to the external pressures and opportunities they face. They often live close to marginal segments, they perceive these segments' unmet needs first-hand, and they have an intuitive grasp of how to meet them. They also have a sense of fairness that drives them to make basic services like education, healthcare, and energy accessible to all. Finally, jugaad innovators believe in what Bill Gates calls 'creative capitalism'—that is, they know how to employ for-profit business models to bring about social change.[4] Jugaad innovators work with these traits to successfully reach the excluded in the following ways.

APPROACHING MARGINAL GROUPS AS WHOLE NEW MARKETS

Jugaad innovators don't merely treat marginal groups as one more segment on which to dump their existing products. Instead, they approach marginal groups as whole new markets that need to be served with entirely new business models. For instance, large technology vendors boast about the accessibility features built into their existing products to enable the physically challenged to use them. But few of these companies come up with new products—let alone whole new business models—dedicated to serve, say, blind people.

A notable exception is Abhi Naha of the cellphone company Zone V. After two decades of executive-level experience in the tech sector, Naha founded Zone V with the express intention of developing cellphones for exclusive use by blind and partially sighted people worldwide.[5] Globally, there are 28.4 crore blind and partially sighted people, two-thirds of whom are women.[6] Naha is particularly determined to empower blind women through mobile technology—especially in developing nations where such women are outcasts and are excluded from educational and economic opportunities.

In 2013, Zone V will introduce three models of cellphones. The first model will be a high-end smartphone with a simplified user interface targeted at elderly people in Europe (and later in the US) with regular eye sight—but which can also be used by blind and partially sighted people. The second will be a mid-range smartphone primarily for blind and partially sighted people in urban areas of emerging markets. And the third will be a basic low-cost phone with valuable features for blind people who live at the bottom of the socio-economic pyramid. All three models will be co-developed and co-marketed with a global network of design, manufacturing, and distribution partners.

Naha estimates the global cellphone market for blind and partially sighted people as well as regular-sighted senior citizens to be more than $1.36 billion (₹ 6,800 crore). Zone V will operate as a for-profit company and will initially target blind and partially sighted people in Western economies with easy to use yet beautifully designed cellphones. Some of the profits from the sales in Europe and the US will help Zone V to create ultra-low-cost phones that will be supplied to blind women in India and Africa on a not-for-profit basis. Abhi Naha is truly a visionary. What else to say of someone who aspires to create a world in which the lack of sight does not mean a lack of vision?

Helping Everyone Climb Up Maslow's Hierarchy of Needs

Jugaad entrepreneurs recognize that even low-income consumers have high aspirations and are eager to climb up Maslow's hierarchy of needs. (According to the American psychologist Abraham Maslow, people face a hierarchy of needs: basic requirements such as food and safety come first, followed by higher level needs such as belonging, status, and esteem, with self actualization at the top.)

Jugaad innovators do not, therefore, short-change low-income consumers on quality: they know that while these consumer are low earners, they are high *yearners*. As such, jugaad innovators strive to offer marginal segments products of value that are nonetheless affordable. For example, as mentioned before, YES BANK has adapted high-end investment banking products for development banking—which, in turn, help MFIs gain access to additional capital so they can offer micro-loans to even more people.

Likewise, Zone V is infusing even its low-cost phones with high-end design to make them more desirable to blind women in developing nations. To that end, Naha has hired Frank Nuovo as Zone V's chief designer. Nuovo is the former Chief of Design of Nokia and the co-founder of Vertu—Nokia's offering for the luxury phone segment (which represents a $1 billion (₹ 5,000 crore) market)—where he remains Principal Designer. While continuing to design diamond-encrusted phones for the super-rich, Nuovo has joined Zone V determined to make luxury affordable and accessible to the masses. In particular, he is designing phones for Zone V that are cool yet inexpensive and that deliver a high-end experience to blind consumers at the bottom of the pyramid—giving them a phone they can be proud to own and that can help elevate their status within their community (see Chapter 3 for more examples of how jugaad entrepreneurs deliver more value at a lower cost for more people).

Although people at the bottom of the pyramid do worry about meeting their basic needs, like food and shelter, they also have *higher order* needs such as being entertained or looking beautiful. Many companies, especially multinationals, fail to see this. Rama Bijapurkar, the Indian marketing guru and author of *Winning in the Indian Market*[7], says: 'Every kid—poor or rich—has a right to be entertained. It is a basic right. Yet Western theme parks, with their steep entry fees, tend to exclude low-income people. Such an exclusive business model won't work in an emerging market like India where 30 crore people still earn ₹ 50 a day—and yet want to be entertained.'[8]

As if speaking directly to this point, Xavier López Ancona, a Mexican entrepreneur, founded KidZania in Mexico City in 1999 to make entertainment more inclusive—as well as increase its educational value. KidZania is a reasonably priced indoor theme park where four to twelve-year-old kids play at being adults in a realistic, safe, and fun environment. At KidZania, kids perform 'real world' jobs—as doctors, TV anchors, firefighters, police officers, pilots, or shopkeepers—and are paid in 'kidZo' currency that they use to buy goods and services. In their role-play, kids get guidance and support from adult 'Zupervisors'.' Built to scale for kids, KidZania is complete with paved roads, cars, buildings, an active economy, and real-world establishments like hospitals, banks, fire stations, and supermarkets. The success of the Mexico City park—1 crore children have visited it to date—encouraged Ancona to open more parks not only in emerging-market cities like Jakarta and Dubai but also in Tokyo, Seoul, and Lisbon. To date, 2 crore people have visited KidZania parks worldwide. Walt Disney Parks and Resorts and Six Flags had better watch out: KidZania is planning its US entry in the near future.[9]

Similarly, in the early 1990s, Heloísa Helena Assis—known as Zica—recognized the basic need of underprivileged women to look beautiful. A former hairdresser who grew up in a family of thirteen children in the *favelas* (urban slums) of Rio de Janeiro, Brazil, Zica was aware that these women couldn't afford to go to expensive beauty salons or spas in cities that charge a premium for services like hair care. She also noticed Brazilian women tended to go to hair salons to straighten their curly hair. Zica thought: 'What if I could come up with a product—and a unique process for applying it—that can enhance Brazilian women's curly hair, rather than straighten it? That would help these women find beauty in their natural looks.' After several experiments on her own curly hair, she came up with the right formula—a cream that could hydrate and relax it and preserve its natural structure without straightening it.[10] She patented her proprietary formula under the name Super-Relaxing. As a logical next step, in 1993, Zica opened a hair salon in Rio de Janeiro named Beleza Natural, where she could test her Super-Relaxing formula on real customers. The formula and the salon were a hit. Zica immediately expanded her business and opened more salons with three other partners.

Beleza Natural currently operates twelve salons, located in Rio de Janeiro, Espírito Santo, and Bahia, primarily targeting low-income women. These salons are all operated by local community women. Each salon serves up to a thousand customers a day, treating up to forty clients at a time through a fast seven-step process. The salons now also sell a complete line of hair care products—developed by Beleza Natural's manufacturing unit CorBrasil in partnership with leading researchers in top Brazilian universities.[11] Beleza Natural currently serves over 70,000 customers and the company's sales revenues are growing at 30 percent a year. Since 2005, Beleza Natural has increased its revenues by 918 percent and has expanded its workforce by 214 percent—today employing more than 1,400 people. 'Above all, we sell self-esteem', explains Assis. 'I saw an opportunity to make all Brazilian women feel beautiful, [regardless of] their financial means.'[12]

CO-CREATING VALUE WITH CUSTOMERS AND PARTNERS THROUGHOUT THE VALUE CHAIN

Jugaad innovators don't view customers as merely passive users of their products and services. Recognizing the diversity of customer needs, they invent new solutions from the ground up by working closely with marginal groups to identify their unique needs. They then engage local communities and partners to set up a grassroots value chain to locally build, deliver, and support their solutions—making these solutions in turn affordable, accessible, and sustainable.

For instance, to effectively serve the 60 crore unbanked Indians, YES BANK is constantly experimenting with new technology-powered inclusive business models that tap a vast network of partners. The YES MONEY service is one such initiative. As part of this initiative, the bank has teamed up with various Payment Platform companies like Suvidhaa Infoserve and Oxigen Services, which offer payment services through about 2 lakh mom-and-pop retail stores in urban and rural areas. YES BANK has helped these companies to deploy a specialized 'domestic remittance' module allowing, for example, migrant workers in cities to send money to their families in far-flung villages through the National Electronic Fund Transfer (NEFT) System. Compared to Money Order remittance services (offered by India Post, a government undertaking), YES MONEY is about five times cheaper and five times faster. YES Money also offers a cost-effective alternative to Western Union. Moreover, the majority of the fees collected are passed back to the Payment Platform company and the retailer—creating value for all partners in the YES MONEY ecosystem. [13]

Like YES BANK, Zone V is positioning its products as tools for economic empowerment rather than for passive consumption. Zone V's phones can, therefore, enable blind women in rural India to manage not only the finances of their households but also those of their neighbours and the village council. In this way, the individual phone becomes a vehicle for driving socio-economic growth in an entire community. To make all this happen, Zone V will rely on a host of partners. It has outsourced its design and manufacturing to contract engineers and manufacturers and relies on non-government organizations (NGOs) like Sightsavers to distribute its phones in emerging markets like India—especially in rural areas. More important, Zone V will create a platform for third-party software developers to develop 'inclusive apps' for its phones. These apps will be available at different price points depending on the customer segment and the phone being used. Naha believes that many mobile app developers will be motivated to create solutions that meet the basic needs of blind people worldwide.

In emerging markets, jugaad innovators often partner with state-level and local governments to make healthcare, education, and financial services more inclusive. For instance, GE Healthcare has signed a performance-based service contract with the government of the Northwestern Indian state of

Gujarat. Under the terms of this public-private partnership agreement, GE-trained partners will operate and maintain all the medical equipment installed in government-run hospitals in the smaller cities of Gujarat. Rural hospitals, for their part, won't need to invest in expensive equipment or scramble to recruit qualified technicians. Nevertheless, they will be guaranteed higher equipment uptime and lower utilization costs—all of which will translate into cost-effective and high-quality care for rural patients.[14]

SCALING UP PERSONALIZED SOLUTIONS WITH TECHNOLOGY

Jugaad innovators cleverly employ technology—especially mobile computing—to reduce the cost of delivering services to marginal segments. They also leverage technology to customize their offerings on a large scale. A case in point is Reuters Market Light (RML), a mobile phone service developed by Thomson Reuters in India. RML delivers to farmers customized and localized weather forecasts, local crop prices, agricultural news and other relevant information (namely relevant government aid schemes), in the form of three SMS messages sent daily to their mobile phones in the local language. Such customized and timely information enables farmers to better plan their activities such as irrigation, fertilizer use, and harvesting. As a result, farmers can better manage risks and improve their decisions regarding when and where to sell their produce to maximize profit. The service costs a mere ₹ 250 for a three-month subscription. As of 2011, some 2,50,000 Indian farmers from over 15,000 villages had subscribed to RML. Thomson Reuters estimates that over 10 lakh farmers across at least thirteen Indian states have benefitted from the RML service. Moreover, farmers have reaped substantial returns from their investment in RML. Some have realized up to ₹ 2,00,000 in additional profits, and savings of nearly ₹ 4,00,000 with an investment of only ₹ 250 in subscription costs.[15]

Another jugaad innovator using technology to bring low-cost services to the masses is Dr Liu Jiren, Chairman and CEO of Neusoft, China's largest IT solution and service provider. Dr Liu, a former professor of computer science, is worried that the Chinese, thanks to sustained double-digit economic growth, 'have accumulated lots of wealth in the past two decades, but have also accumulated lots of diseases as they got richer'.[16] It is estimated that 9 crore Chinese suffer from diabetes and 20 crore may be suffering from cardiovascular diseases. The explosion of chronic diseases—which are particularly devastating for low-income Chinese in rural areas—is forcing the government to invest in a healthcare system that has so far been deficient, or non-existent in the rural areas which lag behind urban areas in medical resources and healthcare infrastructure. But Dr Liu warns: 'If the Chinese government were to build a healthcare system to serve 130 crore Chinese modeled on the US [where healthcare spending is projected to account for 20 percent of GDP by 2020] we will need a huge budget which will soon bankrupt our country. We need an alternative healthcare model that is smart, affordable, and inclusive. We need a model that focuses on—and enables—disease *prevention* rather than treatment.'[17]

For its part, Neusoft has developed several low-cost but high-tech solutions such as affordable health monitoring devices and tele-medicine solutions for rural hospitals to serve low-income Chinese patients. More impressively, Neusoft has developed a cutting-edge wristwatch for chronic disease patients to use as a mobile health monitor. On a regular basis, the watch collects bio indicators from sensors attached to the patient's body. This dynamic data is sent to Health Cloud, a cloud-computing-based expert system. Health Cloud analyzes the data using a healthcare knowledge database and offers customized advice to the patient in terms of exercise plans and diet regime, thus helping the patient make healthy lifestyle changes.[18] For instance, if you are overweight, the system will suggest a three-month jogging plan, monitor and report back your progress daily, and even suggest improvements when needed.

Dr Liu notes that in a rapidly ageing China—where family ties are important and the over-65 population is projected to increase from 13 crore in 2010 to some 22.2 crore by 2030—these wristwatches and home health monitors have become popular gifts from young Chinese to their parents.[19] Through these gifts, young Chinese can remotely track their parents' health—through daily reports on their mobile phones—and proactively tend to their well-being. Dr Liu believes that Neusoft's ability to serve marginal groups, such as the elderly and the rural poor, faster and cheaper by harnessing affordable technologies like cloud computing gives the company an advantage over Western multinationals. He says: 'We don't have the resources of a large multinational corporation, but we identify opportunities in underserved markets early on and execute fast on them by harnessing the power of technology—especially cloud computing, which significantly lowers the cost of service delivery in sectors l ike healthcare.'

Jugaad innovators like Dr Liu successfully include the margin by approaching marginal groups as whole new markets, helping everyone climb up Maslow's hierarchy of needs, co-creating value with customers and partners throughout the value chain, and making clever use of affordable technology to scale up their personalized solutions. As economies around the world become increasingly diverse, however, there is a growing urgency for large companies to pay close attention to the margin.

The Margin is Becoming the Majority

In coming years, 'marginal' segments will no longer be marginal; they will become bigger, possibly *much* bigger. And the number of marginal consumers will increase across a number of dimensions: age, ethnicity, and income.

Take age. In the next fifteen to twenty years, the number of Americans over 65 will double. In the same period, the number of Americans over 85 will triple. This shift will be even more dramatic in Europe. The continent already has nineteen of the world's twenty demographically oldest nations. By 2030, nearly 25 percent of Europeans will be older than 65, up from about 17 percent in 2005. As a result, the US Census Bureau estimates the European Union will by 2030 experience a 14-percent decrease in its workforce and a 7-percent decrease in its consumer populations.[20] All this means that American and European companies will need to tend to a rapidly ageing workforce and learn to serve ageing consumers—many of whom belong to the assertive baby boomer generation which is used to getting what it wants given the sheer strength of its numbers. Although India boasts a young population today, its ageing will accelerate—especially in the South—in coming decades. According to the United Nations Population Division, India's population aged 60 and older is expected to increase drastically from 8 percent in 2010 to 19 percent in 2050. By mid-century, this age group will include 32.3 crore people, which is greater than the total American population in 2012.[21]

The good news is that this senior market is a highly lucrative one. In the UK, the over-fifties spent £276 billion (₹ 20 lakh crore) in 2008, making up around 44 percent of total family spending in Britain.[22] In the US, the over-fifties' annual after-tax income is estimated to be $2.4 trillion (₹ 120 lakh crore), accounting for some 42 percent of all after-tax income.[23] In India, senior citizens are contributing to a boom in several sectors—especially real estate and healthcare. For instance, India is viewed as one the most lucrative markets for remote patient monitoring devices.[24] The bad news is that existing products and services are often not tailored to ageing consumers' needs. Ian Hosking, senior research associate at the Engineering Design Centre at the University of Cambridge's Department of Engineering, points out: 'Ageing populations exhibit an increasing variation in functional capabilities such as vision, hearing, and dexterity. In general these abilities reduce with age. Even though it may seem obvious to design inclusive products, many products are targeted at young, able-bodied users. As a result, they are neither accessible nor desirable to older users. At the same time, the products that we use every day seem to grow ever more complex to operate.'[25] Large companies will miss out on a big market opportunity if they fail to adapt their offerings to the requirements of a rapidly ageing consumer base.

Populations around the world are not only ageing, they are also becoming more diverse and multicultural. For instance, the percentage of children in the US with at least one foreign-born parent rose from 15 percent in 1994 to 23 percent in 2010. Similarly, more than half of the growth in the US population between 2000 and 2010 came from the increase in the Hispanic population, which rose 43 percent to 5.05 crore during that period; these Hispanic consumers are likely to form the majority in states like California within a generation. It is estimated that the Hispanic consumer group has a collective buying power of about $1 trillion (₹ 50 lakh crore).[26] The Census Bureau projects that the share of ethnic and racial minorities will reach 54 percent of the total US population and surpass that of non-Hispanic whites by 2042—eight years sooner than expected.[27]

The demographic makeup of Europe is also bound to change rapidly. Muslims, who currently account for 5 percent of the overall population of the European community (reaching 10 percent in France), are expected to account for 20 percent by 2050.[28] But long before that, countries such as Britain, France, Spain, and the Netherlands will have surpassed that figure. As the working-age population rapidly decreases, European governments will have no choice but to liberalize their immigration policies if they wish to sustain their economic competitiveness. This growing ethnic and cultural diversity of populations around the world will force corporations to innovate their products and services to meet the differing needs of minority consumers.

Another key factor contributing to the diversity of populations is the rise of Generation Y and Z workers, with their idiosyncratic values and expectations. Many studies show that Gen Y and Z employees consider themselves widely misunderstood in the workplace and feel alienated— primarily because the hierarchical structures and top-down communication styles of large corporations are at odds with the collaborative spirit of Gen Y and Z workers. Unless large companies find an innovation mechanism to keep their Gen Y and Z employees fully engaged, these young workers are likely to feel marginalized and leave for organizations that truly capitalize on their creative talents.

Finally, there has been a dramatic shift in income groups around the world. In emerging markets like India, large numbers of consumers are moving out of poverty into the lower middle class. In 2007, McKinsey Global Institute projected that India's middle-class would grow from 5 percent of the population back then to 40 percent over the following two decades, creating the world's fifth-largest consumer market by 2025.[29] But in developed economies like the US, a reverse phenomenon is happening: the lingering recession has pushed more people into relative poverty. Whereas in emerging markets consumers are engaged in a 'race to the top', in mature Western economies consumers are being pulled into a 'race to the bottom'. In 2010, 15.1 percent of Americans (or 4.6 crore people) were living below the official poverty line, the highest level since 1993 (in 2009, the percentage was 14.3 percent).[30]And America's consuming middle class, which accounts for 70 percent of national spending and forms the bedrock of the US economy, is shrinking. According to Pew Charitable Trusts, nearly a third of Americans who belonged to the middle class as teenagers in the 1970s have slipped below it as adults.[31] In India too, there is a widening gap between the affluent and the poor. Indeed, the Indian 'growth story' actually hides a more complex—and worrisome—reality: while educated Indians swell the ranks of the middle-class, the uneducated are falling off the economic ladder and feeling the pinch. For instance, according to Gallup's 2012 Financial Wellbeing Index, 31 percent Indians rate their lives as (financially) 'suffering' in 2012 compared to 24 percent in 2011 and 12 percent in 2006. Merely 13 percent respondents said they are 'thriving' compared to 21 percent in 2006. Finally, 56 percent respondents said they are financially struggling. Those financially suffering or struggling are low-skilled and lower-paid manual workers whereas those thriving are well-educated white-collar workers. Hence, although the Indian middle-class is expanding, there is equally a growing segment of the Indian population that is feeling economically marginalized.

What does all this mean for large corporations? The marginal groups that have traditionally been perceived—and therefore ignored—as the 'long tail' of the consumer economy (that is, as niche segments) are rapidly becoming the 'fat tail' (that is, dominant consumer groups).[32] These groups can no longer be ignored. Companies that actively embrace them, and form their businesses around their needs, are likely to find, just as jugaad innovators in emerging markets are finding, that doing so increasingly makes business sense. Indeed, it will increasingly be possible to include the margin (do good) and make a profit (do well) at the same time. But there are several factors holding back large companies from including the margin in their business strategies. We explore these factors in the next section.

Why Large Companies View Marginal Groups as Unprofitable

Even though marginal segments are increasingly economically important, many large businesses still shy away from serving them for three key reasons, each of which is related to either the unwillingness or the inability of these companies to view marginal groups as profitable.

First, many large companies view creating products and services for segments that are typically marginalized as a social mission rather than a core business opportunity. They tend to use their philanthropic arms to reach out to, say, low-income groups or ethnic minorities. But such exercises invariably become part of companies' corporate social responsibility activities, while the for-profit business focuses on 'mainstream' customers. For instance, many leading Western banks have set up foundations and CSR programmes through which they partner with non-profit organizations like Operation Hope to serve the banking needs of the disenfranchised, yet in their core business these banks continue to serve middle-class and wealthy clients. Similarly, many companies have diversity programmes that celebrate diversity in the workforce and customer base, but they rarely succeed in implementing employee engagement strategies specifically tailored to diverse groups.

Second, large companies' current, often entrenched business models are not designed to meet marginal customers' diverse needs. To truly serve marginal customers and make a profit, companies would need to build entirely new business models specifically tailored to such groups. Unfortunately, most companies are reluctant to do this; they prefer to tweak their existing offerings and business models to serve the diverse needs of marginal customers. Such attempts, being halfhearted, are often doomed to fail. Thus, companies fail to come up with a compelling and unique value proposition for marginal customers.

Third, a short-term outlook prevents large companies' long-term investments in products and services that serve marginal groups. Companies that worry about quarterly performance aren't motivated to invest the time and resources needed to design business models that target marginal segments; the returns on such investments, they feel, are unlikely to materialize for a number of years. The financial services sector is a prime example. According to the FDIC, 6 crore Americans are either unbanked or underbanked.[33] The large banks have yet to address the need of this large marginal group. Rob Levy, manager, Innovation and Research, at the Centre for Financial Services Innovation (CFSI), explains why: 'Some large banks are aware of the market potential that over 6 crore unbanked and underbanked American consumers represent. But to effectively serve those consumers, banks will need to design entirely new products, marketing strategies, and distribution channels to meet the needs of this consumer segment. While, this kind of comprehensive approach to the underbanked market may realize positive returns and strong customer relationships in the long run, it may not yield gigantic profits in the first few years of operation. It can, therefore, be hard for banks to justify such long-term investments to shareholders.'[34]

This reluctance of large companies to include the margin is unfortunate. It means these companies are literally and figuratively leaving money on the table, and exposing themselves to competition from unexpected quarters on many fronts.

Large Companies will Face Increased Competition in Core Markets

As we've noted, with the ranks of those in the marginal segments growing, the 'long tail' is increasingly becoming the 'fat tail'. And as long as large corporations continue to view marginal segments as unprofitable, opportunities will open up for new players to step in and fill the vacuum created in this sizable and growing market. As a result, established companies will soon face competition, even in their core markets of middle-class and affluent consumers, from a range of players.

FRUGAL INNOVATORS FROM EMERGING MARKETS

Companies from emerging markets such as HTC and Haier are already giving established consumer goods companies a run for their money by offering lowcost, high-value cellphones, fridges, and wine coolers to financially stretched consumers around the world. Similarly, established car makers need to worry about the upcoming launch in the US and European markets of Tata Motors' ₹ 1 lakh Nano, as the car is poised to capture the hearts (and wallets) of cost-conscious Western consumers clamouring for affordable, fuel-efficient transportation.

GOLIATHS FROM UNRELATED INDUSTRIES

Leading players across industries are facing competition from big players from other industries who are encroaching on their home turf by serving marginal segments. For instance, Walmart, Inc. is challenging banks on their home turf by opening 1,500 Money Centres that serve many of the basic financial needs of low-income consumers—allowing them to transfer money, buy prepaid debit cards, pay bills, and cash checks (not to mention allowing them to use this cash, along with complimentary coupons, to shop within the same store). Walmart Money Centres are highly successful because they are accessible (they are located very close to where consumers live), intimate (consumers regularly visit the Walmart store for their grocery purchases and trust the brand), and affordable (Walmart charges only $3 (₹ 150) for cashing checks up to $1,000 (₹ 50,000) and only $3 (₹ 150) for buying or reloading its prepaid card).[35]

Encouraged by the success of its Money Centres, Walmart is launching even smaller kiosks called Express Centres in more far-flung locations. As Rob Levy of CFSI notes: 'While many are talking about financial inclusion, Walmart is actually championing it using an innovative business model that eschews product complexity in favour of simplicity and convenience that enhance the user experience.'[36]

NIMBLE START-UPS

By exclusively focusing on mainstream markets, large companies ignore lucrative opportunities in marginal segments and expose themselves to competition by nimbler start-ups. Again, take the financial services sector: not only do incumbents have to contend with a giant retailer like Walmart encroaching on their turf, but they also need to ward off rivalry from nimble start-ups like PayNearMe. PayNearMe helps the 24 percent of American households who have neither a debit nor a credit card to buy stuff on Amazon, purchase bus tickets on Greyhound's website, or pay by cash offline at a 7-Eleven outlet. Danny Shader, a serial entrepreneur who founded PayNearMe, observes that 'the "underbanked" is a giant underserved market. We're making it better, faster, and cheaper for them to transact.'[37] Visa and MasterCard are paying close attention to PayNearMe, given that $1.2 trillion (₹ 60 lakh crore) worth of consumer purchases were conducted using cash in 2010. In India, many start-ups now provide similar hassle-free prepaid card services targeted at low-income citizens who can't avail of a regular debit card since they don't have a regular bank account. For instance, Commonwealth Inclusive Growth Services, established by the Commonwealth Business Council, offers a multipurpose prepaid card that members in underprivileged communities in the Chennai region can use to pay for groceries or even bus tickets. I Manimekalai, member of a self-help group in Chennai, describes the value of such prepaid cards: 'It takes us nearly half a day to visit the bank, get the required signatures and withdraw money. This card will make it a lot easier for us to buy raw materials to make products.'[38]

Marc Andreessen, co-founder of Netscape and general partner of the venture capital firm Andreessen-Horowitz, believes that 'asset-light' tech start-ups—such as PayNearMe, which conducts crores of dollars in financial transactions without owning a single bank branch—are in the process of invading and overturning established industry structures. Andreessen believes that we are in the midst of a radical and wide-ranging technological and economic shift in which software companies are about to take over large swathes of the economy. He notes: 'Over the next ten years, I expect many more industries to be disrupted by software, with new world-beating Silicon Valley companies doing the disruption in more cases than not.'[39] Increasingly, these Silicon Valley entrepreneurs—and start-ups in Indian high tech hotspots like Bangalore, Chennai, and Pune—are targeting marginal segments that have long been ignored by brick-and-mortar companies in capital-intensive sectors such as healthcare, telecom, finance, education, and energy. It is this sharp focus on marginal segments that will lead to big revenue gains and growth for the companies who target them.

How to Make Big Margins by Including the Margin

Jugaad entrepreneurs offer many powerful strategies that large companies can learn from in their attempts to include the margin profitably. Specifically, large companies can adopt the following strategies.

CARRY OUT SOCIAL INCLUSION WITH A BUSINESS MINDSET

Non-profit CSR programmes that serve marginal groups are redundant if your company is also striving to meet the needs of the same groups using a for-profit business model—just as jugaad innovators in emerging markets are doing. To avoid such corporate cultural schizophrenia, corporate leaders need to pull the plug on their CSR efforts and get serious about social inclusion by making it a strategic *business imperative* for all their departments and senior managers. These leaders could emulate Ramón Mendiola Sánchez, CEO of Florida Ice & Farm Co., a large food and beverage producer and distributor in Costa Rica. As explained in Chapter 3, Mendiola merged his corporate, social responsibility, and environmental strategies into a single integrated strategy, which is carried out by employees at all levels in ways that bring benefits to all stakeholders.[40]

Cater to the Expanding Low-Income Consumer Base

As the ranks of low income aspirational consumers grow, large companies that traditionally served more affluent markets will need to radically shift their innovation strategies—or lose out to low-cost rivals. Rather than spending R&D on premium products with high-end features, these companies will need to create value-for-money products that are accessible to the growing low-income consumer base. This is a wise strategy that companies such as the French car maker Renault are currently following. These companies are stepping up their R&D and marketing efforts to launch a slew of products tailored for budget-conscious consumers around the world. For instance, Renault is rapidly extending its low-cost Dacia brand—that includes the Logan, the highly successful sedan that sells for about $10,000 (₹ 5 lakh)—by adding the Logan van, the Logan pickup, and even the Dacia Duster SUV to the portfolio. Aimed at cost-conscious European car buyers, these no-frills Dacia vehicles—manufactured in Renault's factory in Romania—use fewer parts and boast a simplified design, yet are affordable and robust. Low-cost vehicles in the Dacia portfolio have rapidly become Renault's cash cow, contributing to over 25 percent of its sales revenues in 2010, up from 20 percent in 2008. That percentage could be higher in coming years, given that 59 percent of Europeans under thirty—and 54 percent of Europeans over fifty—claim to be ready to buy a low-cost car.[41] Renault envisions expanding its low-cost product portfolio even further in the future by adding more models that will be developed by the company's rapidly-expanding R&D team in

India—a country that, according to CEO Carlos Ghosn, boasts deep expertise in what he calls 'frugal engineering'.[42]

CREATE AN INCLUSIVE WORK CULTURE

As their workforce becomes increasingly diverse and global, companies must ensure that no worker feels marginalized due to age, social background, or job title. Companies must strive to foster an open and inclusive culture anchored by a participative management style. This helps to foster a creative and motivated workforce, one that can tap into different domains of expertise in devising new products and services and that feels empowered and encouraged to do so. ThoughtWorks is one such company that has successfully cultivated a transparent and inclusive work culture. This software consultancy, headquartered in Chicago, has experienced revenue growth of 20 to 30 percent a year, by charging premium fees to its loyal blue-chip clients such as JetBlue, L.L.Bean, and DaimlerChrysler. The company's secret: a flat organizational structure that allows its 1,000 global employees to have an equal say in all major corporate decisions. Roy Singham, founder and chairman, notes: 'We want to be the flattest company in the world. The janitors in China should be the strategic equals of the CEO in Chicago. And how do intellectuals collaborate in the 21st century? Self-organizing in small teams, poly-skilled, decentralized, non-authoritative.'[43] ThoughtWorks' 'hypertolerance' of diversity begins with a stringent recruitment process that ensures, says Singham, that 'no bigot, sexist, or homophobe gets in'. Singham observes, 'In the 21st century, inclusivity won't happen through authority or some artificial 'diversity' program. Rather, the CEO must embody the spirit of inclusivity by nurturing an "obnoxiously" transparent culture where every decision and strategy can be debated openly, without fear.'[44]

RECOGNIZE THAT MARGINAL SEGMENTS ARE NOT MARGINAL MINDS

By labelling marginal customers and employees 'too poor' or 'too old', companies lose an opportunity to tap into the rich knowledge and wisdom these marginal groups might contribute to the organization. Take the baby boomers, for instance. On January 1, 2011, the very first baby boomers started to turn 65, an age beyond which employees are deemed 'unproductive' by most employers. Yet companies such as Boeing and Eli Lilly have recognized that although at 65 their employees' hair may be grey, their 'grey matter' remains of considerable value. Recognizing this fact, in 2003 Procter & Gamble and Eli Lilly (along with Boeing) launched YourEncore.com, an innovation community that connects retired scientists and engineers with organizations seeking to leverage their expertise to solve challenging technical problems. Fifty companies—including many Fortune 500 companies—are now members of the YourEncore network, which provides a great platform for retired scientists to continue doing the work they love by matching them to short-term projects at member companies.[45]

USE TECHNOLOGY TO LOWER THE COST OF INCLUSION

Just like jugaad innovators in emerging markets do, rather than invest in expensive brick-and-mortar delivery infrastructure, companies need to harness the power of social media, cloud computing, and mobile telephony to cost-effectively deliver their products and services to marginal consumers. For instance, US healthcare insurers UnitedHealth Group and Blue Cross and Blue Shield—in partnership with technology vendors such as Cisco—are piloting cost-effective tele-medicine programmes that allow patients in the US states of Minnesota and Colorado to talk to healthcare professionals remotely as a low-cost alternative to expensive in person visits from doctors to patients who live in rural and underserved areas (it's worth noting that the tele-medicine technology used in this US pilot project was developed in Cisco's R&D lab in Bangalore!). If successful, these virtual solutions could be deployed in several other states across the US. According to a 2008 study by the Centre for Information Technology Leadership, a non-profit research centre in Boston, the widespread implementation of tele-medicine solutions could save the US healthcare system more than $4 billion (₹ 20,000 crore) annually just by reducing transfers of patients from one location, such as a nursing home, to provider offices or hospitals.[46] Affordable, accessible tele-medicine solutions also significantly reduce hardship for financially stretched American patients and their families.

PARTNER WITH NON-PROFIT ORGANIZATIONS

Corporations rarely partner with non-profit entities outside their CSR initiatives (initiatives that, as we argued earlier, need to be integrated with the company's core business strategy). But a new generation of non-profit ventures is willing to work with businesses to co-create for-profit business models that improve the lives of marginal citizens while also generating a profit. For instance, the Centre for Financial Services Innovation, a policy research and advisory organization based in Chicago, advises large US banks on how to design inclusive business models that can profitably serve the roughly 6 crore Americans who are either unbanked or underbanked. Likewise, The Centre for Microfinance, housed within the Institute for Financial Management and Research in Chennai, is a non-profit research centre that advises Indian banks on inclusive business models that can improve the accessibility and quality of financial services for the poor—especially by leveraging new technologies such as mobile phones, point of sale devices, and smart cards.

SECURE C-LEVEL BUY-IN TO DRIVE SYSTEMIC BUSINESS MODEL CHANGES

Given that inclusivity requires fundamental and systemic changes in how companies operate, top management's commitment is vital to enabling and sustaining such business model transformation within companies. For instance, GE's Healthymagination programme—aimed at making healthcare services affordable and accessible for the masses—is overseen by CEO Jeff Immelt himself. Through his leadership, Immelt is personally driving a shift in GE's culture from that of an R&D-driven high-end product company to a community-focused inclusive solution provider (see Chapter 8 for more details on GE's Healthymagination initiative).

ADOPT—AND ADAPT—PROVEN BEST PRACTISES FROM EMERGING MARKETS

As we described earlier in this chapter, emerging markets—because of scarcity, diversity, and interconnectivity—are increasingly a breeding ground for solutions that include the margin. If you have learned how to financially include the 60 crore Indians who are unbanked or offer affordable medical treatment to the hundreds of crores of Indians who lack access to basic healthcare, you are likely to have gained valuable insights into how to serve the 6 crore unbanked and underbanked Americans and the 5 crore Americans who lack health insurance.

By using emerging markets as a breeding ground for inclusive innovation, companies can not only grow their businesses in those markets but also learn lessons and develop products and services that they can adapt to serve marginal groups in other emerging markets or even the West. Johnson & Johnson, for example, is currently sponsoring Text4baby, a text messaging service that provides pregnant women and new mothers in low-income families with valuable information about how to care for their health and give their babies the best possible start in life. Text4baby was inspired by successful mobile health initiatives undertaken in emerging markets such as Mexico and Kenya.[47] (In Mexico, VidaNET is a free service that sends text messages to HIV patients to remind them to take their medication on a regular basis.) Text4Baby is literally a lifesaver in the US, where each year 5 lakh babies are born prematurely and nearly 28,000 children die before their first birthday. (According to the World Health Organization, babies born in the US have a greater probability of dying in their first month than babies in much of the developed world.[48]) By late 2011, over 2.6 lakh women had signed up for Text4baby—a number expected to reach 10 lakh by the end of 2012.[49]

EMBRACE INCLUSIVE DESIGN PRINCIPLES

It is easier to factor in inclusivity up front, during the design phase of innovation, rather than to try and retrofit or reengineer existing products and services to appeal to marginalized segments of the market after the fact. To learn these new inclusive R&D skills, companies should consider joining academic initiatives like the Inclusive Design program at the University of Cambridge's Department of Engineering or recruiting graduates from Stanford University's Entrepreneurial Design for Extreme Affordability programme and Santa Clara University's Frugal

Innovation Labs. (We describe these programmes in more detail in Chapter Nine.) In addition to helping Western companies gain access to the next generation of inclusive innovators, these programmes can give Western companies early access to new technical solutions, results of pilot tests in the field, and knowledge of how to go about doing inclusive innovation more generally. For instance, the Engineering Design Centre at University of Cambridge's Department of Engineering is helping organizations such as the BBC, Bayer Healthcare, Roche, Nestlé, Royal Bank of Scotland, Bosch, Siemens, and Marks & Spencer design mainstream products and services that are accessible to, and usable by, as many people as reasonably possible (but especially the elderly) without the need for special adaptation or specialized design. There are already 13 crore people over 50 in the European Union; by 2020, one in two European adults will be over 50. Designing products and services that these consumers love to use is not only socially responsible but also makes great economic sense.

Companies can no longer afford to ignore marginal segments, which are poised to grow in size and significance in the coming decades. Recognizing the commercial potential of these marginal groups, large companies must start designing entirely new products and services that meet their particular requirements—just as Renault-Nissan is doing. To effectively market and distribute these offerings to these segments, companies need to take advantage of technologies such as social media and mobile computing and to forge partnerships with non-profit organizations. More critically, to optimally serve marginal segments in the long run, large companies need to enshrine inclusivity into their corporate culture and their business models, just as Walmart is doing. As Johnson & Johnson did, large companies can jump-start these inclusion initiatives by adopting proven solutions and business practises from emerging markets.

Large companies, however, need to move fast—or else they risk leaving opportunities open for nimble rivals from around the world to jump in. This threat is precisely why consumer goods giant Procter & Gamble is proactively reinventing its business model to serve marginal groups—especially low-income consumers.

How Procter & Gamble Includes the Margin Profitably

For decades, Procter & Gamble (P&G) has concentrated on developing household goods for the vast American middle class. But today the company is changing the way it does research, distribution, and marketing so that it can better serve the needs of cash-strapped Americans. Specifically, P&G wants to build a whole new business by tapping into what it calls 'un-served and underserved consumers'. Thus, for the first time in 38 years, in 2010 P&G launched a new dishwashing soap in the US. The soap had the Gain name and scent, formerly reserved for laundry detergent, and was offered at a bargain price (compared to the company's slightly more expensive Dawn Hand Renewal dish soap). Since 2008, when the recession deepened, P&G's cheaper brands—such as bargain-priced Luvs diapers and Gain laundry detergent—have sold better and posted faster market-share gains than its premium-priced Pampers and Tide brands.[50]

Seeing a clear trend, P&G is stepping up its research into the swelling ranks of low-income American households. In doing so, the company seeks to ward off growing competition from low-cost suppliers across its product lines. Between 2008, when the recession began, and 2011, P&G's fabric-softener sheets business (which includes the Bounce brand) lost 5 percent of its market share to Sun Products and private-label brands. Rivals such as Church & Dwight and Energizer Holdings, which supply the low-cost Arm & Hammer detergent and Schick shaving blades, respectively, are stealing market share from P&G's pricier brands such as Tide and Gillette.

With a sense of urgency, P&G's CEO Robert McDonald is accelerating the company's R&D efforts to come up with a rich pipeline of 'value for money' products that cater to budget-conscious Americans—making this a strategic priority for P&G. 'We're going to do this both by tiering our portfolio up in terms of value as well as tiering our portfolio down', Mr McDonald explains.[51]

Although P&G has successfully served the bottom of the socio-economic pyramid in emerging markets, its executives in the US never imagined they would one day be selling to this segment in America. 'This has been the most humbling aspect of our jobs,' says Phyllis Jackson, P&G's vice president of consumer market knowledge for North America. 'The numbers of Middle America have been shrinking because people have been getting hurt so badly economically that they've been falling into lower income groups.'[52]

Conclusion

The increasing diversity of the workforce and the growing number of low income consumers around the world are forcing companies to find innovative ways to serve marginal segments—segments which now carry more economic weight than ever before. But jugaad innovators don't include the margin on a mere whim or for philanthropic purposes. Rather, innovators like Dr Rana Kapoor of YES BANK include the margin because it makes business sense for them to do so.

Perhaps of greater interest, jugaad innovators are driven to include the margin by passion, intuition, and empathy. Indeed, they pour their hearts into their inclusive innovation initiatives, as they are able to intuitively connect with marginal groups and empathize with their needs. This genuine empathy confers authenticity on their inclusion initiatives and makes these projects more sustainable. Like Bill Gates, jugaad innovators are passionate about creating a system of *inclusive capitalism*—one that can harmoniously reconcile the twin goals of making profits and improving people's lives. Empathy, intuition, and passion are at the core of the final principle that drives jugaad innovation: 'Follow your heart'.

Chapter 7

Principle Six: Follow Your Heart

'Your time is limited, so don't waste it living someone else's life.
Have the courage to follow your heart and intuition. They somehow
already know what you truly want to become. Everything else is
secondary.'

—STEVE JOBS

Unlike Western CEOs, Kishore Biyani doesn't rely on
expensive management consultants to advise him on his
next strategic move. Biyani owns Big Bazaar, one of India's
largest grocery and home goods retail chains or 'hypermarkets'.
When Big Bazaar opened its first store in India, Biyani was
advised to follow the traditional, Western approach to retailing,
using neatly organized aisles and soothing music. But that
format didn't go down well with Indian shoppers who found
it all a bit too sleek and unnatural. After all, Indians are used
to shopping in noisy, disorganized street markets. Biyani then
realized that the Big Bazaar stores should live up to their name:
they must look—and even smell—like bazaars. When we visited
him in his office in Mumbai, he told us, 'Initially we took the
advice of management consultants who made us follow the

Walmart model. But we soon discovered that this didn't work in the Indian context. We realized what we had to do was to be ourselves, and follow our *intuition*.'[1]

Guided by his intuition, Biyani swiftly reconfigured his stores to have the chaotic look and feel of Indian street markets: cluttered aisles, store clerks in casual clothing, and bins of vegetables with some bad items thrown in to make customers feel they had scored when for instance they found the perfect onion. And rather than standardize their offerings across all stores, he made sure that each Big Bazaar outlet stocked a product mix that fit local needs. Further, these needs weren't identified by expensive market researchers, but by regional store managers with an intuitive and empathetic understanding of local preferences.

'Common sense retailing' is what Biyani calls this customer-centric approach. And it's worked. We visited several Big Bazaar stores across India. Typically crowded, they have the feel of a buzzing Moroccan souk. Biyani continues to experiment and tweak his business model. Not surprisingly, Big Bazaar is now India's largest hypermarket.

Jugaad innovators in emerging markets rely more on their intuition than on analysis to successfully navigate a highly complex, uncertain, and unpredictable environment. They use their gut intelligence and innate empathy for customers to innovate breakthroughs that defy conventional wisdom. Their undying passion acts as the fuel that sustains their efforts to make a difference in the lives of the communities they serve.

In this chapter, we discuss why and how corporate leaders, inured to data-driven decision making, can benefit from relying more on their intuition to succeed in an increasingly complex world. Rather than second-guessing what customers want by sitting in a remote R&D lab, innovators in large companies need to immerse themselves in customers' native environment so as to better empathize with customer needs. Most important, we show how, rather than merely seeking to harness their employees' brainpower, large companies can learn to tap into their employees' 'heartpower', thus unleashing the passion of individual employees and channeling it into innovative pursuits that serve a larger purpose.

Your Heart Knows What Your Mind Doesn't

The heart is the seat of passion, intuition, and empathy. Jugaad innovators in emerging markets possess these qualities in abundance. The challenge is twofold: how to develop these qualities in the first place and then how to nurture them. We have found that several key aspects of the complex environment in which jugaad innovators operate make them particularly passionate, intuitive, and empathetic.

Jugaad entrepreneurs are regularly exposed to the harsh conditions in which their fellow citizens live—whether these involve regular electricity failure, water rationing, or poor access to healthcare and education. Whatever they may be, these extreme conditions arouse the empathy of jugaad entrepreneurs, who feel they must do something to improve the often harsh conditions around them. Thus, jugaad innovators don't just sit around after witnessing others' pain; rather, they convert their compassion into passion by seeking solutions to alleviate this pain. Yet these solutions are not charity work—they are built around sound for-profit business models. As such, empathy forms the cornerstone of jugaad innovators' practise of an altruistic form of capitalism that is shaped by enlightened self-interest. Adam Smith captured well the importance of empathy as a vital ingredient of entrepreneurial innovation. In his pioneering work *The Theory of Moral Sentiments,* Smith argued that although man generally tends to be selfish, 'there are evidently some principles in his nature which interest him in the fortune of others, and render their happiness necessary to him, though he derives nothing from it, except the pleasure of seeing it'.[2]

In some cases, jugaad entrepreneurs innovate to meet their *own* needs—and to alleviate their personal pain. For instance, after Venkat Rangan heard his father constantly complain that his brokerage company couldn't execute stock transactions as fast as he liked, Rangan decided to do something about it. He founded INXS Technologies, a software product company based in Chennai, which has developed one of the world's largest mobile trading platforms. The platform, called MarketSimplified, currently helps speed transactions through mobile phones not only for Rangan's father, but also for crores of customers of the world's leading brokerage houses that use MarketSimplified.[3]

Another reason why jugaad innovators follow their hearts—more than their brains—is that they are forced to think on their feet all the time. It's hard—even counterproductive—to logically analyze a highly complex situation and make rational decisions when things are changing constantly. Emerging markets are fast-paced and volatile. Confronted daily with do-or-die situations, jugaad innovators have learned to make decisions on the fly, using their well-honed intuition rather than relying solely on analysis and logic. For instance, as soon as he saw signs that a Westernized retail format for Big Bazaar was faltering, Kishore Biyani quickly dropped it and embraced a new one—without waiting for an opportunity to do market research. If he had failed to respond as quickly as he did by heeding his intuition, it is quite possible that his business would have gone under.

The harsh conditions in emerging markets kindle jugaad innovators' creative empathy and passion, and the unpredictability of the local environment forces them to make rapid-fire decisions based on intuition rather than rational analysis.

The Gutsy Art of Acting on What Feels Right

Jugaad innovators like Kishore Biyani and Venkat Rangan are a self-confident and brave breed: they dare to *act on* what they feel is right. They don't seek validation or approval from customers or investors for their visionary ideas, and they tend to ignore naysayers. They know intuitively what the right solution for an unmet market need is. Only after they have introduced their pioneering solution do others recognize its true value. In other words, jugaad innovators valiantly forge their way into uncharted territory using the heart as a compass.

For instance, Diane Geng and Sara Lam, two Harvard-educated Chinese–Americans eager to reconnect with their ancestral roots, decided to spend time in Chinese villages where 80 crore people or 60 percent of China's population live. In these villages, Geng and Lam noticed that up to 90 percent of the youth dropped out of middle school without any occupational skills—and with a clear disdain for their communities. Geng and Lam also learned that the reason why rural youth either never attended or did not complete high school was not financial difficulty but (1) the irrelevance of the school curriculum to their life needs and (2) ineffective teaching that encouraged rote learning rather than creative thinking. As a result, Chinese villages were deprived of skilled young workers who would otherwise find creative ways to sustain the socio-economic growth of their communities.[4]

Geng and Lam recognized this was going to be a major issue for China, given its rapidly ageing population (by 2030, 16 percent of the Chinese population will be over 65—up from 10 percent in 2011). Driven by empathy, they decided to do something about the situation. Their intuition told them that the solution lay in improving the 'software' of the rural education system—such as curriculum and teacher quality—rather than fixing the 'hardware' such as building more schools and offering scholarships (as most NGOs and government agencies in China do). So Geng and Lam launched the Rural China Education Foundation (RCEF), a community-led grassroots initiative that recruits and works with local teachers in villages. RCEF creates new student-centred curricula that impart life-relevant skills to students, using practise-based teaching and learning methods that foster creativity and keep students engaged. By providing rural youth with a quality education that is practical and relevant to their life needs and skills, RCEF hopes to ensure China's future economic stability.

When asked what drives jugaad entrepreneurs like her to do something bold like RCEF, Lam had this to say: 'A sense of urgent need and mission. A feeling that something must be done. Compassion and an intolerance for injustice. The willingness to take the first step and to do what you can with what you've got. It's easy to think "All I need is this much more funding, or that many more people, then I can start".'[5]

Jugaad innovators also succeed in following their hearts because they rely heavily on their social intelligence to guide their decisions. Jugaad innovators are street smart and possess very high 'cognitive fluency'—which means that, rather than relying on spreadsheets to make decisions, they rapidly process large amounts of sensory information from the real world and improvise decisions in an intuitive and dynamic fashion based on emergent patterns.[6] Jan Chipchase and Ravi Chhatpar, who work for frog, a global design and innovation consultancy, and have interacted extensively with innovators in emerging markets agree. Chipchase is frog's Executive Creative Director of Global Insights, and Chhatpar is Strategy Director at frog and founder of its Shanghai studio. Both point out that, for instance, many Chinese innovators in the consumer electronics sector who practise *zizhu chuangxin*, the Chinese version of jugaad, don't use focus groups to determine ahead of time what features to include in their new products.[7] Rather, they spend a great deal of time on the street, observing what products customers actually use, and learning about which competitors' products are selling well and why. These innovators then use their deep customer insight to prioritize and quickly decide which features to include in their own products. In the process, they gain an intuitive sense of what customers want and can anticipate their needs.

Their deep customer insight also enables jugaad entrepreneurs to connect with customers at an emotional level—and establish higher customer intimacy in the process. Kevin Roberts, CEO of the global advertising agency Saatchi & Saatchi, discusses this very connection in his book *Lovemarks*.[8] Noting that intimacy is a key ingredient of winning over consumers, and highlighting the importance of empathy, commitment, and passion in achieving intimacy, Roberts says: 'It's the thoughtful touch, the surprises, that connect with a consumer's heart.'[9] Jugaad innovators tap into this empathy-based customer intimacy to gain deeper insights into the core issues that customers are grappling with and the broader socio-economic context in which they live. These rich insights allow jugaad innovators to then devise solutions that have a meaningful impact on customers' daily lives.

For instance, Anil Jain, Managing Director at Jain Irrigation Systems Ltd, has come up with a series of innovative solutions that have dramatically improved the productivity of the small-scale Indian farmers who make up a large segment of the Indian population. He attributes this success to the high emotional quotient of his employees: 'We intentionally hire salespeople whom we call "sons of the soil"—that is, people with an agricultural background who can relate to and empathize with the company's customers—the farmers.[10] These employees help elevate transactional customer relationships to transformative relationships. For instance, in their initial interactions with their customers—the farmers—Jain Irrigation's salesmen don't try to 'pitch' solutions to them; rather, they try to instill pride in the farmers by cocreating innovative solutions with them. Such shared innovation is sustainable because it is shaped by empathy and a passion shared by all stakeholders. Thanks to this customer-centric engagement approach, Jain explains, his company has been able to successfully shift its business model from 'contract farming' to '*contact* farming', a model that delivers disproportionately higher value to farmers.

While jugaad innovators trust their intuitions, they also conduct rapid experimentation to validate them. Rather than making forecasts or predictions, jugaad innovators test their intuitions in the real world to get rapid feedback. As such, they use experiential learning (that is, learning by doing) to hone their intuition and innovate continuously over time. Take Bam Aquino's Hapinoy Program in the Philippines, introduced in Chapter 3. The programme empowers women owners of sari-sari, stores (mom-and-pop shops) in the rural islands of the Philippines by identifying new business opportunities for them and giving them the tools and skills needed to capitalize on these opportunities. Aquino told us that although he relies on his intuition to identify what additional services he can bring to the women in the Hapinoy Program's network, he also relies on rapid prototyping to validate his intuition: 'We do lots of small pilots. We drop bad ideas early on and identify good ideas that have legs and focus our efforts on scaling them up'.[11] For instance, the Hapinoy Program recently piloted a project with a large pharmaceutical company to sell its over-the-counter medicine on a per-tablet basis through some of the sari-sari stores in far-flung villages that belong to the Hapinoy network. The pilot was successful, and is now being scaled up across the network.' On the other hand, Aquino had a strong intuition that mobile remittances—sending money to family members via cellphones—would be a great service that the Hapinoy Program could offer throughout its sari-sari store network, but the pilot project revealed some limitations. The organization found that adoption of the mobile remittance service depended on the level of access to banking services—which varied widely from area to area. So the mobile remittance service was deployed selectively in some areas only. Aquino explains: 'We use rapid prototyping to validate our intuitive ideas and reach one of three decisions: kill the idea, selectively scale it up in some parts of our network, or totally scale it up all across our network.' Acting in congruence with their intuitive feelings—and staying true to their passion—gives jugaad innovators such as Kishore Biyani, Diane Geng, Sara Lam, Anil Jain, and Bam Aquino an edge over competitors. And this can lead to eventual success in the marketplace.

Keeping the Fire Alive

How do jugaad innovators manage to sustain their passion? By practising what one might call 'detached engagement'. Although deeply engaged in their innovative projects, jugaad innovators remain detached from the outcomes. They don't let either failure or success affect their passion. For instance, Kishore Biyani didn't allow the failure of his first retail business model to dampen his passion for delivering a better retailing experience to Indian customers; he just moved on and tried other business models.

Jugaad innovators are indefatigable in pursuing their interests because their passion transcends the intellectual and emotional realms: they frequently believe they are carrying out a critical mission that serves a larger purpose. In Indian philosophical terms, jugaad innovators believe they are following their *dharma*—the personal obligations or duties that one is called upon to perform in his or her lifetime with diligence and detachment. Dr Prasad Kaipa, a CEO coach and Senior Fellow at the Indian School of Business, explains: 'Mahatma Gandhi famously said that "Happiness is when what you think, what you say, and what you do are in harmony". By aligning these three elements—thoughts, words, and actions—with heart and spirit, jugaad entrepreneurs derive a sense of fulfillment by serving a larger cause. This is truly the secret of their undying passion.'[12]

Take the case of Dr Devi Shetty, a reputed Indian heart surgeon who treated Mother Teresa. Dr Shetty is the founder of Narayana Hrudayalaya, a heart hospital in Bangalore, India, where hundreds of low-income people receive heart surgery every week. Dr Shetty started the hospital because he believes that, as a physician, he has a moral duty to make healthcare affordable and accessible to everyone, regardless of their caste, creed, religion, or income.[13] It is a compassionate sense of duty that sustains the passion of Dr Shetty and his fellow physicians at Narayana Hrudayalaya. In doing his duty, and being true to his profession, Dr Shetty is clearly following his heart (our website jugaadinnovation.com features a video interview with Dr Devi Shetty in which he discusses his compassionate health delivery model).

Not only are jugaad innovators able to sustain their own empathy and passion, but they also actively seek to ignite the passion and empathy of others. These qualities can be contagious: jugaad entrepreneurs are very good at inspiring employees, customers, and partners to rally around the cause—thus forming 'passion networks'. For instance, to secure his managers' buy-in for his visionary ideas, Big Bazaar's Kishore Biyani doesn't rely on traditional corporate communication tools such as PowerPoint presentations. Instead, he has a 'chief belief officer'—Devdutt Pattanaik—who concocts stories inspired by the rich storehouse of Indian myths to fire up managers' passion and enlist their support for transformational changes in the company.[14] Similarly, driven by his own passion, Bam Aquino is igniting the passion of women entrepreneurs in the Philippines through the Hapinoy Program, which encourages them to dream big and scale up their mom-and-pop stores. The women who succeed in doing so in turn become passionate advocates of Aquino's idea—and the Hapinoy Program—and evangelize it to other women business owners in nearby villages—thus forming a 'passion network' whose ripple effects are felt all across the Philippines.

The World is Too Complex for the Mind Alone to Grasp

In the coming years, corporate leaders—inured to data-driven analysis and rational decision making—will find it helpful, if not crucial, to follow their hearts as much as their brains. In this section, we discuss the reasons why we believe this is likely to be the case.

PURE LOGIC WILL NOT SUFFICE

In an unpredictable environment, companies can't solve problems using data when the problems themselves are ill defined and good data is likely to be unavailable. As Dan Pink argues in *A Whole New Mind*, the left-brain's linear, analytical, computer-like thinking—controlled by what we call our 'mind'—is insufficient to help us decipher, let alone navigate, our increasingly complex and ambiguous world.[15] Rather than relying purely on logic, therefore, Western executives must learn to innovate by also tapping into what Jack Welch calls their 'gut intelligence'—a creative intuition honed by years of experience.[16]

Research in neuroscience, cognitive psychology, and behavioral economics increasingly shows that the emotions play a major role in helping humans solve complex problems in situations of ambiguity and uncertainty. Rather than being untrustworthy, emotion and intuition may actually help people make wiser decisions than if they were guided by rational considerations alone. As Malcolm Gladwell shows in *Blink*, in many cases spontaneous decisions can often be as good as, if not better than, carefully planned and considered ones.[17]

GEN Y EMPLOYEES ARE LOOKING FOR MEANING

Employees today—especially Gen Y or Millennial workers—are no longer motivated by money alone: they want to work for an organization that puts their creative skills to use for a larger cause. Firms that leverage Gen Y's brainpower only to please shareholders are likely to lose out to rivals who channel Gen Y's *heartpower* into innovative projects that actively engage them and benefit the company as well as society at large. In a global survey conducted by EuroRSG among Millennials worldwide, 92 percent of Gen Y—including many Indians aged 18 to 25—agree that the world must change, and 84 percent consider it their duty to drive this change. Nearly 91 percent of young Indians believe their generation has the power to make this change happen—and 86 percent believe that social media will provide the enabling platform to drive this change.[18] With 50 percent of the world's population under the age of 27 (in India half the population is below 25), it is imperative that large companies find creative ways to harness the passion and entrepreneurial dynamism of young people driven to make a difference in the world

CUSTOMERS YEARN FOR AUTHENTIC RELATIONSHIPS

According to Forrester Research, only 5 percent of consumers agree with advertising claims; the other 95 percent consider them to be dishonest and inauthentic. Forrester also found that a growing number of consumers—empowered by peer-to-peer social computing tools like blogs and Facebook—trust other consumers *more* than they trust brands.[19] In the hyper-connected age of Twitter and Facebook, customers can swiftly punish brands that disingenuously attempt to 'sell' to them rather than engage them in a respectful and empathetic relationship. The good news, according to Josh Bernoff and Charlene Li, co-authors of *Groundswell*, is that consumers do trust brands that they feel truly empathize with their needs. The authors argue that the onus lies with companies to demonstrate genuine empathy in their interactions with customers—by respectfully engaging them as value co-creators rather than passive users of their offerings.[20] Indeed, 96 percent of North American consumers are more likely to purchase products from a company that listens to—and acts on—their advice.[21] According to the TNS Digital Life Study, 59 percent Indian consumers are willing to engage with brands in social networks—in contrast with only 25 percent in most western countries.[22]

Unfortunately, many companies don't realize that by encouraging or even allowing employees to follow their hearts and by creating emotionally engaging experiences for customers, they can help drive innovation and growth. And the companies that do recognize this may find it difficult to institutionalize such a culture and make it fundamental to the organization and its practises.

Industrial-Era Business Practises Keep Hearts Locked Out

In the post-industrial experience economy in which complexity is the norm, customers seek intimate and authentic relationships with brands, and Gen Y employees look for meaning in their work, it pays to be empathetic, intuitive, and passionate—and to take advantage of your organization's heart power. Yet large companies have trouble cultivating—and demonstrating—their heart power because they remain attached to industrial-era business practises and structured innovation approaches. These practises and approaches—which overemphasize left-brain thinking and rational behaviour—hinder corporate leaders' ability to make intuitive decisions, and prevent their companies from building empathetic connections with customers and igniting and harnessing the passion of creative employees.

R&D: Isolated and Disconnected from Real-World Customers

R&D engineers who operate in isolated labs do not spend time immersed in the world of customers and thus cannot empathize with them. Further, at many companies, R&D performance is still measured by the number of patents produced (an indicator of left-brain prowess) rather than the quality of the customer experience delivered (an indicator of right-brain empathetic creativity). But as Matt Bross, an American who runs Huawei's R&D, notes: 'There are no breakthrough technologies, only breakthrough *market applications*.'[23] R&D's inventions, groundbreaking or otherwise, will fail at launch if they don't address a well-defined source of customer pain. Understanding customer pain requires empathy for, and collaboration with, customers. Unfortunately, R&D tools and techniques, used for scientific discovery in the lab, were not conceived to capture consumer insights such as latent buyer needs, let alone to dynamically engage end users in designing and testing new products. This explains why 80 percent of new consumer products fail after launch—they often lack market relevance, leading Tim Brown, CEO of IDEO, a top design and innovation consultancy, to conclude: '[R&D] design may have its greatest impact when it's taken out of the hands of designers and put into the hands of everyone.'[24]

FIRMS OFTEN SEEK SAFETY IN NUMBERS—AND SHUN INTUITION

The business world abhors surprises and craves predictability: forecasts, plans, and budgets are all meant to 'control' the future and confer a sense of stability—leaving no room for intuitive improvisation. It is easier for a CEO to justify to investors a decision to invest in a new product or service if the CEO has lots of data to back it up. But investors are less likely to buy into an innovation project if you tell them that it's your gut telling you that the project merits investment.

Companies' overreliance on data—rather than intuition—leads them to make two strategic mistakes. First, they tend to axe many projects too early because they can't find enough data to support their commercial viability. (Conversely, they don't realize that by the time they have collected all the data needed to justify an innovation project, the window of opportunity for commercializing it may already have closed.) Second, companies prefer to invest in incremental innovation rather than breakthrough innovation because the former is easier to justify to investors. This attitude explains why nearly 90 percent of R&D projects in consumer product companies are aimed at sustaining existing products—by developing, for instance, line extensions—rather than investing in new-to-the-market products.[25] This leaves the door open for a competitor to disrupt the market with a groundbreaking offering.

Marketing Executives don't Emotionally Connect with Customers

Marketers often want customers to understand their value proposition, when it should be the other way around. For instance, consumers are sending this message to suppliers of premium consumer goods: 'My values have shifted. I now value simplicity and affordability: can you deliver on that?' But consumer good companies lack the empathy to positively respond to this plea; instead they continue to make and sell high-priced goods to middle-class buyers. The *Credit Suisse India Consumer Survey 2011* reports that 70 percent of Indian consumers surveyed find the current environment conducive for making major purchases, and yet the same consumers are more frugal and value-conscious in their spending—which prompted the Credit Suisse Research Institute, which conducted the survey, to note: '… we find Indian consumers excessively focused on value for money. Image (prestige) and power performance seem to matter the least'.[26] As a result, value-conscious consumers who find their suppliers insensitive to their frugal needs risk taking their business elsewhere. Kevin Roberts warns marketers: 'In the [old] Era of New marketing, it was all about your product. In the Age of Now it is all about the mastery of emotional communication; not manipulation, but of having relationships. In the Age of Now it's all about the single question consumers have of you: "How will you improve my life?" Answering this is to deliver priceless value.'[27]

OUTDATED HUMAN RESOURCE MANAGEMENT DOESN'T ENGAGE NEXT-GENERATION EMPLOYEES

Companies continue to rely primarily on financial incentives (such as bonuses) to motivate their employees rather than giving them the space and time to pursue their passion in a constructive manner.

Not surprisingly, according to the Blessing White Employee Engagement Survey of 2011, only 37 percent of Indian employees work with passion while the remaining workers say they do not feel fully engaged by their jobs. John Hagel, co-chairman of the Deloitte Centre for the Edge and co-author of *The Power of Pull: How Small Moves, Smartly Made, Can Set Big Things in Motion*, offers the following piece of advice to heads of human resource management: 'One thing I would do is to start systematically measuring the passion levels of my employees. I've developed a strong view that one of the keys to motivating individuals is to help them connect to their passion for their profession. Monitoring passion level gives you the ability to provide rapid performance improvement. Passionate people are deeply motivated to improve themselves and drive themselves to the next level of performance.'[28]

How Corporate Leaders Can Follow their Hearts

In an environment that favours more structured and data-driven approaches to innovation, following one's heart in business today poses several challenges for large companies and their managers. By drawing on the experience of jugaad entrepreneurs, however, there are several ways in which corporate leaders can develop a culture of empathy and passion within their companies.

Send Senior Management to 'Empathy Development Boot-Camps'

Empathy is like a muscle; it can be developed in senior executives by exposing them to diverse perspectives. For instance, Allianz Global Investors runs a dedicated training centre in its headquarters in Munich, Germany, where senior executives from Allianz as well as client companies attend training programmes in communication, team building, and leadership—all of which are conducted by visually impaired trainers in the dark or by hearing impaired trainers in a soundproof space.[29] The goal of these programmes is to increase self-awareness among senior executives, the idea being that one cannot empathize with others unless one has direct knowledge of them and one has realized and acknowledged one's own limits.

Ignore Market Researchers and Investors to Innovate Radically

C-level executives need moral courage to follow their hearts—and this often entails ignoring market researchers and investors when it comes to disruptive innovation. Specifically, to avoid getting caught in an inflexible web of structure and demands for data, senior executives shouldn't rely solely on the approval of external stakeholders when launching truly disruptive product and services. Relying on external approval in this way could either delay or altogether prevent corporate leaders from pursuing truly breakthrough ideas. For instance, when developing new products or formulating new strategies, Apple's Steve Jobs rarely bothered to get validation from financial analysts, media pundits, or even consumers. He was more interested in following his heart than merely seeking to please analysts and market watchers.

EMBRACE CUSTOMER-CENTRIC DESIGN PRINCIPLES

R&D engineers and scientists need to get out of their labs and immerse themselves in the environment that surrounds their customers, to truly understand their needs: this is the basis of customer-centric design. As we've noted, companies like Nokia and Intel employ ethnographers who spend months living with underserved customers in emerging markets to identify their latent needs and design meaningful solutions that can make a significant impact on customers' daily lives. These solutions (such as Nokia's 1100, which has sold over 25 crore units worldwide) carry the potential of turning into breakthrough products with huge commercial potential. Firms eager to build their internal skills in human-centreed design can do so by hiring specialized consultancies such as Idiom, IDEO, or frog. Companies that can't afford these design consultants can use social media tools like Facebook and crowdsourcing techniques to engage 'lead users'—that is, the early adopters among consumers. These lead users can help companies identify mainstream customers' unarticulated needs and help co-create new products, services, and experiences that fulfill those needs.[30]

ENGAGE YOUR CUSTOMERS IN A HEART-TO-HEART CONVERSATION

Researchers in fields from neuroscience to psychology, behavioural economics to marketing, all agree that emotions are as powerful a driver of consumer behaviour as rationality and calculation. In many cases, emotions may even be the only driver of consumer behaviour. In others, they may be more dominant. In still others, the emotions may play a complementary and reinforcing role to that of reason.[31] All this has profound implications for CMOs and marketers more generally. In a world where brands have achieved parity on features, price, distribution and even design, engaging customers' emotions becomes a crucial way for marketers to differentiate their offerings from those of others.

Kevin Roberts of Saatchi & Saatchi has long been passionate about engaging customers' emotions. Roberts says that a major breakthrough in his thinking came from the insight that reason leads to conclusions while emotion leads to action. Following this insight, Roberts felt certain that emotional, not rational factors, were the key to the next round of competition and that the future would be won on relationships, not just transactions. This conviction led Roberts to create the notion of 'love marks' to replace 'brands'. He felt certain that 'if people loved something rather than merely liked it, they would be loyal beyond reason, beyond price, beyond recession'. Hence the notion of Lovemarks: a 'future beyond brands, infused with mystery, sensuality and intimacy. Delivering premium margins because people don't merely like them, they love them'.[32]

Starbucks provides another example of this kind of emotional connection with consumers. The company revolutionized how coffee was bought and sold by engaging customers emotionally rather than through price or convenience. Prior to Starbucks, the mass market was mostly about 'instant coffee', bought off the shelf, and with price discounts. But following a trip to Milan, Starbucks' Howard Schultz, who joined as director of retail operations and marketing in 1982, realized that coffee was much more about passion, emotion, and lifestyle than about price, convenience, and a warm drink. By creating a 'third space' between home and work, and using coffee as the means to fill that space, Starbucks was able to engage consumers emotionally and create a global business in the process.

Lululemon Athletica also engages customers at an emotional level. The yoga-inspired athletic apparel company has used this ethos to develop a cult-like following for its high-end yoga gear and generate remarkable sales—over 52 percent compound annual growth in the roller-coaster American economy between 2005 and 2009. It has achieved this largely through the creation of a unique customer-centric culture—built both within stores and through a community-based marketing approach—that is quickly being copied by Nike, Gap, and Nordstorm, among others. The company identifies local yoga ambassadors who embody the 'lulu lifestyle' and outfits them with their gear. Every week, the store pushes aside racks and shelves, and mats are unrolled so these ambassadors can provide free yoga classes in stores. Their easily identifiable red shopping bags are decorated with phrases and aphorisms such as 'breathe deeply' or 'friends are more important than money'. Although yoga has been around for millennia, Lululemon has driven a trend that makes yoga practitioners feel they are a part of a community and a larger vision—and keeps consumers coming back for more.

CREATE 'CENTRES OF PASSION' ACROSS YOUR ORGANIZATION

Firms must empower employees to publicly share and discuss ideas they are passionate about—however controversial and disruptive these ideas may be. And to bring these ideas to life, they must help build communities of customers and partners around them. For instance, frog has launched 'centres of passion' across its global network of design studios where employees can freely discuss their left-field ideas and engage with colleagues, customers, or external partners who share similar passions. Robert Fabricant, Vice President of Creative at frog and the driving force behind this enterprise-wide initiative, explains: 'We want to turn an individual employee's passion into a "community of passion" where people with different perspectives can identify ways to convert their personal passion into a practical reality. These passions are the seeds of transformational solutions that can be used to enhance existing initiatives or launch entire new practise areas. The aim is to create a groundswell movement within frog by cross-pollinating and cross-fertilizing personal passions across our organization.'[33]

Frog has set up a website where its employees can share their passions with the world. In one of these videos, Denise Burton, a frog Fellow, describes her passion: 'Connecting people has always been my passion. Even as a kid, whenever there was a fight in the playground I was the one who always brokered peace among fighting kids and reconnected them. As I grew up, I recognized how technologies like the World Wide Web and RFID can not only help connect [crores of] people but also [crores of] devices together. I always dreamed of "connected experience"—a seamless world where people and devices are interlinked. Even after I joined frog, it long remained a dream. But now I think frog's clients are finally ready for my dream: it's no longer a blue-sky idea. The timing is right to turn "connected experience" into a viable commercial reality.'[34]

ENCOURAGE EMPLOYEES TO TRUST THEIR GUT—AND VALIDATE WITH RAPID EXPERIMENTATION

CEOs need to follow the lead of Kip Tindell, CEO of The Container Store, a leading US house-wares chain, who not only relies on his *own* intuition to guide his business decisions but has also enshrined intuition as one of his company's

'Foundation Principles'. As Tindell explains: 'We just beg and plead and try to get employees to believe that intuition does have a place in the workforce. After all, intuition is only the sum total of your life experience. So why would you want to leave it at home when you come to work in the morning?'[35]

Both Google and Facebook encourage employees to trust their gut by beta-testing their intuitive ideas—and then adopting those that achieve significant customer uptake into their mainstream product line. Despite the power of intuition, it is important to note that however much you trust your intuition, it is unlikely to *always* be right. Therefore, the best way to minimize the risks of investing in the wrong products and services is to test your intuitive ideas early on in the marketplace—and use customer feedback to continually iterate design or drop the offering altogether if customer interest is tepid.

Apple: A Heartpowered Corporation

Steve Jobs, former CEO of Apple, was perhaps the world's most effective practitioner of the 'follow your heart' principle. Jobs helped Apple disrupt the consumer technology industry several times over, first with the iPod and iTunes, then with the iPhone and most recently with the iPad. But Apple didn't do extensive market surveys to come up with the iPad. This may have been just as well, given that many consumers, analysts, and media experts were convinced that there was no market for it. But Jobs had a knack for reading the market and was well known for anticipating customer needs without relying on analysts' predictions or focus groups.

Importantly, Jobs depended on his company's heartpower, as measured by the quality of customer experience delivered, rather than its brainpower, as measured by the number of patents filed. Indeed, it is telling that Apple ranked eighty-first in the 2010 Booz & Company's ranking of companies by their R&D expenditures. As a percentage of its revenue, Apple spends a *fifth* of what Microsoft spends. Yet it is the world's most valued brand today: actually, in the same Booz & Company's study mentioned above, Apple was ranked as the most innovative company in the world.[36] Credit for this goes to three qualities that Jobs consistently demonstrated throughout his career at Apple.

JOBS WAS INTUITIVE

Steve Jobs was always a dreamer who envisioned the future of technology well before competitors—or even customers—did. He let his intuition identify big opportunities and reveal the pathways to seize them (interestingly, according to Jobs's biographer Walter Isaacson, Jobs learned to trust his intuition during an introspective trip to India in 1974).[37] As such, he was able to shape—and lead—entire new markets again and again. For instance, when he returned to Apple in 1997 after a twelve-year absence, he happened to meet a designer named Jonathan Ive. Ive was dejected because his latest invention—a monolithic monitor that had all the computer functions integrated into it—had been rejected by Apple's managers who viewed it as too avant-garde. But Jobs was immediately smitten by Ive's invention—in it, he saw the future. He promised Ive that they were about to start a long-term partnership that would change the world of computing forever. Ive later became Apple's head of design; the invention that Jobs helped bring to market was the iMac.[38]

Because he always followed his intuition, Jobs never sought out or relied on external validation for his decisions—either from investors or customers. In fact, in an interview with *Inc.*

magazine in 1989, Jobs said: 'You can't just ask customers what they want and then try to give that to them. By the time you get it built, they'll want something new.'[39] Jobs practised customer-*minded* innovation, honed by intuition, rather than customer-*driven* innovation, shaped by rationality.

JOBS WAS EMPATHETIC

Steve Jobs never had to purposefully listen to end users to understand their needs. His identification with users was so great that he used himself as Apple's first and foremost customer. And he was often the customer of the future rather than of the present. This helped him design superlative customer experiences not so much to please external users as to please himself. Indeed, it seems as if he spent his entire career trying to address his *own* needs as a technology user, rather than thinking and acting like a technology provider as most of Apple's rivals do. You could call this self-empathy or self-directed compassion.

JOBS WAS OBSESSIVELY PASSIONATE

Steve Jobs wasn't just a passionate leader—he was an *obsessively* passionate one. He was obsessed with delighting customers with amazing products that marry ease of use and superior technical performance—and with over-the-top customer service to boot. His unabashed passion for excellence in everything pushed Apple's employees to outdo themselves and meet his stringent quality expectations. Jobs's perfectionism is enshrined in Apple's product development principles, such as 'Pixel Perfect Mockup' (any prototype needs to be designed hyper-realistically to look and feel as close as possible to the end product) and '10 to 3 to 1' (for every new feature, Apple

217

engineers design without restriction ten entirely different mockups, then narrow them down to three, and eventually settle on a final one).[40] Of course, Jobs's detractors thought that his passion for excellence bordered on insanity (the marble for the floor at the New York Apple store was allegedly shipped to his California office first so he could examine the veins). But as the saying goes, the difference between genius and madness is success.

In his 2005 commencement address at Stanford, Jobs had this to say to the graduating students: 'You can't connect the dots looking forward. You can only connect them looking backwards, so you have to trust that the dots will somehow connect in your future. You have to trust in something—your gut, destiny, life, karma, whatever—because believing that the dots will connect down the road will give you the confidence to follow your heart, even when it leads you off the well-worn path, and that will make all the difference.'[41]

Tim Cook, Steve Jobs's successor, is more operations focused, given his supply chain background—and he seems more driven to managing the present rather than predicting the future. However, Cook may be just what Apple needs now that the role of chief empathy officer and chief intuition officer has shifted from a single individual—Steve Jobs—to thousands of passionate jugaad innovators at Apple. To help these employees channel their ingenuity into shaping the future of computing while maintaining Apple's successful legacy, you need a leader who is solidly anchored in the *present*. Tim Cook might well be just that person.

Conclusion

Jugaad innovators like Kishore Biyani and Steve Jobs are truly gutsy in many respects: they have courage and the willingness to take risks, they trust their intuition, and they are passionate about what they do, believing that they are pursuing a higher cause in the process.

Following one's heart—the seat of empathy, intuition, and passion—is the last of the six principles that jugaad innovators follow. But following these principles alone is insufficient for an enterprise to be able to implement the jugaad approach to innovation. As we explore in the next chapter, to sustain the adoption of jugaad and its six principles, corporate leaders must understand what changes are needed at the *organizational* as well as the individual level.

Chapter 8

Integrating Jugaad into Your Organization

'Company cultures are like country cultures. Never try to change one.
Try, instead, to work with what you've got.'

—PETER DRUCKER

So far, we've shown you the many ways in which practising the six principles of jugaad innovation—seeking opportunity in adversity, doing more with less, thinking and acting flexibly, keeping it simple, including the margin, and following your heart—can help companies generate and sustain breakthrough growth in today's complex environment. But jugaad innovation is not a panacea to be applied to all innovation problems in all situations; despite its clear benefits, it also has some clear limitations. Indeed, jugaad isn't a substitute for the traditional structured approach to innovation most commonly used in companies; rather, jugaad is a useful complement to this approach.

In this chapter, we discuss the advantages and limitations of jugaad innovation and the contexts in which it is best applied.

We describe how companies can combine the agile and resilient spirit of jugaad with more structured approaches to innovation, and how they can prioritize the jugaad principles they need to adopt most urgently.

When Does Jugaad Work Best?

The relevance—and ultimate success—of any new business tool, practise, or approach depends on the context in which it is applied. When adopting any new tool or approach, companies should not apply it indiscriminately in all circumstances but selectively, in situations where the tool or approach is most appropriate. Companies must demonstrate similar discernment when implementing jugaad innovation—applying it in specific contexts that best lend themselves to this approach. We have found that jugaad innovation delivers the most impressive results when it is practised in complex and volatile environments with the following characteristics:

- *Rapid changes*: Jugaad has particular potency in highly volatile settings where product life cycles are shorter, demographic patterns are shifting, competition can come from anywhere, or governments are constantly changing policy and unleashing new regulations. For instance, the fast-paced consumer electronics industry, with its short product life spans, requires flexible thinking and rapid-fire action, which jugaad innovation can handily deliver.

- *Widespread resource scarcity*: Jugaad is most relevant to companies, sectors, or countries where capital is limited and access to natural resources is constrained. For example, the resource-hungry food and beverage industry as well as the automotive sector—confronted with scarcity of water and oil—need jugaad innovation to revamp their supply chains so they can do more with less.

- *Frugal and diverse customers*: Jugaad can be most powerful in markets where cost-conscious customers are seeking affordable products and want them to be tailored to their particular needs. For instance, the consumer products and healthcare sectors need jugaad innovation to discover ways to include marginal segments and build empathetic and personalized relationships with their customers.

- *Industry immaturity*: Jugaad is important in sectors that are still nascent and where market mechanisms and industry standards aren't established. For example, for companies that operate in sunrise sectors like clean tech and biotech—which are highly unpredictable—jugaad innovation can help them seek opportunity in adversity, turning it to their advantage.

- *Exploding interconnectivity*: Jugaad has relevance in industries that are undergoing a technology revolution and where free social media tools and ubiquitous cellphones are making communication cheaper and collaboration easier. Banks, for instance, can apply jugaad innovation to devise inclusive business models that leverage mobile technologies to cost-effectively serve the 60 crore Indians who are unbanked.

These extreme conditions typically have been more prevalent in emerging markets like India, China, and Brazil than in the US or Europe. As we discussed in previous chapters, however, Western economies have also begun to exhibit many of these aspects of scarcity, diversity, unpredictability, and interconnectivity. Given these developments, jugaad may be just what the doctor ordered for large companies around the globe: a pill that can boost their immune system, ward off complexity, and help them innovate and grow. But how should big corporations that have implemented or are about to implement a structured approach to innovation go about dealing with jugaad? Should they abandon the structured approach altogether? Or should they integrate it with the jugaad approach? If they choose to do the latter, how should they integrate the two approaches?

The Hammer versus the Screwdriver

Despite the limits of the structured approach to innovation—particularly in complex, unpredictable contexts—companies shouldn't abandon these traditional structures and processes as they still hold value in certain conditions. Rather, companies with structured approaches to innovation—built around big budgets, large R&D teams, and standardized and linear product development processes—should expand their innovation toolkit with jugaad. As the global environment gets ever more complex, companies will need more than a single tool to deal with complexity. Instead of always using a hammer to deal with problems, they might find it useful to use a screwdriver too from time to time. If the structured approach to innovation is the hammer, then jugaad could well be the screwdriver.

The key issue for companies, therefore, is to know when to use the hammer and when the screwdriver. For that, they need to understand the capabilities and benefits of both tools and how they complement each other. The traditional structured innovation approach brings three major benefits:

- *Volume-oriented economies of scale*: Large R&D teams and vast supply chain resources enable companies to scale up new products and distribute them to crores of undifferentiated customers. As such, structured

223

innovation—when successfully executed—delivers volume-oriented economies of scale for standardized products and services in homogenous markets.

- *Infusion of 'hard' capital*: Structured innovation favours 'big risks, big rewards' R&D projects undertaken by companies with huge resources. As we explained earlier, many of these mega-budget projects fail. Yet the few projects that do succeed can occasionally lead to disruptive technologies or groundbreaking products (such as blockbuster drugs) that can help companies increase revenues and profits and expand market share—generating 'hard' capital and tangible assets that can be reflected in the balance sheet.

- *Efficiency*: Standardized processes like Six Sigma can help companies execute innovation projects more effectively and efficiently, provided the environment is stable.

The jugaad approach extends these benefits by bringing additional value in the following ways:

- *Value-oriented economies of scope*: As populations grow more diverse and markets become more fragmented, jugaad enables companies to tailor solutions to the specific needs of multiple customer segments. Jugaad innovation helps deliver more value to individual customers in heterogeneous markets.

- *Infusion of 'soft' capital*: We are entering a post-material era in which employees and customers are seeking meaning more than material benefits per se. By adopting jugaad, companies can unleash the passion of employees and engage customers in meaningful relationships. In this way, companies can accumulate 'soft' capital—namely, 'higher employee productivity and customer loyalty. These intangible assets will sustain the company's competitive edge, as they are harder for competitors to replicate than more tangible assets, like technology.

- *Flexibility*: In an increasingly volatile business environment, managers need to think on their feet to overcome unexpected challenges. The resilient jugaad mindset can help managers overcome harsh constraints by improvising robust solutions using limited resources.

To summarize: jugaad is like a booster, extending a company's ability to cope with volatility and do more with less in highly constrained settings. Ultimately, in order to simultaneously deal with low-volatility, resource-rich settings as well as high-volatility, resource-constrained settings, companies need to have *both* sets of capabilities: the volume-oriented economies of scale, hard capital, and efficiency of the structured approach to innovation, as well as the value-oriented economies of scope, soft capital, and flexibility of jugaad.

The challenge for companies is to know when to apply which approach—that is, when to use the hammer and when the screwdriver. This, in turn, requires leaders to create an organizational context in which both approaches can exist in harmony without favouring one over the other at all times. Tim Leberecht, Chief Marketing Officer of frog, a global design and innovation consultancy, observes, 'Companies need to give themselves the freedom to swing to both extremes—that is, from highly structured innovation to free-flowing jugaad—rather than settling in the middle trying to achieve an elusive "balance".'[1]

Such organizational flexibility can be visualized metaphorically as a pendulum whose dynamic movement enables companies to explore a wide range of options to meet the innovation requirements of the rapidly evolving marketplace. For leaders, this means they need to cultivate the wisdom to know when to be like Miles Davis and improvise innovation and when to be like Leonard Bernstein and orchestrate it.

Managing the creative tension between jugaad innovation and a structured approach can prove disruptive. Bringing in the new approach can conflict with companies' existing organizational structures and practises such as resource-intensive R&D models, time-consuming product development processes, mass-marketing techniques, and hierarchical management structures. Yet this creative tension between the 'yin' (structured) and 'yang' (unstructured) aspects of innovation is healthy and worth nurturing: it can even yield tremendous benefits for organizations. In an increasingly complex world, managing polarities—that is, extremes—is rapidly becoming a core competence for corporate leaders worldwide. And there is no better way to develop it than by integrating jugaad into their organizations and learning how to balance and integrate multiple—and conflicting—approaches to innovation.

How GE Successfully Integrates Jugaad and Six Sigma

GE, a large conglomerate that heavily relies on structured approaches like Six Sigma, has managed to integrate the jugaad approach into its existing organization and, in the process, learned to swing with this 'innovation pendulum'. There is a strategic reason behind this. The $150 billion (₹ 750,000 crore) industrial goliath that employs 3 lakh people worldwide is striving hard to become agile and resilient in the face of growing complexity. The company is doing so by shifting its business model from that of an R&D driven company to that of a customer-focused organization.

GE's radical transformation is driven by CEO Jeffrey Immelt. Unlike his predecessors—such as the legendary Jack Welch—who had an operations or engineering background, Immelt's background is in sales and marketing, the first CEO with such a background in GE's 120-year history. Because he has spent most of his career interacting with customers, Immelt understands intuitively the importance of being customer-focused, agile, and responsive. In particular, through extensive interaction with customers, Immelt gained the following important insight: GE's customers no longer value just how well GE engineers its products, but also how well GE *serves* them throughout the product life cycle. Plus they expect GE to deliver these quality products and services faster and cheaper.

For GE, this means that the ability to sense and respond swiftly to customers' requirements is as critical to success as engineering prowess is—if not more so. Recognizing that this new market reality calls for higher speed, agility, and cost-efficiency, Immelt is encouraging every GE employee to innovate and think differently by adopting the frugal and democratic principles of jugaad. And, as we'll now describe, this push is working.

In no country is GE's organizational transformation more visible than India. GE set up India's first hydropower plant way back in 1902. Currently, all of GE's global businesses in manufacturing, services, and technology have operations in India. GE employs 14,500 people across India and generates about ₹ 14,000 crore in revenues in the country. GE's Indian subsidiary also exports over ₹ 5,000 crore in products and services.

GE Healthcare, one of GE's units, is a clear example of the massive cultural transformation GE is undergoing—and the resulting benefits. GE Healthcare operates in the West and in emerging markets like India, in an industry that is extremely complex, super-competitive, highly regulated, and undergoing a great deal of change. Despite these challenges, GE Healthcare is managing to innovate by successfully practising the six principles of jugaad to compete and win in a complex world of adversity, scarcity, and unpredictability. (NB: In the next few paragraphs, we refer to GE Healthcare as GE.)

GE SEEKS OPPORTUNITIES IN ADVERSITY

PET/CT scanners are high-end devices used for cancer diagnosis and treatment. The devices themselves are expensive. They also require a cyclotron—which is as costly as a PET/CT scanner—to generate a radioisotope called fludeoxyglucose (FDG) that is injected into patients to help produce the diagnostic images that can precisely locate the disease. In India, large hospitals have traditionally imported FDG for use with their PET/CT equipment. But this process is expensive and time-consuming—and quite beyond the reach of small-town and rural hospitals. Seeing an opportunity in these adverse circumstances, GE worked with private diagnostic centres and local airlines to domestically produce FDG and deliver it within hours to small-town hospitals around the country.[2] This just-in time supply chain for FDG delivery is now fully operational and is being scaled up. In addition, GE has tied up with Nuclear Healthcare, an Indian owned company, to set up a network of 120 advanced molecular imaging centres all across India by 2015. These types of affordable and accessible solutions for early cancer detection are of huge value to India where cancer is one of the leading causes of death and growing alarmingly fast. The number of cancer patients, currently about 25 lakh, are expected to increase five-fold by 2025.[3]

Despite the challenges of working in a country like India, where logistics can be highly unreliable, GE has succeeded in making high-quality cancer diagnosis and treatment available to even low-income communities across the country. Terri Bresenham, President & CEO of GE Healthcare India, says: 'We are trying to debunk the myth that you can't innovate in a regulated sector like healthcare. Of course you can—if you can reframe regulation not as a constraint but an opportunity to innovate. But your innovation can't be just about developing new technology products; it must also be about *new business models* for making that technology affordable and accessible to more people.'[4]

GE DOES MORE WITH LESS

GE recognized that its bulky and expensive electrocardiogram (ECG) devices were unaffordable for physicians in emerging markets like India, China, and Africa. The company also realized that these devices were impractical in these markets, as doctors could not carry them on their motorbikes or bicycles when visiting patients in far-flung villages. Plus, villages often didn't have electricity to power these ECG devices. Recognizing the problem and aware of the need for this device in rural areas, GE's researchers in India invented in 2008 the MAC 400—a portable electrocardiogram that costs one-tenth and weighs one-fifth of its current equivalent in Western markets. The compact MAC 400—priced at $1,000 (₹ 50,000)—boasts of a super-long battery life and uses several off-the-shelf components. Its rugged printer, for instance, is an adapted version of the portable ticket machine used in Indian bus kiosks. As a result, MAC 400 is easy to use and maintain in dusty rural environments and delivers more value at a lower cost.[5]

After successfully deploying MAC 400 in emerging markets such as India and China, GE rolled out this FDA-approved device in the US for applications such as emergency roadside assistance.[6] After introducing MAC 400 in 2008, GE outdid itself in 2010 by launching the MAC i, an ECG device that is lighter than MAC 400 and is priced at around $500 (₹ 25,000)—bringing the cost of ECGs down to just $0.20 (₹ 10) each.[7]

GE THINKS AND ACTS FLEXIBLY

GE's clients are increasingly reluctant to pay crores of dollars up front for big-ticket items like power turbines, aircraft engines, and medical equipment. This reality has forced GE to think flexibly. Accordingly, the company has transformed its business model from that of a product supplier to that of a total solutions provider, offering clients more financing options in the process. In particular, rather than selling its products outright, GE also now rents them out using a 'pay as you go' pricing model. Alternatively, the company works with partners to operate and maintain products for a fee under a performance-based service contract. For instance, in India, GE Healthcare has implemented a flexible pricing model known as 'pay-per-scan' that enables frugal medical diagnostic centres to rent GE's diagnosis equipment like CT scanners—instead of buying them at a high price—and pay a variable fee depending on the total number of scans conducted each year.[8]

GE is also demonstrating its flexible thinking by revamping its relationship with government bodies. While many large companies complain about escalating government regulations—and thus view the government as a barrier to increasing business performance—GE is forging win-win public-private partnerships (PPP) with governments worldwide. For instance, in India, GE has partnered with state and local governments and specialized service providers that operate diagnostic imaging facilities equipped with GE's equipment at public hospitals—especially in rural areas. Such a win-win PPP model has helped increase the efficiency of state-run hospitals that don't need to invest in expensive equipment or scramble to recruit qualified technicians—and yet can provide affordable and high-quality care for rural patients.[9]

GE is not only empowering its executives to think flexibly, but also enabling them to *act* flexibly. Indeed, GE has started redesigning its rigid, top-heavy organizational structure to allow for jugaad innovators in its regional units to sense and respond to local opportunities faster. In particular, the heads of GE operations in emerging markets—such as Terri Bresenham, CEO of GE Healthcare India—are being given latitude to make strategic decisions without seeking approval or resources from headquarters.[10] Now these regional leaders can quickly fund and execute promising jugaad ideas, such as the just-in-time delivery of FDG to hospitals and clinics equipped with PET/CT scanners.

GE Keeps it Simple

Having traditionally over-engineered products, GE's R&D teams are now learning the virtues of simplicity. GE's top engineers found that physicians in rural areas of emerging markets like India, who use only a thermometer and stethoscope, had no use for their bulky, hard-to-use ultrasound machines. Yet these physicians were not technology averse—they all carried cellphones. With this information, GE's engineers had a jugaad idea: what if they could design an ultrasound machine as compact and simple to use as a cellphone? The result was Vscan, a portable ultrasound device that weighs merely one pound, is as small as a smartphone, and has a user interface as simple as an iPod's. Vscan has been a huge success in both developed countries as well as in emerging markets. Immelt believes this simple but powerful device will one day become as indispensable to physicians as the thermometer and stethoscope. Indeed, a study conducted by Scripps Health validated Vscan's ability to accurate diagnose structural heart conditions. The study called Vscan the greatest invention since the two-hundred-year-old stethoscope (which was invented in 1816), because Vscan allows the physician to 'see' a patient's heart, leading to more accurate diagnoses. Dr Eric J. Topol, chief academic officer at Scripps Health and principal investigator on the study, explains: 'Approximately 2 crore echocardiograms are conducted in the US every year, each costing $1,500 (₹ 75,000) or more and requiring a return appointment for a hospital or clinic echo labouratory for an extended session of about forty-five minutes. A pocket echocardiogram [like the Vscan] could significantly reduce costs and improve the quality of the patient experience.'[11]

GE INCLUDES THE MARGIN

In 2009, GE launched Healthymagination—a strategic initiative overseen by Immelt that aims to make high-quality healthcare affordable and accessible to more people, especially underserved communities around the world. As part of Healthymagination, GE has, for instance, partnered with P&G, Johnson & Johnson, Anthem, and UnitedHealthcare to pilot a government-funded community program in Cincinnati, in the US State of Ohio, that aims to improve health delivery while reducing costs. Cincinnati's health statistics are alarming: over 12 percent of the population lacks health insurance while the mortality rate is higher than the national average—causing health spending to increase at 8 percent annually. The Beacon Community programme will set up an electronically connected, citywide healthcare system called HealthBridge that aims to reduce the cost of care and improve quality and efficiency metrics targeted at diabetes, primary care, childhood asthma, and congestive heart failure. If this grassroots model in Cincinnati is successful, GE intends to apply it to other communities across the US—thus making healthcare accessible to marginal segments. As part of the Healthymagination initiative, GE is making its low-cost, easy-to-use devices like the MAC 400 and Vscan more widely available to less specialized community health workers—such as those in rural areas of the US.[12]

GE FOLLOWS ITS HEART

GE has traditionally served business customers such as airlines, hospitals, factories, and governments. But given his commercial background, Jeff Immelt recognized the importance of developing empathy for *end users*—those whom its business clients serve. To that end, Immelt has tasked Beth Comstock, GE's chief marketing officer, with increasing GE's emotional quotient by engaging these end users in a meaningful dialogue. Comstock is now connecting GE's left-brain R&D engineers more closely with end users through an empathy-building initiative called 'market back'—that is, first identify end users' needs, and then co-create new solutions, in partnership with business customers and partners. These market back solutions are designed from the ground up in local markets rather than being pushed down by senior executives in headquarters, so they fit specific local contexts better. They are quickly rolled out and tested using immediate customer feedback. For instance, GE's R&D engineers are immersing themselves in village clinics in India and Bangladesh to develop empathy for rural patients and understand how to come up with healthcare solutions that are affordable and accessible for low-income communities worldwide. As Comstock notes: 'Global perception and expectation of innovation is changing and businesses would be short-sighted not to change with it. And that means looking at innovation in both the science lab and the 'real world' lab. From the top-down to the masses-up. And from pure profit to profit with a purpose. Companies that embrace this new model for innovation today will be better positioned for growth tomorrow.'[13]

By internalizing the six principles of jugaad, GE is developing the flexible and inclusive mindset needed to improvise empathetic solutions that are affordable and sustainable for a larger number of people. But where does Six Sigma fit into all this? Six Sigma enhances—and helps magnify—the value of GE's jugaad inventions. In particular, GE leverages structured Six Sigma processes, first to improve the *quality* of its jugaad inventions so they meet international standards (in the same way it obtained FDA approval for its MAC 400 and Vscan devices), and then to rapidly *scale up* these jugaad inventions—taking advantage of GE's impressive global manufacturing and distribution capabilities—so they can be made available to a larger number of customers worldwide, thus accelerating the market adoption of jugaad inventions.

In sum, GE is a successful example of how a large company, by embracing jugaad, can think flexibly, act nimbly and harness the ingenuity of its vast base of employees, customers, and partners to drive breakthrough innovation and growth. More important, GE has shown how to mesh the bottom-up, unstructured approach of jugaad innovation with a more traditional, structured approach to innovation in the context of an advanced global organization.

But GE is not alone in achieving this synergistic blend. Hundreds of organizations are effectively integrating jugaad into their organizations—enabling them to innovate faster, better, and cheaper. And so too can you and your company. But to make the most of jugaad, you need to prioritize your efforts to adopt this new frugal and flexible approach to innovation.

Getting Started with Jugaad

Jugaad can disrupt business as usual—for the better. As with any disruptive change, however, companies can adopt jugaad in one of two ways: in one fell swoop or in small chunks. Some large corporations such as 3M, Future Group, GE, PepsiCo, Renault-Nissan, Siemens, Tata Group, and Unilever have the resources, willpower and visionary leadership needed to reinvent the *entire* organization around the six jugaad principles. But the majority of large companies—and their leaders—may be intimidated by the thought of such a wholesale adoption. For those companies and their executives we offer two suggestions:

1. *Prioritize the jugaad principles you need to adopt*: Not all jugaad principles are of equal importance to all organizations. At the corporate level, you need to let industry dynamics and your company's strategic requirements determine which of the six jugaad principles is most critical for your business success. For instance, if you are a premium retailer that sells luxury items, doing more with less and including the margin may not be of critical relevance; however, keeping it simple may be crucial to streamlining the service experience for high-end customers. If you are a consumer goods supplier like Hindustan Unilever or Godrej, you may choose to primarily do more with less by creating new frugal products for buyers whose purchasing power is waning. Similarly, large companies in industries undergoing major change, such as pharmaceuticals and automotive (think of Ranbaxy and Maruti), would be wise to seek opportunity in adversity and think and act flexibly in order to radically reinvent their obsolete business models.

At an individual level, your functional role may determine the critical mix of jugaad principles that will add most to your career. For instance, we would suggest to marketing executives and R&D directors—who tend to think with the logical left brain—that they follow their hearts in engaging customers and co-creating solutions that delight them. Human resource managers may also find the 'follow your heart' principle relevant to their jobs. According to the Blessing White Employee Engagement Survey of 2011, only 37 percent of employees in Indian corporations feel engaged at work. At such a time, HR managers need to create a work environment that encourages employees, especially free-spirited Millennials, to pursue their passion in the workplace—just as companies like 3M, SAP Labs India, and TCS are doing.[14]

2. *For each principle you choose to adopt, aim first for the low-hanging fruit*: Once you have decided which principles are of strategic importance to you, you can adopt each of them in small, manageable stages. If 'keep it simple' appeals to you, you can begin by simplifying the design of your products and making them easier to use and maintain—as Siemens did by launching their SMART initiative. If, on the other hand, you are willing to be bold, you can do what Philips did: simplify *all* your business processes and your *entire* organization—but especially your customer interactions. Likewise, if you are attempting to 'do more with less' you can demonstrate frugality by first *reusing* components across existing product lines—just as GM is doing with its 'global (vehicle) platforms' initiative. Later, you can develop your frugal mindset by emulating GE—that is, by designing entirely new, very affordable, high-quality products. Finally, if you are an enlightened Indian bank wishing to 'include the margin'—that is, the 60 crore Indians who

are unbanked or underbanked—you can first partner with an organization like the IFMR-Centre for Micro Finance and pilot financial inclusion solutions in a few Indian cities before scaling them up nationally. Of course, you would have to hurry as you do this, because nimble Indian start-ups like EKO India Financial Services are already encroaching on your turf by offering basic banking services to underserved communities using technologies like mobile banking and smart cards.

In our companion website (www.jugaadinnovation.com) we showcase additional tools that can help you prioritize how you implement jugaad and guide you in how to do so effectively.

Prioritizing and adapting the six principles most relevant to your business will help you build buy-in for jugaad across the organization and successfully integrate its most relevant principles into your enterprise—enabling you to use jugaad as a powerful tool to accelerate innovation and growth. The most critical factor, however—one that can make or break the successful adoption of jugaad in an organization—is leadership. Without strong commitment and backing from senior leaders, starting with the CEO, a potent yet disruptive approach like jugaad will fail to take hold in organizations accustomed to the structured approach to innovation.

Driving Jugaad Adoption: The CEO's Agenda

Ultimately, jugaad won't take hold in a corporation without active support from the very top. Growth-seeking CEOs have a key role to play in driving the adoption of jugaad across their enterprise. Based on our knowledge of many companies' experiences, we've created a list of dos and don'ts for CEOs seeking to integrate jugaad into their organizations.

Don't Try to Implement Jugaad in a Systematic, Top-Down Fashion

In these recessionary times, CEOs may view jugaad as a silver bullet for driving innovation-led growth. They may be very tempted to adopt—and even impose—jugaad as a new 'best practise' that can quickly be implemented in a top-down fashion. Yet such an attempt is more likely than not to fail. You don't roll out jugaad across your organization the same way you roll out a Six Sigma process or an enterprise software tool. Jugaad is neither a process nor a tool nor a scientific method that can be deployed in a top-down way. In spirit and practise, jugaad is closer to a fluid art and culture than a rigorous science. More important, an *organization* doesn't practise jugaad; rather, the *individuals* in that organization do so. CEOs need to exercise restraint, enabling the ingenuity that lies dormant in each one of his or her employees to emerge on its own and flourish in a bottom-up fashion.

Do Celebrate Your Existing Jugaad Innovators

Rather than trying to institutionalize jugaad, CEOs should seek instead to identify—and celebrate—those maverick employees who already think and act like jugaad innovators. These mavericks are the 'outliers' who defy corporate policies and guidelines to come up with groundbreaking inventions. By publicly celebrating their achievements, CEOs can send a signal to other employees that it's OK to think and act flexibly or do more with less or include the margin. But CEOs should also acknowledge—and even celebrate—the failures of jugaad innovators—to also send the signal that failure in the pursuit of innovation is fine. For instance, Google's ethos celebrates both success and failure. Google's executive chairman Eric Schmidt explains that his company is a risk-tolerant organization where 'it's absolutely OK to try something that's very hard, have it not be successful, and take the learning from that.'[15]

DO PERSUADE SKEPTICAL EMPLOYEES BY CREATING A SENSE OF URGENCY

CEOs of large companies may find it difficult to convince some employees in their firms to embrace jugaad innovation. These employees may lack the appropriate context to properly appreciate these principles and their relevance in today's complex world. For instance, R&D teams that may be accustomed to abundant resources and devoted to pushing the technology frontier for its own sake, may find it hard to relate to the jugaad principles of do more with less and keep it simple. Here is some anecdotal evidence to that effect: after attending our workshop on jugaad, a senior executive at a Fortune 500 company pointed to the hundreds of cars in his company's vast parking lot and said, 'Look: all I see is abundance, not scarcity. Why should I bother doing more with less?' Nevertheless, engineers and scientists love challenges. And CEOs can appeal to this competitive spirit by setting R&D teams challenges that are both socio-economic and technological. These challenges will foster a sense of urgency by creating artificial constraints that favour the emergence of jugaad ideas and 'good enough' solutions. For instance, inspired by Ratan Tata (who came up with the idea for a ₹ 1 lakh car), Renault-Nissan's CEO Carlos Ghosn, who famously coined the term 'frugal engineering' in 2006, is challenging his French and Japanese engineers to match and even exceed the cost, performance, and speed of his Indian engineers. In one instance, Mr Ghosn asked an R&D team each from France, Japan, and India to come up with an engineering solution for the same technical problem. The three

R&D teams came up with solutions of equal quality—yet the Indian engineers' solution cost only one-fifth of what the French and Japanese engineers had developed.[16] Jean-Philippe Salar, a Frenchman who heads Renault's Design Studio in Mumbai, notes that Renault's R&D and marketing leaders in headquarters are learning to appreciate the flexible and frugal mindset of Indian engineers—who think and act like jugaad innovators do.[17] Indeed, as frugal engineering becomes key to competing and winning in the recessionary economies of the West, these Western executives want to embrace the principles of jugaad in France.

DON'T PATENT JUGAAD INVENTIONS—MONETIZE THEM

As the jugaad culture blossoms in companies, it is bound to unleash a torrent of inventions—conceived by thousands of ingenious employees. Rather than trying to patent them all—which will only cost time and money—companies should focus on *monetizing* the most promising ideas by commercializing them at speed. In this area, Asian companies are ahead of Western companies in their perception of and approach to intellectual property (IP)—as exemplified by Neusoft, China's largest IT solution and service provider. Dr Liu Jiren, Chairman and CEO of Neusoft, explains: 'When we introduced our first software in China, it was immediately copied by other Chinese rivals. That's when we realized that even if I had patented an idea, someone else could have come up with a better idea. So we shifted our focus from patenting a single big idea to generating a multitude of ideas and then executing on our ideas as fast as possible. The faster we can monetize our ideas, the better positioned we will be vis-à-vis our competition.'[18] Ananth Krishnan, Chief Technology Officer of Tata Consultancy Services (TCS), shares Dr Liu's viewpoint on IP: under Krishnan's leadership, TCS has become selective about patenting only those inventions that are fully aligned with the company's long-term business strategy. In addition, TCS is enabling active collaboration among its R&D and business units to accelerate the commercialization of its jugaad inventions. Neusoft and TCS want to avoid the mistake made by Western tech powerhouses like Xerox that were prolific inventors who failed to monetize their inventions. Compare the enlightened attitude towards IP of Dr Liu and Ananth Krishnan with the practises more typical of technology companies in Silicon Valley. Companies in the Valley tend to place greater emphasis on patenting a single big idea and desperately trying to defend it against competitors—an obsession that often leads to unending lawsuits and counter lawsuits for patent infringement. Jugaad isn't about who has the best ideas, but who is the best at *executing* ideas.

Do Use 'Innovation Brokers' to Cross-Pollinate and Synergize Jugaad Ideas

Although 'letting a hundred jugaad ideas bloom' is a great way to harness the ingenuity of all employees, there's a danger that companies may miss out on bigger opportunities that could emerge by recombining and integrating multiple ideas in a synergistic solution. To avoid forming 'islands of creativity', CEOs need to create an 'innovation brokering' function tasked with cross-pollinating and cross-fertilizing jugaad ideas across teams.

For instance, after dabbling in Six Sigma and finding that it stifled innovation, 3M swiftly returned to a more jugaad approach to innovation (see Chapter Two). Now Chief

Technology Officer Fred J. Palensky oversees the cross-fertilization of jugaad ideas produced by fiercely independent inventors across the company as a whole. According to Palensky, 3M allows all technical members in its R&D group to invest 15 percent of their time and efforts in programmes, interactions, teaching and learning in areas totally outside their core activities. To enable collaboration and cross-pollination of ideas across business units, 3M has launched more than 300 joint innovation programmes that span multiple divisions. As Palensky points out: 'All of this creates a community of collaboration and ensures that everybody has some skin in the innovation game. And because our senior leaders have grown up in this culture, they continue to nurture and protect this highly collaborative, enterprising environment.'[19]

Do Apply Jugaad to Formulate Robust Strategies

When John F. Kennedy gave voice to the bold vision of putting a man on the moon, he refrained from formulating the precise means by which to achieve that vision. Instead, he allowed the means to emerge organically through the creative input and interplay of the scientific community. Similarly, CEOs must paint a bold vision for their company's future and then trust that employees will tap into the jugaad spirit to come up with the appropriate strategy for realizing this vision. For instance, although the vision to launch a ₹ 1 lakh car was conceived by Ratan Tata, the precise means to execute this vision were developed by employees at Tata Motors who were passionate about building a comfortable and affordable car for the masses.

Do Use Web 2.0 Collaboration Tools to Harness Customer and Partner Creativity

CEOs should extend the adoption of jugaad beyond the limits of their organization and seek out bright ideas from jugaad innovators in their customer and partner communities as well. To do so, they should invest in social media technologies to engage customers and partners in a dialogue on key issues of relevance to the company. Such grassroots collaboration can help identify challenging problems and generate counter-intuitive solutions.

For instance, HCL, IBM, and TCS regularly conduct 'jamming' sessions involving hundreds of employees and partners. These intensive brainstorming sessions—powered by social media tools—help identify major socio-economic problems, like global warming and the healthcare crisis, as well as promising ideas that can be developed to tackle these problems. Similarly, design houses such as frog and Idiom are now practising crowd sourcing: using social medial tools, they are inviting jugaad innovators in cyberspace to put their brains together to solve vexing problems that afflict corporations and societies alike, worldwide.[20] These issues range from the mundane exploration of 'how to make a user-friendly fridge' to more serious stuff like how to increase the number of registered bone marrow donors to help save more lives.

Bold, creative leadership is vital for the successful adoption—and integration—of jugaad in an organization. Rather than imposing jugaad as the best practise *du jour*, CEOs should strive to *facilitate* the adoption of jugaad as a grassroots movement that evolves organically and voluntarily. In doing so, CEOs will increase the stickiness of jugaad in the organization so it can deliver sustainable value to the company.[21]

Conclusion

Many corporations, such as GE, Godrej, PepsiCo, Renault-Nissan, SAP, Suzlon, and Tata Group are adopting jugaad practises and integrating them into their existing innovation approaches. But we believe that jugaad isn't applicable only to corporations, it also has relevance to non-governmental organizations (NGOs), governments, and society at large. Indeed, entire nations stand to gain from adopting a jugaad approach to innovation. Interestingly, after having lost touch with their jugaad roots, a growing number of grassroot entrepreneurs in the West—especially ordinary citizens and Generation Y—have already begun to apply jugaad to address major issues in their societies that are related to areas such as healthcare, energy, and education. As a result, a whole jugaad *ecosystem* is emerging in the US and Europe, with the backing of forward-thinking government agencies and academic institutions. In the next chapter, we describe how corporations that operate in India, both domestic and multinational, can learn from Western efforts in this arena. Specifically, we look at how Indian corporations can support—and benefit from—the groundswell innovation movement unfolding across the globe, a movement that is heralding the birth (and rebirth) of jugaad nations worldwide.

Chapter 9

Building Jugaad Nations

'The highest and best form of efficiency is the spontaneous cooperation of a free people.'

—Woodrow Wilson

The jugaad movement is rapidly gaining traction in the West. While some Western organizations are adopting jugaad to catalyze innovation and growth, increasingly jugaad is also being practised by a broad spectrum of individuals and groups in the West. Led by creative citizens, Millennials, forward-thinking entrepreneurs, venture capitalists, and non-profit organizations, a whole jugaad innovation ecosystem is emerging—to help Western societies improvise frugal and flexible solutions to problems of complexity and scarcity. Larger institutions in the US and Europe—such as governments and universities—are actively supporting the emergence of such an ecosystem—and contributing to its sustainability. This emerging ecosystem not only creates an environment for grassroots entrepreneurs in the West to thrive in, but also helps Western corporations in their own attempts to practise jugaad innovation. Indeed, corporate leaders in India—seeking to leverage jugaad in their organizations—can learn from such jugaad innovators in Western economies. By joining the *external* grassroots movement, Indian companies can accelerate their *internal* adoption of jugaad—and profit from it handsomely.

The Ingenuity Economy

The developed world, like the emerging world, is facing its own problems in areas such as healthcare, education, finance and community development. Western governments, with their bloated budgets and bureaucracies—and faced with financial meltdown—are severely constrained in their efforts to solve these problems. In such a context, entrepreneurial citizens from all walks of life in the West are increasingly taking matters into their own hands. With a flexible and frugal mindset, these citizens are seeking to address the vexing problems their societies face rather than waiting for their governments to do so.

For example, across the US, ordinary American citizens are coming up with innovative solutions to deal with challenges in healthcare, energy, and education. These citizen innovators are the Ben Franklins (see Chapter 1) of the 21st century: they rely on pure American ingenuity to improvise simple yet practical solutions to the problems afflicting their communities. They innovate not in a fancy R&D lab, but in their homes and on the streets, doing more with less. Examples of such citizen innovators in the West include the following:

- *The Frugal Housebuilder*: In the aftermath of Hurricane Katrina, Zach Rosenburg and Liz McCartney founded the St. Bernard Project in New Orleans to make homebuilding efficient, 'unfettered by prior processes and structure, by reducing construction time by 30 percent and costs by up to 15 percent'.[1]

- *The Inclusive Doctor:* Dr Vivian Fonseca, an Indian-origin professor of medicine at Tulane University in New Orleans, helped develop an SMS-based diabetes control solution for elderly and low-income patients that is simple to use and cost effective.[2]

- *The Resilient Lawyer:* After graduating from law school, Brooke Richie launched the Resilience Advocacy Project to train young kids from underprivileged communities in New York to give their peers free legal advice—allowing them to discover new economic opportunities that can help them break out of multigenerational poverty.

- *The Passionate Educator:* Lily Lapenna has created MyBnk, the UK's first independent, peer-led youth banking program approved by the national banking regulator. In doing so, Lapenna is developing the next generation of financially literate and entrepreneurial citizens. Such literacy will be crucial as the UK economy struggles to avoid another recession. In just five years, thanks to its partnership with dozens of schools and youth organizations, MyBnk has evolved from a pilot project to now reach thirty-five thousand 11-25 year olds in underprivileged neighbourhoods of London. These tech-savvy youth learn about managing money and the basics of entrepreneurship through cellphone-based games.[3]

Millennials Launch the DIY Revolution in the West

The groundswell jugaad movement unfolding across the US and Europe is receiving particular support—and active participation—from the Millennials, aka Generation Y. These

North American and European youth, who have witnessed massive corporate layoffs and scandals, are cynical about large enterprises and no longer believe in job stability. They prefer to start their own companies and be their own bosses—thus becoming a do-it-yourself (DIY) generation. According to a survey conducted by The Affluence Collaborative, 40 percent of those in Generation Y plan to launch their own business, and 20 percent already have.[4] But these budding Generation Y entrepreneurs are frugal and think and act flexibly, like the fictional MacGyver. They are big believers in doing more with less. Rather than running big R&D departments, the new DIY start-up generation makes extensive use of social media tools like Facebook in an open source model to co-create new products and services with their friends around the globe.

Nobody embodies the frugal and flexible mindset of this 'do-it-yourself' generation better than Gen Y'er Limor 'Ladyada' Fried. An MIT-trained engineer, Fried is a pioneer of the open-source hardware (OSHW) movement.[5] Members of this movement—mostly geeky engineers—make the source code of the electronic products they design available for free on the Web: anyone can download the code and use it to build their own products using off-the-shelf components. Any improvements or additions to the code are shared with other members of the larger community who improve the modified code and share it again with other members—and so the cycle repeats itself. This collaborative method of creation allows the entire community to do more for less—that is, create more products at a low cost, and with a reduced timeline, because members don't have to build a code from the ground up every time they start a new project—they can simply reuse a code that is already freely available. Fried's nickname 'Ladyada' is a tribute to Lady Ada Lovelace, a 19th-century English countess with a gift for mathematics. Lovelace is widely regarded as the first computer programmer in the world, having written perhaps the first algorithm intended to be processed by a machine (Charles Babbage's Analytical Engine).[6] Like Lovelace, Fried is a maverick. When Microsoft launched the Kinect, a motion-sensing input device for the Xbox 360 video game console, Fried organized a $2,000 (₹ 1 lakh) challenge for open source Kinect drivers. When Microsoft reacted by deeming the challenge an unacceptable modification to their product, Fried responded by raising the prize to $3,000 (₹ 1.5 lakh). Microsoft eventually relented and recognized that the Kinect drivers developed by the open source community were of high quality—and very likely far cheaper to develop than investing crores of dollars in R&D. Commenting on this bottom-up innovation, *Wired* magazine wrote: 'When DIYers combine those cheap, powerful tools with the collaborative potential of the Internet, they can come up with the kinds of innovations that once sprang only from big-budget R&D labs.'[7]

Fried is a prototypical jugaad innovator. From her modest studio in Manhattan, Fried—who labels herself a 'citizen engineer'—churns out high-impact gadgets whose source code is immediately made available on her personal web site, www.ladyada.net. Her noteworthy inventions include Minty MP3, a portable music player whose body is essentially an Altoids box (you get 'fresh' music with it), and the MONOCHRON clock, a device which displays a 'Retro Arcade Table Tennis for Two' (à la PONG, the popular 1970s video game) while telling the time.

Fried also operates an e-commerce site—adafruit.com—that sells the kits and parts for the projects featured on ladyada.net along with other cool open source electronic products. In August 2011, adafruit.com hit the 100,000th customer mark. Reacting to this milestone, Fried and her teammates wrote on the website: 'We'd like to thank all our customers that got us here and we look forward to the next 100,000 chances to make the world a better and smarter place through electronics, engineering and sharing!' Fried would have made the original Lady Ada proud.

In 2011, Fried received a dual honor: she was named among the Most Influential Women in Technology by *Fast Company* and was featured on the cover of *Wired* magazine.[8] She was the first female engineer ever—and maybe the first ever jugaad innovator—to appear on the magazine's cover. Like many Gen Y'ers, Ladyada has a natural proclivity for jugaad innovation that enables her to improvise frugal and flexible solutions to even the most complex problems.

Next-Gen Entrepreneurs Reshape Entire Industries

A new wave of flexible-minded jugaad innovators in the US and Europe—many of them belonging to Generation Y—are turning the conventional practises of many industries upside down and creating affordable and sustainable products and services that are accessible to more people in the process. Here are some of the ways that jugaad entrepreneurs in the West are reshaping entire industries.

Making Education Playful

Several Western entrepreneurs are trying to put the fun back into education by making coursework more engaging, if not outright entertaining. These attempts are targeted mainly at Generation Z, a cohort that is more at ease playing with Nintendo and interacting on Facebook than learning through boring old textbooks.

For instance, the Khan Academy is making the intimidating subject of mathematics cool (and fun) for thousands of students worldwide. The 'academy' is, in fact, a virtual campus founded by Sal Khan, an MIT-trained former hedge-fund analyst

(Khan's father is from Barisal, Bangladesh and his mother from Kolkata). In 2006, to assist his cousin in New Orleans with her math homework, Khan created and uploaded onto YouTube some rudimentary video tutorials on how to do algebra. His videos quickly went viral. Within days, they were downloaded by thousands of people—students, teachers, and parents—from all over the world. Emboldened by this success, Khan began posting more math tutorials on YouTube. Tens of thousands of users devoured them in no time. Eventually, Khan quit his comfortable financial analyst's job to dedicate all his time to the Khan Academy. His mission was to provide 'a free world-class education to anyone anywhere'. Today, the Khan Academy offers more than 2,400 short lessons—ranging from ten to twenty minutes each—on a slew of topics ranging from algebra to venture capital. Anyone with a web browser can access them all—for free![9]

Students from West Virginia to Uganda to Vietnam are downloading Khan's videos (all of which he has produced himself) in ten different languages. The huge success of these online tutorials is due to five factors:

1. They are free and easy to access.
2. They are simple to use.
3. They are not time-consuming—by watching Khan's videos, you can learn, in less than twenty minutes, algebra basics that might take two hours to learn in a classroom setting.
4. They are highly engaging, given Khan's conversational style.
5. You can watch them and learn at your own pace without feeling left out or falling behind as in a physical classroom.

In a nutshell, the Khan academy delivers more value at a lower cost for more students worldwide—something that the traditional education system has struggled to accomplish. It's not surprising that Bill Gates has called the Khan Academy 'a glimpse of the future of education'.

Ntiedo Etuk is another entrepreneur who's making education fun and engaging for young people. Etuk founded DimensionU in New York to create web-based computer games that teach the fundamentals of mathematics, literature, and other essential subjects. The competitive nature of these games provides an incentive for students to play even after school hours. And so they do homework without even realizing that they are doing so![10]

DELIVERING QUALITY HEALTHCARE TO CRORES

As of this writing, 5 crore Americans lack medical insurance. The US spends twice as much per person on healthcare annually as Japan, Canada, or Germany and still ranks lower in health indicators. Sensing an opportunity, a growing number of jugaad entrepreneurs in private and public organizations are trying to deliver higher-quality healthcare to more people at a lower cost in the US.

For instance, the Centres for Medicare & Medicaid Services—run until recently by Donald Berwick, a Harvard-educated physician—is helping make the bloated healthcare system more lean. Berwick is doing this by rewarding hospitals and doctors not for the number of procedures they do or the drugs or tests they recommend but for bringing about tangible improvements in patients' health. As he explains: 'How *much* doctors and hospitals do has become more important than how *well* they do.' Berwick is trying to change this state of affairs. Thanks to his initiatives, last year alone, the Centres saved

Medicare $36 million (₹ 180 crore) and earned physicians $29 million (₹ 145 crore) in bonuses and cost savings.

Berwick is also eager to improve the quality of healthcare by making it safer. For instance, one in seven Medicare patients is hurt during a hospital stay. 'Too many Americans are being harmed by the care that is supposed to help them', Berwick points out. Rather than imposing any solutions to make health delivery safer, Berwick is encouraging hospitals to come up with jugaad innovations to keep patients safe. For instance, he lauds the cardiac intensive care unit at Children's Healthcare of Atlanta at Egleston for coming up with a deceptively low-tech jugaad innovation: a quiet zone where nurses can place medication orders without being interrupted, even during emergencies. The quiet zone was created after the hospital discovered that distracted staff members were making dangerous mistakes while ordering medicine. Berwick believes such simple and frugal innovations are what are needed to make healthcare safer, better, and affordable for more Americans.[11]

ENABLING FINANCIAL INCLUSION

As we've mentioned, 6 crore Americans are unbanked or underbanked, with poor access to traditional financial services. Banks have traditionally lacked the incentive to serve these financially excluded groups as they were deemed unprofitable. And the global economic recession has only made banks even more conservative. But even as Wall Street retreats further from Main Street, hordes of entrepreneurial start-ups are rising to the challenge by conjuring up inclusive—and profitable—business models to deliver financial services to underbanked Americans.

Says Ryan Gilbert, CEO of one such start-up: 'The 'too big to fail' banks are today, simply put, 'too scared to lend' to worthy consumers, due to the higher costs associated with serving non-prime consumers. There is hope, however...'[12] Gilbert's start-up BillFloat represents precisely that hope. By providing lower cost, short-term consumer credit for bill payments, since 2009 BillFloat has helped thousands of consumers across the country avoid exorbitant late fees, overdraft charges, service termination, and high-interest payday loans. The continued economic downturn, combined with banks contracting the amount of available credit, makes the need for services like BillFloat greater than ever for Middle America.

Plastyc is another start-up making financial services affordable and accessible to the masses. Leveraging the power of the Internet and social networks, Plastyc offers 24×7 access to FDIC-insured virtual bank accounts and prepaid Visa cards. Cardholders cannot overdraft on these cards, as they can spend only money they have added beforehand. As a result, there are no late fees and no risk of going into debt. Plastyc's virtual accounts can be accessed from anywhere via the Internet or cellphone. Its iBankUP portal and UPside prepaid cards offer better services (at lower prices) than brick-and-mortar bank checking accounts, with more ways to receive money and no risk of spending more than you actually have.

Most impressively, jugaad innovators in financial services are catalyzing a seismic shift in Western societies: they are inculcating frugal thinking and behavior among spendthrift Western consumers by making *saving* more rewarding and fun than *spending*. For instance, Plastyc's prepaid cards have built-in automated savings—backed by generous rewards and no maintenance fees—to encourage even people with tight budgets to save more.

Says Patrice Peyret, CEO of Plastyc: 'Underbanked and low-income people have the hardest time saving money because they don't have much of it, they have limited access to traditional savings accounts, and interest rates are too low to generate meaningful rewards. Our goal is to turn savings into a habit by making it simple, automatic and rewarding.'[13]

For consumers who lack the motivation or ability to save alone and want to save with friends or partners toward a shared goal, PiggyMojo offers a web-based savings tool that uses text messages, social networks, and linked transfers from checking to savings accounts to enable a system of 'impulse savings' rather than impulse spending. Here's how it works: First you set a goal for saving; for instance, a serious emergency fund or a more fun 'Adopt a Pet'. Then you start saving toward that goal. Whenever you overcome the impulse to buy something—like, say, a ₹ 100 mocha latte—you text or tweet 'I just saved ₹ 100' to friends and family, who then cheer you on. And when your friends and family save, you get a message too—thus creating momentum and a virtuous cycle. At the end of each week, you transfer the amount you 'saved' that week from your checking to savings account. By giving you an incentive to save 'in the moment' and reinforcing your decision with positive feedback from various sources, PiggyMojo makes saving satisfying and fun.[14]

ELEVATING ENTERTAINMENT TO HIGH ART—WITHOUT BREAKING THE BANK

The so-called 'creative' industries, like gaming and Hollywood, often churn out safe, relatively uninspiring sequels that consume huge budgets. In contrast, frugal artists are now making games and films that are truly creative and cost much less to develop.

Consider the case of Jason Rohrer, a game developer. Rohrer lives with his wife and three kids on a modest ranch in Las Cruces in the middle of the New Mexico desert where he creates ingenious, meaningful games with high experiential value that he gives away for free (or charges a modest fee for downloading). Rohrer and his family do not own a car; they ride bicycles. They have no insurance or mortgage; they do have a fridge, but turn it off during winters [Jason suggested we do NOT refer to his family as 'The Rohrers' but just 'Rohrer's family']. This family of five has voluntarily capped its yearly expenses at $14,500 (₹ 7.25 lakh)—which represents the family's total annual budget. [Jason explained that while they can't control their income—which is variable—they do control spending, living off an annual budget (expenses) of $14,500 (₹ 7.25 lakh)]. Rohrer's highly variable income—generated from modest sales of his software and donations—is a far cry from the six-digit salaries earned by top software developers in large gaming companies like Zynga.

Rohrer's frugality also extends to his professional life. His 'studio' is actually a tiny office in his home where he relies on a few ageing computers (including an 11-year-old laptop that his sister gave him) to develop his mind-expanding games. 'Frugality', he told us, 'is indeed a business decision for me. Whenever I'm in a corporate environment, I'm bowled over by the sheer amount of waste that is part of the everyday routine!'[15]

Rohrer's fans love his games because they feel 'real'—not because of hyperrealistic graphics (which would typically cost a fortune to develop) but because their stories ring true and feel genuine. Rohrer infuses his games with his own life experiences, and this in turn gives his characters and storylines authenticity. His creations deal with complex sociocultural topics such as marriage, the desire to become an artist, or balancing personal aspirations with family commitments. Whereas in commercial games superhuman heroes mindlessly shoot down monsters, aliens, and criminals, Rohrer's thoughtful characters struggle to overcome their inner demons and cope with personal dilemmas.[16]

The sophistication of the stories in Rohrer's games stands in striking contrast to the frugal simplicity of their user interface: the interface is typically minimalist, even slightly 'retro', with no whiz-bang special effects like 3D. His games are rendered in low-resolution graphics—the same ones found in arcade-style games—with characters that look like pixelated gnomes. The frugal look and feel of Rohrer's games hasn't stopped them from rapidly achieving cult status among users worldwide. In 2007, within months of its free online release, Passage—Rohrer's first major game that tackled mortality as its main theme—went viral and achieved a cult-like status among top game developers. The game was even lionized by the *Wall Street Journal* and *Esquire*, which both hailed Rohrer as the pioneer of an entirely new genre of gaming that was closer to 'high art' than entertainment.

Clint Hocking, creative director at Ubisoft, the world's fourth-largest game developer, is a big fan of Rohrer's. Hocking has publicly criticized his industry for failing to innovate the way indie developers like Rohrer do—developers who are making 'games that matter'. Says Hocking: 'These games have used what is innate to games—their interactivity—to make a statement about the human condition. And we in the industry seem not to be able to do that.'[17]

Thoughtful jugaad-minded individuals like Jason Rohrer live frugally while creating high-art games that are rich in meaning: they deliver better experiential value at less cost for more users. This grassroots movement toward DIY and doing more with less is catching on beyond individuals in the West and is being backed by an unlikely party: governments.

Western Governments Are Joining the Jugaad Bandwagon

In several Western nations, governments that used to promote big-ticket R&D projects and top-down innovation policies are recognizing the limits of these growth strategies—especially in a recessionary climate. As a result, visionary American and European policy makers are investing in—and supporting—bottom-up innovation programmes. These programmes are specifically designed to empower and harness the ingenuity of jugaad innovators at the community level to address pressing socio-economic issues.

In the US, the Obama administration has launched several initiatives to stimulate community-led innovation. Perhaps the most significant of these is the White House Office of Social Innovation and Civic Participation (SICP), which was set up by President Obama in early 2009 with an explicit mission to enable social inclusion and spur bottom-up innovations by grassroots entrepreneurs in healthcare, education, and energy. President Obama noted, 'The best solutions don't come from the top-down, not from Washington; they come from the bottom-up in each and every one of our communities.'[18] SICP acts as a catalyst to enable such community-driven solutions.

For instance, SICP collaborates with federal agencies to develop incentive-based tools—such as innovation funds, prizes, and other social capital market structures—to channel resources toward community solutions that have *already* achieved demonstrable success, with the goal of helping scale them up. In addition, SICP also acts as an innovation broker by facilitating the cross-fertilization of proven best practises across communities. Finally, SICP helps shape new public-private partnership models that will pave the way for the government to creatively engage the private sector in co-creating innovative solutions that address shared problems at the community level.

For instance, SICP coordinates the Social Innovation Fund—a public-private partnership model launched with $50 million (₹ 250 crore) seed capital from the US Congress. The fund identifies and supports the most promising, results-oriented community programmes led by grassroots jugaad innovators that can be replicated in other communities facing similar challenges.[19] It focuses on high-priority areas for the country's socio-economic development: education, healthcare, youth development, and economic opportunity. The fund also partners with foundations and corporations that commit matching resources, funding, and technical assistance. One of the fund's inaugural awardees is Venture Philanthropy Partners (VPP), founded by Mario Marino, with a vision of applying a venture approach to philanthropy. VPP leads the youth CONNECT initiative—a pioneering network that brings together government, private philanthropy, and non-profit organizations to dramatically improve socio-economic opportunities available to low-income youth (aged fourteen to twenty-four) in the Washington, DC region.

Sonal Shah, the first director of the SICP, explained to us: 'The US has traditionally approached innovation with top-down policies that focused on improving the *inputs* of the innovation system—like R&D spending—without bothering about improving the *output*—i.e., the impact of the innovation on our socio-economic development. The SICP was set up to catalyze a new paradigm of innovation that is bottom-up and incentive-based. Rather than legislating innovation policies in a top-down fashion—the old 'stick' approach—SICP is creating *incentives* for driving positive changes at the grassroots community level—the 'carrot' approach. Innovations in emerging markets are happening in a bottom-up fashion led by grassroots innovators, like jugaad entrepreneurs in India.

We are helping develop a similar grassroots model in the US to effectively address our pressing socio-economic issues. Rather than debating whether America deserves a big or small government, we should all focus our efforts on building a 'democracy' with lower-case 'd': grassroots democracy is what America is all about.'[20]

Efforts by the US federal government, such as the SICP, are being matched by projects undertaken by state and local governments. For instance, policy makers in economically depressed cities are boosting incentives to attract and retain jugaad innovators who can help reinvigorate ailing local economies. The Merrimack Valley in Massachusetts—one of the most economically depressed regions in the US—has partnered with the Deshpande Foundation to launch the Merrimack Valley Sandbox, hosted by the University of Massachusetts in Lowell. The Sandbox brings together local colleges, non-profit organizations, and corporations to boost entrepreneurship among students and professionals and to cultivate local leadership through mentoring and seed funding programmes. These jugaad entrepreneurs and leaders work with local authorities to identify and develop highly relevant solutions that bring benefit to their communities. Gururaj 'Desh' Deshpande, the serial technology entrepreneur who heads the Deshpande Foundation, was appointed by US President Barack Obama as Co-Chairman of the National Advisory Council on Innovation & Entrepreneurship in June 2010 (Deshpande is the only India-born member in the council). Deshpande says: 'For innovation to have impact, it needs relevance. Innovation plus relevance equals impact. Innovation is getting trapped at MIT and in intellectual circles. [But] not everybody needs to try to be MIT or Harvard. They can define a new role of developing relevance and doing things that are good for local business.'[21] It is worth noting that the Merrimack Valley Sandbox in the US is inspired by—and modelled along the lines of—a similar project initiated much earlier by the Deshpande Foundation in Hubli, Karnataka. Applying a 'bottom-up' approach, the Hubli Sandbox engages with local not-for-profits, academics, organizations, and entrepreneurs to co-create effective and scalable models of development in the northern Karnataka region.

Across the Atlantic, the British government is also keen to encourage jugaad innovators. In mid 2010, we were invited to Number 10 Downing Street to meet Rohan Silva, a Senior Policy Advisor to Prime Minister David Cameron. Silva had read our *Harvard Business Review* blog on jugaad and wanted our perspective on how the British government could 'do more with less'—a theme dominating UK politics as Cameron attempts to replace 'Big Government' with 'Big Society' and empower communities and citizens in the process.[22] Silva explained that Cameron wants to see more jugaad entrepreneurs flourish in the UK, and that he wants to encourage bottom-up solutions for making healthcare, energy, and education affordable and accessible to all.

The reasons behind this are obvious. In the UK, public sector borrowing rose to £175 billion (₹ 13.7 lakh crore) or 12.4 percent of GDP in 2009—a peacetime record and the highest level of borrowing of all developed economies.[23] This dire situation has forced the UK government to launch several initiatives—particularly in areas such as healthcare and education—that seek to deliver more value for citizens at less cost and 'include the margin'. For instance, the 'Free Schools' initiative empowers grassroots groups of parents and local citizens to start their own schools, which make decisions on staffing and curriculum design independently of local authorities. These schools will receive public funds based on how many students enroll, with those from poor families attracting a premium. The attempt here is to make public money go further and to shake up the state system while also being more inclusive.

Not to be outdone by the British, the French government is also encouraging more citizens to become jugaad innovators and catalyze growth. With unemployment stuck at 10 percent, the French government is expanding efforts to liberalize France's highly regulated economy and make life easier for entrepreneurs (after all, the word *entrepreneur* is French). Thus on January 1, 2009, the French government launched the 'auto-entrepreneur' initiative to allow professionals to register their small businesses online in just a few minutes and benefit from a simplified and generous tax structure, thus bypassing France's labyrinthine bureaucracy and convoluted tax system. Since its launch, more than 7 lakh French citizens have become jugaad innovators by signing up for the auto-entrepreneur program.[24]

France is already familiar with Système D, the French expression for jugaad-like improvised innovation. The D in Système D is short for *débrouillard,* which refers to a flexible, quick-thinking, and resourceful person who is able to extract himself from any predicament.[25] Système D is a tribute to those French entrepreneurs who rely on their ingenuity and resourcefulness to build their new businesses in spite of France's notorious bureaucracy. Now, with the auto-entrepreneur initiative sanctioned by no less than the French government itself, the country is poised to see jugaad innovation spread more broadly in the coming decade.

Such government-led initiatives to catalyze growth by enabling jugaad are receiving generous support from philanthropists and funding bodies. For instance, the New Economy Initiative for Southeast Michigan (NEI) is a unique philanthropic initiative launched in 2008 by the Ford Foundation and others. NEI partners have together committed $100 million (₹ 500 crore) to be spent over an 8-year period to accelerate the transformation—driven by nimble jugaad entrepreneurs—of the industrial economy of metropolitan Detroit (home to America's once mighty carmakers) into an innovation-based economy. NEI is also supported by the Kauffman Foundation, one of America's largest foundations devoted to entrepreneurship development. In a similar vein, Venture for America (VFA)—launched in 2012—offers $100,000 (₹ 50 lakh) each to graduates of top universities to launch their start-ups in the inner cities of Louisiana and Tennessee and contribute to local economic development. Finally, 'crowd-funding' sites like Kickstarter.com enable grassroots entrepreneurs across the US to raise funds from the general public online within days or weeks.

Jugaad has the potential to represent the truest and most creative expression of a democracy: one in which innovation is led by the people, for the people, and with the people. One could call this Democracy 2.0, a form of government in which interconnectivity and diversity are leveraged to build resilient, equitable, and sustainable societies that can meet all the challenges of complexity. A growing number of visionary policy makers in the US and Europe are encouraging Democracy 2.0 to flourish by setting up the right incentive systems and grassroots institutions to promote jugaad innovation and growth.

Training Future Jugaad Innovators

Leading American and European universities are also playing their part in creating jugaad nations. They are doing so through programmes that imbue the next generation of engineers and managers with a jugaad mindset and its associated principles. Specifically, these programmes are creating future leaders who can think and act flexibly, do more with less, keep things simple, and include the margin. By internalizing the principles of jugaad, these future leaders will be able to design and deliver affordable and sustainable solutions that are relevant not only for developing nations but also for developed economies in the West. These academic programmes are training Western youth to think and act like jugaad innovators.

STANFORD UNIVERSITY'S 'ENTREPRENEURIAL DESIGN FOR EXTREME AFFORDABILITY'

At Stanford University, one of the most popular courses at the business school teaches aspiring entrepreneurs how to raise capital for their start-ups. But a growing number of MBAs are now also enrolling in 'Entrepreneurial Design for Extreme Affordability', a course on frugal innovation taught by Professor James Patell and his colleagues David Beach and Stuart Coulson.

As noted by Paul Polak, author of *Out of Poverty*, 90 percent of the world's products and services are designed for 10 percent of the world's population—to meet the desires, rather than actual needs, of the richest people on earth.[26] Professor Patell's course aims to correct this imbalance. Over a 6-month period, students from across disciplines—engineering, business, medicine, public policy, even law—work intensively in teams to design, prototype, and commercialize products that cost a fraction of those available in the US market—and address the real needs of 90 percent of the world's population. Rather than reinventing the wheel, students are encouraged to use inexpensive, readily available, eco-friendly materials when developing their products. For instance, one team used local, recyclable parts to make infusion pumps for resource-constrained hospitals in Bangladesh at one-thirtieth of their current cost in the West. Not only is the pump inexpensive, it is also of a quality required for FDA approval. Jane Chen, Linus

Liang, Naganand Murty, and Rahul Panicker—introduced in Chapter 3—are alumni of Professor Patell's program and co-founders of Embrace, which has developed low-cost infant warmers for use in both emerging markets like India and developed economies like the US.

Professor Patell explained to us how these frugal design techniques lend themselves to application in the US itself. For instance, one of his student teams is using sustainable architectural practises to build affordable solar greenhouses for the White Mountain Apache Tribe in Eastern Arizona. All the materials that go into these structures are 100 percent locally sourced, making them cheaper to build. Native American youth then use these greenhouses to grow fruits and vegetables using traditional agricultural practises. Thus, the greenhouses not only revitalize the local economy, they also help preserve local cultural history. Professor Patell proudly says, 'Whatever my students make may seem cheap, but we ensure it is classy, useful, sustainable, and of high quality.'[27] In sum, the approach delivers a lot more with a lot less (see jugaadinnovation.com for video interviews with Professor Patell, his students who participated in the White Mountain Apache Tribe project, and Jane Chen, CEO of Embrace).

SANTA CLARA UNIVERSITY'S FRUGAL INNOVATION LABS

At the heart of Silicon Valley, the School of Engineering and the Centre for Science, Technology, and Society at Santa Clara University are jointly training—through the newly-formed Frugal Innovation Labs—a new generation of engineers who won't be rushing to Facebook or Google for jobs after they graduate. Rather, these students are acquiring new competencies in engineering and management to help them design simple, affordable, and accessible solutions—based on technologies like mobile computing—that address the socio-economic needs of underdeveloped communities in areas such as clean energy, clean water, and public health. The students are taught how to innovate under severe constraints—by doing more with less. They are also trained in how to boost the 'appropriateness' of their frugal solutions by taking into account the specific needs of underserved communities as well as their unique sociocultural context.

For instance, one student team worked closely with HealthPoint Services India to improve delivery of clean water in rural communities. Healthpoint Services owns and operates a network of medical clinics—known as E Health Points (EHPs)—and clean water access points known as Waterpoints. EHPs provide families in Indian villages with basic health services—delivered via tele-medicine. While most Waterpoints are attached to EHPs, some are freestanding stations located away from EHPs in places where they are more accessible to users. The commercial sale of clean water through Waterpoints generates a steady revenue stream that helps subsidize the health services delivered in the clinics. Unfortunately, Waterpoints are currently operated manually by local operators—who many not always be attentive or honest while managing these stations. The student team from Santa Clara University is helping address this problem by designing and implementing a telemetry solution that can totally automate water distribution at Waterpoints—enabling HealthPoint Services, in the process, to rapidly scale up the number of EHPs as well as Waterpoint units across rural India.[28]

Radha Basu, who heads the Frugal Innovation Labs at Santa Clara University, points out that these affordable solutions developed by her students can be deployed not only in emerging markets but also in developed nations like the US that are increasingly confronted with the problems of scarcity. 'For most Western firms, upwards of 50 percent of growth in the next decade will come from emerging markets. Yet none of the [more traditional] technologies developed here in Silicon Valley are appropriate to the needs of emerging market consumers,' notes Basu. 'Western firms need to acquire new core competencies—that we are teaching here—to not only design high-quality and low-cost products but also develop appropriate *business models* and partnership strategies to make and distribute these frugal products to the masses in emerging markets. By developing these new competencies, Western firms can not only be successful in emerging markets, but even in developed economies like the US, which are confronted with scarcity due to the deepening economic recession.'[29]

UNIVERSITY OF CAMBRIDGE'S INCLUSIVE DESIGN PROGRAM

In the UK, the Engineering Design Centre at the University of Cambridge's Department of Engineering is going one step further than its counterparts across the Atlantic. Rather than merely training undergraduates to design products that are accessible to, and usable by marginalized Western consumers (such as the elderly), the Centre, in partnership with the Faculty of Education at Cambridge, has piloted its programmes for 11-to 14 year-old students in a number of schools.

Ian Hosking, a senior research associate at the Centre, explains: 'We have seen that students at a very young age can genuinely engage with the issue of ageing and create highly innovative solutions. Studies have shown that very young children are particularly good at divergent thinking—i.e., they are able to combine unrelated concepts from diverse domains and come up with unusual solutions in the process. Divergent thinking is key to creative problem solving. Sadly, this ability seems to get lost as children get older and go through an education system that does not always foster creative skills. We have formed a very successful partnership with Bill Nicholl at the Faculty of Education who is a leading expert in creativity. Working together we hope to reverse this process somewhat and bring the creative spark back into these children's lives.'[30]

Called Designing Our Tomorrow (or DOT for short), this innovative program has developed resources for teachers to teach an inclusive approach to design. This includes using elements from the Inclusive Design Toolkit (www.inclusivedesigntoolkit.com) that undergraduates in universities—as well as designers in companies—can use to develop products and services that address the needs of marginal consumers in an ageing population. DOT therefore prepares school children not only for a university education but also for when they enter the workforce.

Moreover, DOT doesn't stop at education in the classroom. The output from one of the pilot schools was of such a high standard that Hosking's team arranged for the students to present their work—the design of cutlery solutions for the elderly—to a major UK retailer. Hosking says: 'When I saw what the kids were doing, I was blown away. Their understanding of the issues related to ageing was quite impressive. I wanted them to present their work to this retailer, not just because it would be a good experience for them but also because their ideas had genuine commercial potential for the retailer as well. This is something that we want to extend in the future to enhance the relevance of what they are being taught.'[31]

The potential of DOT is spreading with interest from other countries and the team is currently piloting the resources in one of these countries that is considering a national roll-out.

DESIGN FOR AMERICA

Design for America (DFA) is a network of student-led studios—spanning US universities like Columbia, Stanford, Northwestern, and the University of Oregon at Eugene—that is using interdisciplinary design to revitalize US cities. DFA's goal is to form a 'new generation of "creative activists" equipped with the mindset and skills to create social impact in local communities across the US'.[32] Fifty DFA studios are expected to pop up across the US in the next five years to address big challenges in education, healthcare, and the environment.

Yuri Malina, the 21-year-old co-founder of DFA, told us: 'DFA was started with the observation that if you are a young American engineer or designer, you don't need to buy a $1,000 (₹ 50,000) plane ticket to go to Africa or India to do development work. There are enough problems to solve right in your backyard—be it making healthcare safer and affordable, education better, or finding renewable energy solutions. Whether you live in San Francisco, Boston, or Chicago, you can apply your creative insights not just to design the next iPod or a pair of cool sunglasses, but rather to fix problems in your own neighbourhood.'[33]

DFA members work on 'super-local' projects—meaning that all projects undertaken are located in neighborhoods accessible within the radius of a fifteen-minute bike ride from their studio. For instance, in his first project, Malina worked with a local hospital in Chicago to design a portable 'roll-on' hand sanitizer for busy physicians and nurses so they can clean their hands on the go. This is a highly practical innovation, given that, according to the Centres for Disease Control and Prevention, approximately 20 lakh people in the US get a hospital-acquired infection (HAI) each year. Of those, roughly 1 lakh die prematurely from this infection.[34]

Many of the engineers and designers graduating from the academic programmes just described are likely to become the social entrepreneurs of tomorrow. These graduates are likely to use their frugal engineering skills to address the basic needs of underserved communities—by fixing unreliable electricity and transportation networks, making healthcare delivery more inclusive, and setting up sustainable water and sanitation systems. But a growing number of these graduates are also likely to join Fortune 500 companies and help ignite the jugaad spirit in these organizations as they seek to enable bottom-up innovation to address needs in global markets, the increasing scarcity of resources in the West, and growing global complexity more generally. Either way, these next-generation jugaad innovators will not operate in isolation. Given their great fondness for and deftness with social networking media, these innovators are sure to link up with like-minded innovators elsewhere, including in the emerging world—thus accelerating the rise of a global community of jugaad innovators.

The Rise of a Global Community of Jugaad Innovators

As innovators connect with jugaad innovators in other parts of the world, especially in emerging markets, this process is helping to cross-pollinate creative ideas across regions. In time, this global community of jugaad innovators could combine, say, American and Indian ingenuity to frugally and sustainably address the major challenges facing humanity. In this section, we highlight just a few of the many organizations and initiatives now at work in creating such a globally integrated network of jugaad innovators.

ASHOKA AND SKOLL FOUNDATION

Both of these non-profit organizations actively support thousands of jugaad entrepreneurs worldwide—especially in emerging economies like India—by giving them funding and training to address major socio-economic challenges. Having invested heavily in developing the capabilities of these individual entrepreneurs, Ashoka and Skoll Foundation are now keen to promote collaboration among these entrepreneurs by integrating them into virtual communities. To that effect, these organizations have actively invested in social networking platforms—such as Ashoka's AshokaHub and Skoll Foundation's Social Edge—to cross-fertilize ideas and best practises among jugaad entrepreneurs across five continents.

ENDEAVOR

This non-profit organization has developed an unrivalled global network of seasoned business leaders who provide mentorship and strategic advice to high impact jugaad entrepreneurs around the world—especially in emerging economies. Linda Rottenberg founded Endeavor fourteen years ago, after an Argentinian taxi cab driver with a PhD in physics asked her: 'How can I possibly start my own company when I don't even have a garage?'[35]

THE STANFORD-INDIA BIODESIGN PROGRAM

This initiative brings together physicians, engineers, and designers from the US and India to co-create affordable, user-friendly medical devices that can be deployed not only in

India, where hundreds of crores of citizens lack access to basic healthcare, but also in the US, where 5 crore Americans lack medical insurance. Recently, a team of physicians, engineers, and designers at Stanford collaborated with their counterparts at the Indian Institute of Technology and the All India Institute of Medical Sciences in New Delhi to conceptualize and develop a low-cost bone drill—a device that, in less a minute, delivers life-saving fluids directly into the bone marrow of victims of accidents whose veins have collapsed. The device costs a mere $20 (₹ 1,000) compared to $300 (₹ 15,000) for the equivalent devices available in the US.[36]

NEW YORK CITY'S NEXT IDEA INNOVATION COMPETITION

Actively promoted by New York City's Mayor Michael Bloomberg, Next Idea is an annual competition that invites teams of students from leading business and engineering schools in Europe, Asia, and Latin America to develop business plans for bold jugaad projects that will be executed in New York City and bring major socio-economic benefits to the city. The NYC Next Idea 2009–2010 edition was won by an entrepreneurial team from the Indian Institute of Technology, Madras (IIT-M), that has devised a new system to allow utility companies and energy producers to store and distribute energy safely and efficiently through remote sites across New York's five boroughs—thus helping avoid a repeat of the 2003 blackout that crippled the city.

The New York City Next Idea competition, as well as the other initiatives just mentioned—Ashoka, Skoll, Endeavor, Stanford-India Biodesign—all aim to connect jugaad innovators in the US with their counterparts in other countries, cross-fertilizing promising ideas across geographical boundaries to address common socio-economic issues. One person who is highly enthusiastic about this effort is Alec Ross, Senior Advisor for Innovation to Secretary of State Hillary Clinton. A former entrepreneur, Ross is Secretary Clinton's 'tech guru'. With more than 3,70,000 followers on Twitter, Ross is leading the US State Department's efforts to find practical technical solutions for some of the globe's most vexing problems in healthcare, poverty, human rights, and ethnic conflict.

Speaking to us, Ross said: 'Everyone is talking about the shift of power from West to East. But the real shift of power happening now is from big institutions to small institutions. Hierarchical power structures and top-down innovation models are being replaced by networked power structures and bottom-up innovation approaches. To thrive in the new multi-polar world, America must relinquish its insular view of innovation and start brokering and facilitating global networks of grassroots innovators who can co-create solutions to global problems we all share.'[37]

How Indian Companies Can Profit From the Groundswell Jugaad Movement

This emerging grassroots jugaad ecosystem—made up of activist citizens, socially minded entrepreneurs, forward-thinking governments, universities, and innovation-funding bodies—can help corporations in India, both domestic and multinational, to accelerate their own adoption of jugaad by tapping into the innovation ecosystem that is growing in India and across the world. Here are some ways Indian companies can contribute to the *groundswell* jugaad movement unfolding worldwide—and profit from it.

SUPPORT GRASSROOTS JUGAAD INNOVATORS TO REVITALIZE LOCAL ECONOMIES

Western CEOs have begun to realize that they have the power to spur demand for their goods and services by supporting grassroots innovators who are striving to revitalize local economies. To do so, these companies have begun to partner with government bodies like the White House's SICP and non-profit organizations to harness the creative power of grassroots jugaad innovators in catalyzing community development. Indian companies can learn from these Western counterparts. For instance, Charles Schwab Bank has partnered with the Centre for Financial Services Innovation (CFSI) to launch the Bay Area Financial Capability Innovators Development Lab.[38] This initiative offers peer learning and review opportunities to grassroots jugaad entrepreneurs in the Bay Area in Northern California who are using innovative approaches to make financial services available to the 6 crore unbanked and underbanked Americans. Similarly, large financial institutions in India could partner with non-profit organizations like the IFMR-Centre for Micro Finance to experiment with innovative business models that leverage technologies such as mobile phones and smart cards to make financial services affordable and accessible to the 60 crore unbanked Indians.

Further, Indian companies should emulate pioneers like Godrej and GE Healthcare India who are linking up with grassroots entrepreneurs to distribute their low-cost products and services to customers at the bottom of the pyramid. Even better, Indian corporations should follow the lead of Marico and Future Group that are funding initiatives to recognize grassroots entrepreneurs and help scale up their inventions by leveraging their companies' own supply chain assets. For example, the Marico Innovation Foundation was set up in

2003 to enable social organizations to apply innovation as a key tool to help scale up their social impact across India. The Foundation also runs the Innovation for India Awards—which are bestowed every year upon innovators across the public, private, and non-profit sectors whose projects and businesses are making a real difference to Indian society at large. In 2010, the Future Group—headed by Kishore Biyani—tied up with the National Innovation Foundation (NIF) and the Department of Science & Technology of the Government of India to form an innovation lab called 'Khoj Lab' that will create and support grassroots innovators and create a marketplace for their inventions—making their products accessible to the 22 crore customers who visit Future Group nationwide retail outlets annually.[39]

Similarly, Microsoft and Google are funding Code for America—a non-political organization that offers fellowships to web professionals to develop applications that can help financially stretched city governments in the US become more open and efficient in responding to citizens' needs. Code for America will replicate successful web applications across multiple US cities as a way to improve governance and socio-economic development nationwide. Inspired by Code for America, one can imagine in the near future the top Indian IT service providers—Cognizant, HCL, Infosys, TCS, and Wipro—forming a joint initiative to create open-source software that can be used by the 2,65,000 gram panchayats across India to improve local governance and accelerate rural development.

Indian companies should also consider partnering with the National Innovation Council (NIC) chaired by Sam Pitroda to support grassroots innovation initiatives. For instance, Indian corporations could co-invest in the ₹ 5,000 crore 'India Inclusive Innovation Fund' that the NIC is currently setting up to financially support grassroots jugaad entrepreneurs who have ideas—or have already devised innovative solutions—for addressing pressing socio-economic issues in their local communities.

USE SOCIAL POWER TO INNOVATE FASTER, BETTER, AND CHEAPER

The groundswell jugaad movement is facilitated by social media tools such as Facebook and Twitter. These tools enable activist citizens—especially Millennials—to instantly organize into large online communities that bring about major change at warp speed (such as toppling governments in the Middle East or exposing corporations that indulge in inappropriate business practises). Many Western companies are increasingly tapping into the social power of these virtual communities of jugaad innovators. As David Kirkpatrick, author of *The Facebook Effect*, puts it: 'Social power can help keep your company vital. Newly armed customer and employee activists can become the source of creativity, innovation, and new ideas to take your company forward.'[40]

Ford is one company that is harnessing social power to great benefit by integrating social media into every aspect of how it designs, builds, and markets its products. 'Digital suffrage is upon us,' observes Venkatesh Prasad, who leads Ford's product social networking efforts. 'Everyone has a right to a byte of the action, and we have embraced this might of the byte within Ford, through the use of internal and external social networks.'[41] For instance, ahead of the launch of its Fiesta subcompact car in 2010, Ford invited one hundred active bloggers—many of whom were Millennials—to test-drive the car and regularly post videos and unfiltered impressions on YouTube, Twitter, and their individual blogs. Ford's jugaad innovation in marketing—dubbed 'Fiesta Movement'—paid off: it generated 70 lakh YouTube views and 4 crore Tweets (mostly favourable). The grassroots media campaign generated great awareness among young car buyers for Fiesta; it also helped Ford shed its stodgy image and reposition itself as a 'cool' automaker. The Fiesta has since become of one of Ford's best-selling cars ever: within ten months of its launch, the Fiesta had conquered one-fifth of the subcompact car segment in the US. Scott Monty, Ford's head of social media, explains, 'Ford doesn't have a social media strategy—it's a business strategy supported by social media.'[42]

Similarly, tech-savvy Indian companies like Nokia India and Tata Motors are harnessing social media to collect ideas from customers and partners and speed up the innovation process by making it open and democratic. For instance, via its forum.nokia.com social media site, Nokia enables Indian software developers and 'lead users' (i.e., mobile enthusiasts among customers) to contribute ideas and software code for developing the next breakthrough Nokia product. Similarly, well ahead of its official launch of Nano in 2009, Tata Motors set up a rich social media platform to interact with potential customers—enabling these end users to view, evaluate, and even personalize the Nano online. Tata Motors is now actively engaging with customers through Facebook and Twitter (the Nano Facebook page has a fan base of nearly 10 lakh!). Interestingly, a growing number of end users engaging with Tata Motors via these social networking sites are from small towns and even villages across India.

RECRUIT JUGAAD INNOVATORS FROM TOP INDIAN AND WESTERN CAMPUSES

Indian companies seeking to strengthen their jugaad innovation skills—such as doing more with less and including the margin—can find those valuable skills in the next generation of American and European graduates from programmes such as Stanford's Entrepreneurial Design for Extreme Affordability and the University of Cambridge's Inclusive Design program. GE Healthcare India, for example, has partnered with Embrace, a start-up co-founded by four graduates of the Stanford program, to commercialize Embrace's portable infant warmer through GE's own vast distribution network in India. But Indian firms don't need to travel far: they can also find such next generation graduates in Indian academic institutions such as IIT Madras and the National Institute of Design(NID) that are leading the way in terms of imparting not only frugal engineering and designs kills to their students but also the commercial skills and networks needed to scale up their jugaad inventions. For example, IIT Madras has set up the Rural Technology and Business Incubator (RTBI) whose mission is to design, pilot and incubate scalable business ventures with a rural focus. Similarly, NID operates the National Design Business Incubator(NDBI) which incubates many design-based start-ups with a social mission.

Indian companies should hire such flexible-minded students with entrepreneurial instincts to create frugal and sustainable solutions aimed at serving the growing number of thrifty and eco-conscious Indian consumers. For instance, Indian pharmaceutical companies and medical device makers could engage student entrepreneurs at NDBI in devising innovative solutions for making healthcare safer, more affordable, and accessible to underserved communities in rural India.

HARNESS INGENUITY ACROSS BORDERS WITH GLOBAL INNOVATION NETWORKS

The global economy is growing ever more connected, thanks to social media tools like Facebook—enabling talented jugaad innovators in both Western and emerging markets to co-create breakthrough solutions that no single region can develop on its own. The Stanford-India Biodesign Program described earlier exemplifies such a synergistic and *polycentric* innovation model.[43] Indian companies must integrate themselves into these global networks of jugaad innovators to take advantage of the unique skills, ideas, and opportunities available across multiple regions. For example, Xerox, Procter & Gamble, and TCS, each orchestrate global innovation networks that integrate the creativity of jugaad entrepreneurs in India with the talent of their R&D teams in Europe and the US to co-create high-quality and affordable products and services for global markets.[44]

Other Indian companies have much to gain from following suit and linking their own R&D teams with jugaad ecosystems in India and elsewhere.

A Prosperous World of Jugaad

The world is increasingly confronted with scarcity and unpredictability. As cash-strapped governments become increasingly unable to deal with these challenges on their own, ordinary citizens, forward-thinking entrepreneurs, venture capitalists, and non-profit organizations are stepping into the breach. These grassroots jugaad innovators are using their flexible thinking to improvise frugal solutions to vexing socio-economic problems in healthcare, education, financial services, and community development. However, as described in this chapter, governments are not standing idly by. From the US to the UK, France and India, central and local governments are busy initiating programmes to support and accelerate the grassroots jugaad movement. Universities too are joining in these efforts. Keenly aware of the problems of scarcity and volatility afflicting their economies, several higher education institutions in the US, Europe and India are training a new breed of designers, engineers, and managers to create next-generation products and services that can deal with scarcity in a frugal and sustainable manner.

All this is good news for corporations over the world, and especially in India: now they can speed up their internal adoption of jugaad by connecting with this grassroots innovation movement unfolding across nations. By integrating their own organizations into local as well as global networks of jugaad innovators, companies can become resilient organizations that think frugally, act flexibly, and generate breakthrough growth. The sooner they do so, the better—not only for them, but also for a world in a battle against scarcity of time and resources. For the challenges this brave new world poses, jugaad innovation offers a powerful solution.

Notes

Chapter 1

1. Professor Anil Gupta, Indian Institute of Ahmedabad, personal interview with Simone Ahuja, January 9, 2009.
2. Mansukh Prajapati, personal interview with Simone Ahuja, January 9, 2009.
3. 'Infrastructure 2011'. Urban Land Institute and Ernst & Young, 2011.
4. 'Forbes lists Top Seven 'Rural Indians'.' [http://news.in.msn.com/business/article.aspx?cp-documentid=4579411]. November 15, 2010.
5. 'Stretching the Rupee to the Maximum'. [http://indiandream.blogspot.com/2007/05/stretching-rupee-to-maximum.html]. May 4, 2007.
6. V. Muniz, 'Campana Brothers'. [http://bombsite.com/issues/102/articles/3040]. 2008.
7. Segal, A. 'China's Innovation Wall: Beijing's Push for Homegrown Technology'. *Foreign Affairs*, September 28, 2010.
8. Daniels, S. 'Making Do. Innovation in Kenya's Informal Economy'. [http://www.analoguedigital.com/docs/makingdo-download-lores.pdf]. 2010.

9. Neuwirth, R. 'The Shadow Superpower'. *Foreign Policy*, October 28, 2011.

10. Radjou, N. 'Let "indovations" bloom'. *MINT*, November 12, 2012. [http://www.livemint.com/2011/11/12005055/Let-8216indovations8217.html].

11. 'Benjamin Franklin, Entrepreneur'. [http://www.benfranklin300.org/etc_article_entrepreneur.htm].

12. 'Franklin Stove'. [http://web.mit.edu/invent/iow/franklin.html].

13. Bellis, M. 'The Inventions and Scientific Achievements of Benjamin'. [http://inventors.about.com/od/fstartinventors/ss/Franklin_invent_2.htm].

14. Franklin, B. *The Autobiography of Benjamin Franklin: 1706–1757*. Bedford, MA: Applewood Books, 2008.

15. Jaruzelski B., Loehr, J., and Holman, R. 'The Global Innovation 1000: Why Culture is Key'. *strategy+business*, Winter 2011.

16. Jaruzelski B., Dehoff, K., and Bordi, R. 'The Booz Allen Hamilton Global Innovation 1000: Money Isn't Everything'. *strategy+business*, Winter 2005.

17. Key Industry Facts About PhRMA. [http://www.phrma.org/about/key-industry-facts-about-phrma].

18. Hirschler, B. 'Last Chance for Sickly Pharma to Deliver on R&D'. [http://www.reuters.com/article/2011/02/10/pharmaceuticals-rd-idUSLDE71912R20110210]. February 10, 2011.

19. Schaper, E. V. 'How Novartis Plans to Avoid the "Patent Cliff"'. [http://www.businessweek.com/magazine/how-novartis-plans-to-avoid-the-patent-cliff-08042011.html]. August 4, 2011.

20. 'Contribution of the Automotive Industry to the Economies of All Fifty States and the US'. [http://www.cargroup.org/pdfs/association_paper.pdf]. April 2010.

21. Gardner, G. 'GM cars: Good December sales can't make up for poor 2010'. *The Christian Science Monitor*, January 5, 2011.

22. Isidore, C. 'Big Three want more money in bailout'. [http://money.cnn.com/2008/12/02/news/companies/automakers_plans/index.htm]. December 4, 2008.

23. Bunkley, N. 'G.M. Repays US Loan, While Chrysler Posts Improved Quarterly Results'. *New York Times*, April 21, 2010; 'The US Motor Vehicle Industry: Confronting a New Dynamic in the Global Economy'. Congressional Research Service, March 26, 2010.

24. 'Six Sigma: So Yesterday?' [http://www.businessweek.com/magazine/content/07_24/b4038409.htm]. June 11, 2007.

25. Pascale, R., Sternin, J., and Sternin, M. The Power of Positive Deviance: How Unlikely Innovators Solve the World's Toughest Problem. Boston, MA: Harvard Business School Press, 2010.

26. Gladwell, M. *Outliers*. Boston, MA: Little, Brown, and Company, 2008.

27. Hindo, B. 'At 3M, A Struggle Between Efficiency and Creativity'. *Bloomberg Businessweek,* June 11, 2007.

28. Tellis, G., Prabhu, J., and Chandy. R. 'Radical Innovation Across Nations: The Preeminence of Corporate Culture'. *Journal of Marketing*, 2003, *73*(1), 3–23.

29. McDonald, B. 'Touching Lives, Improving Life: Why Innovation Matters and How to Make It Work'. [http://www.pg.com/en_US/downloads/company/purpose_people/touching_lives_improving_life.pdf]. December 2008.

30. Jana, R. 'Facebook's Design Strategy: A Status Update'. [http://designmind.frogdesign.com/articles/facebook-s-design-strategy-a-status-update.html].

31. Kirkpatrick, D. 'Social Power and the Coming Corporate Revolution'. *Forbes*, September 26, 2011, p. 72.

32. The acronym BRICs (Brazil, Russia, India, and China) was coined by Goldman Sachs chief economist Jim O'Neill in a 2001 paper entitled 'The World Needs Better Economic BRICs'.

33. Wilson, D., Purushothaman, R. 'Dreaming With BRICs: The Path to 2050'. *Global Economics Paper No. 99*, Goldman Sachs, October 1, 2003.

34. 'Ernst & Young Rapid Growth Markets Forecast (RGMF)'. [http://www.ey.com/IN/en/Newsroom/News-releases/Ernst-and-Young-Rapid-Growth-Markets-Forecast]. October 24, 2011.

35. 'South Asia: India'. [https://www.cia.gov/library/publications/the-world-factbook/geos/in.html]. October 21, 2011.

36. Dr Liu Jiren, Chairman and CEO, Neusoft, personal interview with Navi Radjou, September 15, 2011.

37. Abi Naha, CEO, Zone V, personal interview with Navi Radjou, June 23, 2011.

38. The Best Buy–supported television series *Indique: Big Ideas from Emerging India* ran on PBS stations in 2010.

Chapter 2

1. 'Access to Electricity'. [http://www.iea.org/weo/electricity.asp]. 2010.

2. Tulsi Tanti, Chairman and Managing Director, Suzlon Energy, personal interview with Navi Radjou, November 14, 2011.

3. *Doing Business in a More Transparent World. Economy Profile: India.* Washington, DC: The World Bank and the International Finance Corporation, 2012.

4. *Doing Business in South Asia 2007.* Washington, DC: The World Bank, 2007.

5. *Rural Roads. A Lifeline for Villages in India.* The World Bank, 2000.

6. Majumdar, B. 'India's Poor Healthcare a Threat to Growth: Report'. [http://in.reuters.com/article/2009/09/16/idINIndia-42468920090916]. September 16, 2009.

7. Granito, A. '80 percent of Indians Live on Less Than $2 a Day: WB'. [http://www.livemint.com/articles/2007/10/16235421/80-of-Indians-live-on-less-th.html]. October 16, 2007.

8. 'Population Below Poverty Line'. *The World Factbook.* [https://www.cia.gov/library/publications/the-world-factbook/fields/2046.html].

9. Ratemo, J. 'Airtel Kenya Unveils New Online Payment System'. *Business Daily*, November 4, 2011; 'High Costs Keep Patients Out of Hospitals'. *Xinhua News Agency.* November 23, 2004.

10. 'The Difference Defines Us: The DNA of the Entrepreneur'. *Exceptional*, Ernst & Young, July-December 2011.

11. Radjou, N., Prabhu, J., Kaipa, P., Ahuja, S. 'How Reframers Unleash Innovation in Their Companies (And Beyond)'. [http://blogs.hbr.org/cs/2010/07/how_reframers_are_unleashing_a.html]. July 13, 2010.

12. Dr Prasad Kaipa, CEO coach, personal interview with Navi Radjou, November 3, 2011.

13. Radjou, N., Prabhu, J., Kaipa, P., Ahuja, S. 'How To Ignite Creative Leadership In Your Organization'. [http://blogs.hbr.org/cs/2010/05/how_to_ignite_creative_leaders.html]. May 19, 2010.

14. Comments collected from Professor Anil Gupta, who spoke at 'Innovation in India and China. How to Create Value from Emerging Markets'—a conference hosted by the Centre for India & Global Business at Judge Business School, University of Cambridge, on May 19–20, 2009.

15. Thakor, P. 'Villager from Guwahati gave MIT tech ideas'. *DNA*, December 10, 2010.

16. We collected initial details on Enrique Gómez Junco and his company Optima Energía through our interview with Fernando Fabre, president of Endeavor—a non-profit organization that provides mentorship and strategic advice to high-impact jugaad entrepreneurs such as Junco around the world. Additional details were provided later by Junco himself.

17. 'IFC Investment in Optima Energia Supports Energy Efficiency in Mexico's Hotel Sector'. Press release from International Finance Corporation, October 21, 2009.

18. 'Our Entrepreneurs. Enrique Gómez Junco'. [http://www.endeavor.org/entrepreneurs/enrique-gomez-junco/169].

19. 'Mexico: Optima Energia's Novel Business Model Helps Mexican Hotels Reduce Energy Costs'. [http://www.ifc.org/ifcext/gms.nsf/AttachmentsByTitle/CaseStudyOptima/$FILE/Optima.pdf]. 2010.

20. 'Infosys and Wharton School Announce the Wharton Infosys Business Transformation Awards 2006 for North America

and Latin America'. [http://wwwstage.wharton.upenn. edu/whartonfacts/news_and_events/newsreleases/2006/ p_2006_11_570.html]. November 13, 2006.

21. 'I.M.F. Slashes Growth Outlook for US and Europe'. [http:// www.nytimes.com/2011/09/21/business/global/imf-slashes-growth-outlook-for-us-and-europe.html]. September 20, 2011.

22. 'Borrower defaults at 10-yr high as demand wanes', The *Times of India*, Apr. 4, 2012.

23. 'Economic growth slows down to 6.1 percent; lowest in 2 years', *The Indian Express*, Feb. 29, 2012

24. Edgerton, J. 'Automakers Agree to 54 MPG Standard'. *CBS MoneyWatch*, July 29, 2011.

25. Elliott, L., Kollewe, J. 'Germany Faces Up to Problem of Ageing Workforce'. [http://www.guardian.co.uk/world/2011/mar/17/ new-europe-germany-retirement-pensions-exports]. March 17, 2011.

26. 'Facebook: India to power future growth', The *Times of India*, Feb. 2, 2012.

27. *Water Scarcity & Climate Change: Growing Risks for Businesses & Investors*. A Ceres Report authored by the Pacific Institute, February 2009.

28. 'India faces intense competition in pursuit of $25bn export goal'. [http://www.in-pharmatechnologist.com/Ingredients/ India-faces-intense-competition-in-pursuit-of-25bn-export-goal].

29. Hamel, G. *The Future of Management*. Boston, MA: Harvard Business School Press, 2008.

30. Stelter, B., Vega, T. 'Ad Money Reliably Goes to Television'. *New York Times*, August 7, 2011.

31. Richardson, A. *Innovation X: Why A Company's Toughest Problems Are Its Great Advantage*. Jossey-Bass, 2010.

32. Mookerji, N. 'Flipkart aims for 10-fold growth in revenue in FY12', *Business Standard*, Dec. 27, 2011.

33. Menkes, J. *Better Under Pressure*. Boston, MA: Harvard Business School Press, 2011.

34. Overby, C. S. The Essentials of Consumer-Driven Innovation. Best Practises Report, Forrester Research, May 26, 2006.

35. Neff, J. 'P&G's Buzz-Building Networks Thrive in Age of Social Media'. *Ad Age*, October 10, 2011.

36. 'New Procter & Gamble Survey of Moms Shows Teens Need More Input from Their Parents When it Comes to Spending'. *New York Times,* September 8, 2011.

37. Fleschner, M. 'Best Friends'. [http://www.sellingpower.com/magazine/article.php?i=1168&ia=6273].

38. Hagel, J. III, Brown, J. S., and Davison, L. 'Shaping Strategy in a World of Constant Disruption'. *Harvard Business Review*, October 2008.

39. 'Salesforce.com Announces Fiscal Second Quarter Results'. [http://www.salesforce.com/company/news-press/press-releases/2011/08/110818.jsp]. August 18, 2011.

40. 'Salesforce.com Announces Fiscal Third Quarter Results'. [http://www.salesforce.com/company/news-press/press-releases/2011/11/111117.jsp]. November 17, 2011.

41. Hardy, Q. 'A Leader in the Cloud Gains Rivals'. *New York Times*, December 11, 2011.

42. Ried, S., and Kisker, H. *Sizing the Cloud*. Forrester Research report, April 21, 2011.

43. 'Why is *Behind the Cloud* a Great Book for These Times?' [http://www.salesforce.com/behindthecloud/].

44. 'Psychological Capital: What Lies Beneath'. *Rotman Magazine*, Fall 2008.

45. 'Meeting of minds'. [http://www.danonecommunities.com/en/content/meeting-minds].

46. Radjou, N. and Kaipa, P. 'Do Multinationals Really Understand Globalization?' [http://www.businessweek.com/globalbiz/content/aug2010/gb2010086_282527.htm]. August 6, 2010.

47. 'Developing Employees' Autonomy And Efficiency'. [http://www.danone.com/en/axes-strategiques/developing-employees-autonomy-and-efficiency.html].

48. Global Knowledge Management at Danone. Case No. 9-608-107. Boston, MA: Harvard Business School, 2008; Shanine, K.,

Buchko, A., and Wheeler, A. R. 'International Human Resource Management Practises from a Complex Adaptive Systems Perspective: An Exploratory Investigation'. International Journal of Business and Social Science, Vol. 2 No. 6; April 2011.

49. 'Our Values'. [http://www.danone.com/en/company/values. html].

50. Barclay's 'Back To School' Consumer Conference—Transcript. [http://finance.danone.com/phoenix.zhtml?c=95168&p=irol-presentations].September 7, 2011; 'Sustainable Development'. [http://www.danone.com/en/sustainable-development.html].

51. '2010 Growth First—Interview with Franck Riboud, CEO of Danone'. [http://www.danone.com/en/company/strategy. html].

52. Sharma, S. 'For Danone, innovation is way forward in India', DNA, Mar. 10, 2012.

53. Grameen Danone, Yunus Centre web site, [http://www. muhammadyunus.org/Social-Business/grameen-danone/].

54. The Dannon Company: Marketing and Corporate Social Responsibility. Case No. 9-410-121. Boston, MA: Harvard Business School, 2010.

55. Maney, K., Hamm, S. and O'Brien, J. M. *Making the World Work Better—The Ideas That Shaped a Century and a Company*. Upper Saddle River, NJ: IBM Press, 2011.

56. Goldman, D. 'HP decides to keep its PC business'. *CNNMoney*, October 27, 2011.

57. Lohr, S. 'Even a Giant Can Learn to Run'. [http://www.nytimes. com/2012/01/01/business/how-samuel-palmisano-of-ibm-stayed-a-step-ahead-unboxed.html]. December 31, 2011.

58. 'Samuel J. Palmisano. Computer History Museum'. [http:// www.ibm.com/ibm100/us/en/lectures/what_changes_and_ what_endures.html]. August 4, 2011.

59. Radjou, N. 'TCS's Client-Focused Innovation Network Sets The Bar High For Global IT Service Providers', Forrester Report, Feb. 13, 2007.

60. Hopkins, M. 'The Unstructured Information', *Forbes India*, Apr. 27, 2012.

61. 'A Century of Innovation'. [http://solutions.3m.com/wps/portal/3M/en_WW/History/3M/Company/century-innovation/].

62. Goetz, K. 'How 3M Gave Everyone Days Off and Created an Innovation Dynamo'. [http://www.fastcodesign.com/1663137/how-3m-gave-everyone-days-off-and-created-an-innovation-dynamo]. Feburary 1, 2011.

63. Hindo, B. 'At 3M, A Struggle Between Efficiency and Creativity'. *Bloomberg Businessweek*, June 11, 2007.

64. Ibid.

65. Salter, C. 'The Nine Passions of 3M's Mauro Porcini'. *FastCompany*, October 2011, p. 128.

66. Mauro Porcini, Head of Global Strategic Design, 3M, personal interview with Simone Ahuja and Navi Radjou, October 7, 2011.

67. Ibid.

68. Ibid.

69. Singh, S. '3M Bets on India-Style Innovation'. *Forbes India*, Oct. 18, 2011.

70. Marc Gunther, M. '3M's Innovation Revival'. [http://money.cnn.com/2010/09/23/news/companies/3m_innovation_revival.fortune/index.htm]. September 24, 2010.

71. Jaruzelski B., Loehr, J., and Holman, R. 'The Global Innovation 1000 Why Culture is Key'. [http://www.strategy-business.com/article/11404?pg=all]. October 25, 2011.

Chapter 3

1. Farber, D. 'GE CEO Jeff Immelt: India, Globalization and the Economics of Scarcity'. ZDNet, July 6, 2007.

2. Gustavo Grobocopatel, CEO, Los Grobo, email exchange with Navi Radjou, September 26, 2011.

3. 'The World Factbook. Field Listing: Land Use'. [https://www. cia.gov/library/publications/the-world-factbook/fields/2097. html]

4. Los Grobo: Farming's Future? Case No. 9-511-088. Boston, MA: Harvard Business School, 2010.

5. 'Entrepreneurs Speak Out. A Call to Action for G20 Governments. Country Digest: Argentina'. Report produced by Ernst & Young for the G20 Young Entrepreneur Summit, October 2011.

6. 'Entrepreneurs Speak Out. A Call to Action for G20 Governments. Country Digest: Africa'. Report produced by Ernst & Young for the G20 Young Entrepreneur Summit, October 2011.

7. 'India Lags China in R&D Spending: Sibal'. *Financial Express*, March 13, 2008.

8. 2001 Talent Shortage Survey Results. ManpowerGroup, 2011.

9. Zeng, M. and Williamson, P. J. *Dragons at Your Door: How Chinese Cost Innovation Is Disrupting Global Competition.* Boston, MA: Harvard Business School Press, 2007.

10. Mas, I., and Radcliffe, D. 'Mobile Payments Go Viral: M-PESA in Kenya'. The Capco Institute Journal of Financial Transformation, Journal 32, 2011.

11. Hughes, N., and Lonie, S. 'M-PESA: Mobile Money for the 'Unbanked'.' *innovations*, Special Edition for the GSMA Mobile World Congress 2009, MIT Press, 2009.

12. Strategic Outsourcing at Bharti Airtel Limited. Case No. 9-107-003. Harvard Business School. Boston, MA: Harvard Business School, 2006.

13. Dholakia, R. R., Anwar, S. F. and Hasan, K. (eds.) *Marketing Practises in Developing Economy: Cases from South Asia.* New Delhi, India: PHI Learning, 2010.

14. Prahalad, C. K. *The Fortune at the Bottom of the Pyramid.* Upper Saddle River, NJ:Wharton School Publishing, 2004.

15. FAQs. Hapinoy website. [http://hapinoy.com/faqs.html].

16. Weinstein, J. 'Awakening a "Sleeping Giant", Microfranchise as a Distribution Platform'. [http://www.nextbillion.net/blog/awakening-a-sleeping-giant]. February 15, 2011.

17. Bam Aquino, President, MicroVentures Inc., personal interview with Navi Radjou, September 16, 2011.

18. Doggett, S. 'Low Cost "Revolo" Hybridization Kit Could Boost India's Presence in Gas-Electric Arena'. Autoobserver.com, September 13, 2010.

19. Ravi Pandit, CEO, KPIT Cummins Infosystems, personal interview with Navi Radjou, January 5, 2010.

20. 'Trailblazers, Shapers and Innovators—Model of Success from the Community of Global Growth Companies'. The World Economic Forum, 2011.

21. John, S., and Sood, V. 'Cleaner, Greener, Cheaper'. *Mint*, July 29, 2010.

22. Steen, M. 'Portable Baby Warmer Goes from Classroom Project to Nascent Organization'. *Stanford Business Magazine*, Autumn 2011.

23. 'Embrace—how it works'. [http://embraceglobal.org/main/product?section=howitworks].

24. Jane Chen, CEO, Embrace, personal interview with Navi Radjou, September 2, 2011.

25. Schrage, M. 'Procurement's Best-Priced Deal May Stifle Innovation.' Harvard Business Review Blog, December 1, 2011.

26. Assocham: India's rural consumer durable market to grow 40 percent in 2011-12, CommodityOnline, Dec. 26, 2010.

27. Pop Quiz: Can Indra Nooyi Revive PepsiCo?, Knowledge@Wharton, Mar. 28, 2012.

28. Bharat Stage emission standards, [http://en.wikipedia.org/wiki/Bharat_Stage_emission_standards].

29. Szczesny, J. 'India Likely to Become World's Third-Largest Car Market by 2020', *The Detroit Bureau,* Jun. 14, 2011.

30. Berfield, S. 'Hip Eyewear: Warby Parker's New Spectacles'. *Bloomberg Businessweek*, June 30, 2011.

31. 'India's Online Booksellers Try to Write a New Chapter', *India Knowledge@Wharton*, Jul. 29, 2010.

32. John Maeda, President of the Rhode Island School of Design, personal interview with Navi Radjou, November 1, 2011.

33. Bradner, L. *Five Ways CPG Marketers Are Fighting the Recession.* Forrester Research report, July 16, 2009.

34. *Redefining the Future of Growth: The New Sustainability Champions.* Geneva, Switzerland: World Economic Forum, 2011.

35. Ramón Mendiola Sánchez, CEO of Florida Ice & Farm Co., personal interview with Navi Radjou, December 19, 2011.

36. 'Special Report—The race to the modern 5,000 euro car'. [http://www.autobrief.com/autobrief/?lng=en-us&mode=art_one&aid=635&rid=0]. June 5, 2007.

37. Ghosh, R. 'Ghosn back to praising "frugal engg"'. *DNA*, October 30, 2007; Sehgal, V., Dehoff, K. and Panneer, G. 'The Importance of Frugal Engineering'. *strategy+business*, Summer 2010.

38. Welch, D. 'The Leaner Baby Boomer Economy'. *Bloomberg Businessweek*, July 23, 2009.

39. Binkley, C. 'Beyond Bridal: Vera Wang's New Look'. *Wall Street Journal*, December 15, 2011.

40. Byron, E. 'As Middle Class Shrinks, P&G Marketing Aims High and Low'. *Wall Street Journal,* September 12, 2011.

41. Sharma, S. 'At Godrej, ChotuKool spawns major business strategy', *DNA*, Dec. 5, 2011.

42. McGregor, J. 'GE: Reinventing Tech for the Emerging World'. *Bloomberg Businessweek*, April 17, 2008.

43. Huston, L., and Sakkab, N. 'Connect and Develop: Inside Procter & Gamble's New Model for Innovation'. *Harvard Business Review*, March 2011.

44. Radjou, N. and Prabhu, J. 'Mobilizing for Growth in Emerging Markets', *MIT Sloan Management Review*, Spring 2012.

45. Indra Nooyi, Chairman and CEO, PepsiCo Inc., personal interview with Navi Radjou, January 21, 2010.

46. Jana, R. 'India's Next Global Export: Innovation'.*Bloomberg Businessweek,* December 2, 2009.

47. PepsiCo 2010 Annual Report. [http://pepsico.com/Download/PepsiCo_Annual_Report_2010_Full_Annual_Report.pdf].

48. Ibid.

49. York, E. B. 'Dr Mehmood Khan Taking on the PepsiCo Nutritional Challenge'. *Chicago Tribune*, June 20, 2011.

50. Tanmaya Vats, head of Global Value Innovation Centre, PepsiCo Inc., personal interview with Navi Radjou and Jaideep Prabhu, October 3, 2011.

51. 'PepsiCo: Our Commitment to Sustainable Agriculture Practises'. [http://pepsico.com/Download/PepsiCo_agri_0531_final.pdf].

52. Ibid.

53. Radjou, N., and Prabhu, J. 'PepsiCo and GE Are Innovating in India'. *Bloomberg Businessweek*, November 9, 2010.

54. 'Frito-Lay Unveils "Near Net Zero" Manufacturing Facility'. [http://www.pepsico.com/PressRelease/Frito-Lay-Unveils-Near-Net-Zero-Manufacturing-Facility10052011.html]. October 5, 2011.

Chapter 4

1. Sinha, K. 'India's diabetes burden to cross 100 million by 2030'. The *Times of India*, December 14, 2011.

2. Dr V. Mohan, Chairman of Dr Mohan's Diabetes Specialities Centre, personal interview with Simone Ahuja, December 15, 2008. [Please note that 'specialities' is used here in British English]

3. Dr Harish Hande, founder, SELCO, personal interview with Simone Ahuja, December 23, 2008.

4. Abrar, P. 'Solar entrepreneur Harish Hande's Solar Electric Light Company taps rural schools, homes'. *The Economic Times*, December 16, 2011.

5. Ravi Kant, Non Executive Vice Chairman, Tata Motors, personal interview with Jaideep Prabhu and Navi Radjou, June 18, 2010.

6. A K Bhattacharya. 'Singur to Sanand'. *Business Standard*, August 6, 2011.

7. Baggonkar, S. 'Tata Motors goes on Nano overdrive'. *Business Standard*, November 10, 2011.

8. Zeng, M. and Williamson, P. J. *Dragons at Your Door: How Chinese Cost Innovation Is Disrupting Global Competition*. Boston, MA: Harvard Business School Press, 2007.

9. 'Haier India targets ₹ 1,500 crore sales, top-5 entry', *The Times of India*, Jun. 7, 2011.

10. Zhang, R. 'Creating New Business Models'. [http://www.daonong.com/g/2011EN/Columns/20110915/32691.html]. September 15, 2011.

11. Colvin, G. 'Zhang Ruimin: Management's next icon'. *Fortune*, July 25, 2011.

12. Madden, N. 'Why It's OK to Wash Potatoes in a Washing Machine'. *Ad Age*, February 3, 2010.

13. Backaler, J. 'Haier: A Chinese Company That Innovates'. *Forbes*, June 17, 2010.

14. Professor Carol Dweck, Stanford University, personal interview with Navi Radjou, September 9, 2011.

15. Dweck, C. *Mindset: The New Psychology of Success*. New York: Random House, 2006.

16. Dr Prasad Kaipa, CEO coach and leadership expert, personal interview with Navi Radjou, November 3, 2011; Kaipa, P. 'The flip side of signature strength'. *SiliconIndia*, April 2007.

17. Shashank Samant, President, GlobalLogic, personal interview with Navi Radjou, August 17, 2011.

18. Doreen Lorenzo, President, frog, personal interview with Navi Radjou, August 24, 2011.

19. Hammond, A., Kramer, W. J., Tran, J., Katz, R., and Walker, C. 'The Next 4 Billion: Market Size and Business Strategy at the Base of the Pyramid'. [http://www.wri.org/publication/the-next-4-billion]. March 2007.

20. Pfeiffer, P., Massen, S., and Bombka, U. 'Serving the Low-Income Consumer: How to Tackle This Mostly Ignored

Market'. [http://www.atkearney.com/index.php/Publications/
serving-the-low-income-consumer.html].

21. Prahalad, C. K. *The Fortune at the Bottom of the Pyramid*.
Upper Saddle River, NJ: Wharton School Publishing, 2004.

22. Christensen, C. *The Innovator's Dilemma: When New
Technologies Cause Great Firms to Fail*. Boston, MA: Harvard
Business School Press, 1997.

23. Khaliq, A. A., and Thompson, D. M. 'The Impact of Hospital
CEO Turnover in US Hospitals'. Final Report prepared for the
American College of Healthcare Executives (ACHE), February
2006.

24. 'Majority of American Workers Not Engaged in Their Jobs'.
[http://www.gallup.com/poll/150383/majority-american-
workers-not-engaged-jobs.aspx]. October 28, 2011.

25. Hardy, Q. 'Google's Innovation—And Everyone's?' *Forbes*, July
16, 2011.

26. Harford, T. *Adapt: Why Success Always Starts with Failure*.
New York, NY: Farrar, Straus and Giroux, 2011.

27. Zhang, L. *R&D at Huawei*. Beijing, China: China Machine
Press, 2009.

28. Hardy, Q. 'Google's Innovation—And Everyone's?' *Forbes*, July
16, 2011.

29. Hemp, P., and Stewart, T. A. 'Leading Change When Business
Is Good'. *Harvard Business Review*, December 2004.

30. Palmisano, S. 'Our Values at Work on Being an IBMer'. IBM
website. [http://www.ibm.com/ibm/values/us/].

31. Lohr, S. 'Can Apple Find More Hits Without Its Tastemaker?'
[http://www.nytimes.com/2011/01/19/technology/
companies/19innovate.html]. January 18, 2011.

32. Battelle, J. 'The 70 Percent Solution'. *Business 2.0,* December
1, 2005.

33. Kirkpatrick, M. 'Leader of Google Maps to Launch Multiple
New Mobile Apps Inside Google'. *New York Times*, January
14, 2011.

34. V. R. Ferose, MD, SAP Labs India, personal interview with Navi
Radjou and Jaideep Prabhu, December 26, 2011.

35. Radjou, N., Prabhu, J., Kaipa, P., and S. Ahuja. 'Indian Tales of Inclusive Business Models'. *Harvard Business Review* Blog, January 5, 2011.

36. Kal Patel, Partner at VantagePoint Capital Partners and former president, Asia, Best Buy, personal interview with Navi Radjou and Simone Ahuja, August 11, 2011.

37. Hamm, S. 'Big Blue's Global Lab'. *Bloomberg Businessweek*, August 27, 2009.

38. Levy, S. 'Jeff Bezos Owns the Web in More Ways Than You Think'. *Wired*, December 2011.

39. 'How to be a High-Impact Entrepreneur: Ten Rules for Defeating Risk and Launching a Successful Start-Up'. Study conducted by Endeavor's Centre for High-Impact Entrepreneurship, 2011.

40. 'Google to Pull Plug on Power Meter and Health Services'. *Newsmax.com*, June 24, 2011.

41. 'Best Buy Shuts China Stores to Focus on More Profitable Brand', *Bloomberg News*, February 21, 2011.

42. Fowler, G. 'The Man Who Got Us to 'Like' Everything'. *Wall Street Journal*, August 13, 2011.

43. Jana, R. 'Facebook's Design Strategy: A Status Update'. *design mind*, August 2, 2011.

44. 'P&G Sets Two New Goals for Open Innovation Partnerships Company Seeks to Triple the Impact of Connect + Develop'. Press release, Procter & Gamble website, October 28, 2010.

45. 'Why US Newspapers Suffer More than Others'. The State of the News Media 2011: An Annual Report on American Journalism, Pew Research Centre's Project for Excellence in Journalism, 2011.

46. Strupp, J. 'New York Times' R&D Team Seeks Next Big Thing'. *Editor & Publisher*, December 10, 2009.

47. Garber, M. 'The New York Times' R&D Lab Has Built a Tool That Explores the Life Stories Take in the Social Space'. Nieman Journalism Lab website, April 22, 2010.

48. Fiore, J. 'Welcome to beta620'. [http://beta620.nytimes.com/2011/08/07/intro-beta620-post/]. August 7, 2011.

Chapter 5

1. 'Neonatal Mortality and Newborn Care in India'. [http://mchstar.org/pdf/neonatalMortalityAndNewbornCareInIndia.pdf].
2. 'Innovative Local Technology Warms the Prospects for India's Vulnerable Infants'. Lemelson Foundation website. [http://www.lemelson.org/programmes-grants/developing-country-program/recognition-and-mentoring-programmes-ramps/india/sathya-jeg].
3. Oshima, K. 'Plastic Bottles Light Up Lives'. *CNN World*, August 30, 2011.
4. McGeown, K. 'How Water Bottles Create Cheap Lighting in Philippines'. BBC, September 18, 2011.
5. 'Nokia's cheap phone tops electronics chart'. [http://uk.reuters.com/article/2007/05/03/us-nokia-history-idUKL0262945620070503].
6. Keating, J. 'The AK-47 of the Cell-Phone World'. *Foreign Policy*, January/February 2011.
7. Lakshman, N. 'One Laptop per Child Lands in India'. *Bloomberg Businessweek*, August 4, 2008.
8. Raina, P., and Timmons, H. 'Meet Aakash, India's $35 'Laptop'.' India Link, *New York Times*, October 5, 2011.
9. Ahmed, M. 'Mobile web becomes a reality'. *The Financial Express*, December 1, 2011.
10. Chima, C. 'Hands On: India's $35 Aakash Android Tablet Lands in America' (exclusive). *MobileBeat*, October 26, 2011.
11. Ushahidi—Frequently Asked Questions (FAQ). [http://www.ushahidi.com/about-us/faq].
12. Giridharadas, A. 'Africa's Gift to Silicon Valley: How to Track a Crisis'. *New YorkTimes*, March 13, 2010.
13. 'Why do inclusive design?' [http://www.inclusivedesigntoolkit.com/betterdesign2/why/why.html].

14. 'Indian Consumers Willing to Pay More for Technology and Banking Industry Brands that Offer Elegantly Simple Experiences and Interactions', siegel+nagel press release, Feb. 16, 2011.

15. Capps, R. 'The Good Enough Revolution: When Cheap and Simple Is Just Fine'. *Wired Magazine*, August 24, 2009.

16. Glock, A. 'Back to Basics: Living with 'Voluntary Simplicity'.' *O, The Oprah Magazine*, January 2009.

17. Markowitz, E. M., and Bowerman, T. 'How Much Is Enough? Examining the Public's Beliefs About Consumption'. *Analyses of Social Issues and Public Policy*, DOI: 10.1111/j.1530-2415.2011.01230.x. [http://onlinelibrary.wiley.com/doi/10.1111/j.1530-2415.2011.01230.x/abstract].2011.

18. 'Corporate R&D Spending Rebounds in 2010, Finds Booz & Company Global Innovation 1000 Study'. [http://www.booz.com/global/home/press/article/49852237]. October 24, 2011.

19. Maeda, J. *The Laws of Simplicity (Simplicity: Design, Technology, Business, Life)*. Cambridge, MA: MIT Press, 2006.

20. Radjou, N. 'R&D 2.0: Fewer Engineers, More Anthropologists'. [http://blogs.hbr.org/radjou/2009/06/rd-20-fewer-engineers-more-ant.html]. June 10, 2009.

21. Radjou, N. *Transforming R&D Culture*. Forrester Research report. March 20, 2006.

22. 'The Simplicity Imperative'. [http://www.newscentre.philips.com/main/standard/about/news/speechespublications/archive/2004/article-3188.wpd]. January 9, 2004

23. Ang, J. 'Philips: Sense & Simplicity'. [http://designtaxi.com/article/100322/Philips-Sense-Simplicity/].

24. Tischler, L. 'The Beauty of Simplicity'. *Fast Company*, December 19, 2007.

25. John, S. 'India will soon see Jugaad 2.0', *The Times of India*, Apr. 7, 2012.

26. 'Delivering 'sense and simplicity'.' Philips corporate web site. [http://www.philips.com/about/company/brand/brandpromise/index.page].

27. 'Simplicity Advisory Board'. Philips corporate web site. http://www.philips.com.my/philips5philipsmy/about/brand/simplicityadvisoryboard/index.page].

28. Tischler, L. 'The Beauty of Simplicity'. *Fast Company*, December 19, 2007.

29. 'The highest number ever of annual iF product design awards for Philips'. [http://www.newscentre.philips.com/main/design/news/press/2011/if2011.wpd.] February 8, 2011.

30. Khan, P. 'Safety pin | Colourful, child friendly syringes', *MINT*, Oct. 16, 2009.

31. 'The Seed of Apple's Innovation'. *Bloomberg Businessweek*, October 12, 2004.

32. 'Siemens 2011'. [http://www.siemens.com/press/pool/de/homepage/the_company_2011.pdf]. October 2011.

33. 'Siemens to expand market share in emerging markets'. Siemens corporate press release, June 28, 2011

34. 'Innovations for the entry level'. [http://www.kpmg.de/WhatWeDo/26472.htm].

35. Lamont, J. 'The age of 'Indovation' dawns'. *Financial Times*, June 15, 2010.

36. 'New Approaches for China'. [http://www.siemens.com/corporate-technology/en/research-areas/smart-and-cost-innovation.htm].

37. 'Innovations for the entry level'. [http://www.kpmg.de/WhatWeDo/26472.htm].

38. Dr Mukul Saxena, senior vice-president and head of Siemens Corporate Research and Technologies, Siemens India, personal interview with Jaideep Prabhu and Navi Radjou, March 26, 2010.

39. 'Innovations for the entry level'. [http://www.kpmg.de/WhatWeDo/26472.htm].

40. Ibid.

41. 'Siemens to expand market share in emerging markets'. Siemens corporate press release, June 28, 2011.

42. 'Less is More'. The World in 2012, *The Economist*, p. 132;Loescher, P. 'Strategies to save the only planet we have'.

[http://blogs.reuters.com/great-debate/2011/11/03/strategies-to-save-the-only-planet-we-have/]. November 3, 2011.

43. 'Principles of Universal Design'. [http://www.ncsu.edu/ncsu/design/cud/about_ud/udprinciples.htm].

44. 'Universal Design'. OXO corporate website. [http://www.oxo.com/UniversalDesign.aspx].

45. 'OXO gives Universal Design a shot in the arm'. [http://www.core77.com/blog/object_culture/oxo_gives_universal_design_a_shot_in_the_arm_13772.asp]. June 16, 2009.

46. Gertner, J. 'How Do You Solve a Problem Like GM, Mary?' *Fast Company*, 2011.

47. Ibid.

48. 'Better by design'. *The Economist* Technology Quarterly, September 15, 2005.

49. 'Simplicity and Enterprise Search'. Google white paper.

50. Tischler, L. 'The Beauty of Simplicity'. [http://www.fastcompany.com/magazine/100/beauty-of-simplicity.html]. December 19, 2007.

51. '100 Greatest Movies, TV Shows, and More'. [http://www.ew.com/ew/article/0,,20312226_20324138,00.html].

52. Kate Aronowitz, Director of Design at Facebook, email exchange with Navi Radjou, December 13, 2011.

53. Jana, R. 'Facebook's Design Strategy: A Status Update'. *design mind*, August 2, 2011.

54. Ibid.

Chapter 6

1. Dr Rana Kapoor, CEO, YES BANK, personal interview with Simone Ahuja and Navi Radjou, January 7, 2010.

2. Anand, M., and Bhuva, R. 'Banking on Innovation'. *Outlook Business*, September 19, 2009.

3. Ibid.

4. Gates, B. 'Making Capitalism More Creative'. *Time*, July 31, 2008.

5. Abhi Naha, CEO, Zone V, personal interview with Navi Radjou, June 23, 2011.

6. 'Visual impairment and blindness'. [http://www.who.int/mediacentre/factsheets/fs282/en/]. October 2001.

7. Bijapurkar, R. *Winning in the Indian Market: Understanding the Transformation of Consumer India*. Singapore: John Wiley & Sons (Asia), 2008.

8. Rama Bijapurkar, Marketing Consultant, personal interview with Navi Radjou and Jaideep Prabhu, November 18, 2010.

9. Rubinstein, D. 'Playing Grown-Up at KidZania'. *Bloomberg Businessweek*, May 19, 2011.

10. We collected details on Heloísa Helena Assis (known as Zica) and her company Beleza Natural through Endeavor—a non-profit organization that provides mentorship and strategic advice to high-impact jugaad entrepreneurs such as Zica around the world.

11. Smith, G. 'Brazil's Coming Rebound'. *Bloomberg Businessweek*, August 6, 2009.

12. 'Our Entrepreneurs. Heloísa Helena Assis'. Endeavor website. [http://www.endeavor.org/entrepreneurs/helo percentC3 percentADsa-helena-assis/96].

13. Details on YES MONEY were provided to us by Ajay Desai, Chief Financial Inclusion Officer, YES BANK.

14. 'GE Healthcare and Government of Gujarat Sign MOU for First of Its Kind Public & Private Partnership Model for Healthcare in the Country'. Press release, GE Healthcare, August 2, 2008.

15. Prakash, S. and Velu, C. 'Reuters Market Light: Business Model Innovation for Growth'. [http://www.india.jbs.cam.ac.uk/opinion/pieces/downloads/2010/prakash_reuters.pdf]. February 2010.

16. Dr Liu Jiren, Chairman and CEO, Neusoft, personal interview with Navi Radjou, September 15, 2011.

17. Ibid.

18. 'Neusoft Unveils Health Cloud Strategy'. [http://www.sinocast.com/readbeatarticle.do?id=68980]. December 22, 2011.

19. 'Emerging Focus: Ageing Population in Emerging Market Economies'. *Euromonitor*, May 5, 2010.

20. Hewitt, P. S. 'Depopulation and Ageing in Europe and Japan: The Hazardous Transition to a Labour Shortage Economy'. [http://library.fes.de/pdf-files/ipg/ipg-2002-1/arthewitt.pdf]. January 2002.

21. India's Ageing Population, Population Reference Bureau, March 2012. [http://www.prb.org/Reports/2012/india-older-population.aspx].

22. 'The "Grey Pound" Set to Hit £100bn Mark'. Press release, Age UK, April 7, 2010.

23. '50+ Fact and Fiction'. Immersion Active. [http://www.immersionactive.com/resources/50-plus-facts-and-fiction/].

24. Dolan, B. 'Patient monitoring device market to hit $8B in 2017', *MobiHealthNews*, Mar. 26, 2012.

25. Ian Hosking, Senior Research Associate at the Engineering Design Centre at the University of Cambridge's Department of Engineering, personal interview with Jaideep Prabhu and Navi Radjou, September 8, 2011.

26. Abelson, J. 'Suds with splash'. [http://articles.boston.com/2011-06-12/bostonworks/29650542_1_hispanic-population-p-g-hispanic-consumers]. June 12, 2011.

27. Roberts, S. 'In a Generation, Minorities May Be the US Majority'. *New York Times*, August 13, 2008.

28. Michaels, A. 'A fifth of European Union will be Muslim by 2050'. *The Telegraph*, August 8, 2009.

29. 'Tracking the growth of India's middle class', *McKinsey Quarterly*, August 2007

30. Censky, A. 'Poverty Rate Rises in America'. *CNN Money*, September 13, 2011.

31. Eichler, A. 'Middle-Class Americans Often Fall Down Economic Ladder: Study'. *Huffington Post*, September 7, 2011.

32. Anderson, C. *The Long Tail: Why the Future of Business Is Selling Less of More*. New York, NY: Hyperion, 2006.

33. 'National Survey of Unbanked and Underbanked Households'. Federal Deposit Insurance Corporation, December 2009.

34. Rob Levy, Manager, Innovation and Research, Centre for Financial Services Innovation (CFSI), personal interview with Navi Radjou, Jaideep Prabhu, and Simone Ahuja, September 9, 2011.

35. Ibid.

36. Ibid.

37. Levy, A. 'PayNearMe Targets 'Underbanked' Americans'. *Bloomberg Businessweek*, May 10, 2011.

38. 'Now, a prepaid card for groceries, bus tickets', *The Times of India*, Oct. 9, 2009.

39. Andreessen, M. 'Why Software Is Eating the World'. *Wall Street Journal*, August 20, 2011.

40. Ramón Mendiola Sánchez, CEO of Florida Ice & Farm Co., personal interview with Navi Radjou, December 19, 2011.

41. Moffett, S. 'Renault's Basic Car Detours'. *Wall Street Journal*, February 2, 2011.

42. Ghosh, R. 'Ghosn back to praising "frugal engg"'. *DNA*, October 30, 2007; Sehgal, V., Dehoff, K. and Panneer, G. 'The Importance of Frugal Engineering'. *strategy+business*, Summer 2010.

43. Kirkpatrick, D. 'The socialist state of ThoughtWorks'. *CNNMoney*, March 17, 2008.

44. Roy Neville Singham, Founder and Chairman, ThoughtWorks, personal interview with Navi Radjou, October 26, 2011.

45. Lallos, L. 'Your Encore Keeps Retirees in the Game'. *Bloomberg Businessweek*, April 15, 2010.

46. Ho, A. H. 'The Telehealth Promise: Better Healthcare and Cost Savings for the 21st Century'. Report prepared by the AT&T Centre for Telehealth Research and Policy at the University of Texas Medical Branch, May 2008.

47. Sandhu, J. S. 'Opportunities in Mobile Health'. *Stanford Social Innovation Review*, Fall 2011.

48. Rettner, R. 'US newborn death rate tied with Qatar'. Msnbc. com, August 30, 2011.

49. Miller, N. S. 'National Texting Program for New Moms Continues Growth'. *Pediatric News Digital Network*, December 9, 2011.

50. 'As Middle Class Shrinks, P&G Marketing Aims High and Low'. *Wall Street Journal,* September 12, 2011.
51. Ibid.
52. Ibid.

Chapter 7

1. Kishore Biyani, CEO, Future Group, personal interview with Simone Ahuja, October 30, 2008.
2. Smith, A. *Theory of Moral Sentiments*. Amherst, NY: Prometheus Books, 2000.
3. Venkat Rangan, co-founder and CEO, INXS Technologies, personal interview with Navi Radjou, December 28, 2010.
4. 'Diane Geng and Sara Lam'. [http://www.echoinggreen.org/fellows/diane-geng-and-sara-lam]. 2007.
5. Ibid.
6. Alter, A. L., Oppenheimer, D. M., Epley, N., and Eyre, R. N. 'Overcoming Intuition: Metacognitive Difficulty Activates Analytic Reasoning'. *Journal of Experimental Psychology: General*, November 2007, *136*(4), 569–576.
7. Jan Chipchase, Executive Creative Director of Global Insights, frog, and Ravi Chhatpar, Strategy Director, frog, personal interview with Navi Radjou, August 26, 2011.
8. Roberts, K. *Lovemarks: The Future Beyond Brands*. New York, NY: Power House Books, 2004.
9. Roberts, K. 'Magic Time'. [http://www.saatchikevin.com/Magic_Time/]. June 14, 2011.
10. Comments made by Anil Jain, managing director, Jain Irrigation Systems Ltd., at the World Economic Forum's Annual Meetings of the New Champions 2011 in Dalian, China, September 15, 2011.
11. Bam Aquino interview (see ch. 3, n. 17).
12. Dr Prasad Kaipa, CEO coach and Senior Fellow at the Indian School of Business, personal interview with Navi Radjou, November 3, 2011.

13. Dr Devi Shetty, founder of Narayana Hrudayalaya, personal interview with Simone Ahuja and Navi Radjou, December 14, 2009.

14. Radjou, N. 'Future Group's Mythological Marketing'. *Harvard Business Review* Blog Network, September 15, 2009.

15. Pink, D. *A Whole New Mind: Moving from the Information Age to the Conceptual Age*. New York, NY: Riverhead Hardcover, 2005.

16. Welch, J., and Byrne, J. *Jack: Straight from the Gut*. New York, NY: Business Plus, 2003.

17. Gladwell, M. *Blink: How Little Things Can Make a Big Difference*. New York, NY: Back Bay Books, 2002.

18. 'Millennials: The Challenger Generation'. *Prosumer Report, EURORSG*, 2011, *11*.

19. Kim, P. *Consumers Love To Hate Advertising*. Forrester Research report, November 26, 2006.

20. Li, C., and Bernoff, J. *Groundswell: Winning in a World Transformed by Social Technologies*. Boston, MA: Harvard Business School Press, 2008.

21. *Smart CRM For CPG Manufacturers*. Forrester Research Brief, May 29, 2002.

22. TNS Digital Life Study 2012 [http://www.tnsdigitallife.com].

23. Radjou, N. *Transforming R&D Culture*. Forrester Research report, March 20, 2006.

24. Comment made by Tim Brown, CEO of IDEO, at the 2011 State of Design conference, April 2011.

25. Liu, Y. and Cui, T. H. 'The Length of Product Line in Distribution Channels'. *Marketing Science*, Vol. 29, No. 3, May-June 2010, pp. 474-482.

26. India Consumer Survey 2011, Credit Suisse Research Institute, Jan 17, 2011.

27. Roberts, K. 'Why Lovemarks Are More Valid Than Ever, or Welcome to the Age of Now'. *Ad Age*, February 14, 2011.

28. Ludwig, A. 'John Hagel on Empowerment, Management Fears, and Social Software in Business'. *Forbes*, September 7, 2011.

29. 'HR development of the future'. [https://www.allianz.com/en/press/news/company_news/human_resources/news_2011-03-29.html]. March 29, 2011.

30. Hippel, E. v., Ogawa, S., and de Jong, J.P.J. 'The Age of the Consumer-Innovator'. *MIT Sloan Management Review*, Fall 2011.

31. Brooks, D. *The Social Animal: The Hidden Sources of Love, Character, and Achievement*. New York, NY: Random House, 2011.

32. Roberts, 'Magic Time' (see n. 9).

33. Robert Fabricant, creative director, frog, personal interview with Navi Radjou, September 22, 2011.

34. 'Connected Experiences—Denise Burton, frog Fellow, Austin'. [http://www.frogdesign.com/about/centres-of-passion.html].

35. Tindell, K., and Bryant, A. 'Three Good Hires? He'll Pay More for One Who's Great'. *New York Times,* March 13, 2010.

36. 'Corporate R&D Spending Rebounds in 2010, Finds Booz & Company Global Innovation 1000 Study'. [http://www.booz.com/global/home/press/article/49852237]. October 24, 2011.

37. 'I learned intuition in India: Steve Jobs'. [http://www.indianexpress.com/news/i-learned-intuition-in-india-steve-jobs/864708/.] October 24, 2011.

38. Kuang, C. 'What Can Steve Jobs Still Teach Us?' *Fast Company*, 2011.

39. Steve Jobs's interview with *Inc.* for its 'The Entrepreneur of the Decade Award'. [http://www.inc.com/magazine/19890401/5602.html]. April 1, 1989.

40. Walters, H. 'Apple's Design Process'. *Bloomberg Businessweek*, March 8, 2008.

41. '"You've got to find what you love",' Jobs says'. [http://news.stanford.edu/news/2005/june15/jobs-061505.html]. June 14, 2005.

Chapter 8

1. Tim Leberecht, Chief Marketing Officer, frog, personal interview with Navi Radjou, August 5, 2011.
2. Radjou, N., and Prabhu, J. 'PepsiCo and GE Are Innovating in India'. *Bloomberg Businessweek,* November 9, 2010.
3. 'Nueclear Healthcare Ltd (NHL) and GE Healthcare join hands in the fight against cancer'. [http://www.nueclear.com/NHL_GE.html]. December 10, 2011.
4. Terri Bresenham, President & CEO of GE Healthcare India, email exchange with the co-authors, January 3, 2011.
5. McGregor, J. 'GE: Reinventing Tech for the Emerging World'. *Bloomberg Businessweek*, April 17, 2008.
6. Jana, R. 'Innovation Trickles in a New Direction'. [http://www.businessweek.com/magazine/content/09_12/b4124038287365.htm]. March 11, 2009.
7. Chandran, R. 'In India, for India: medical device makers plug in'. [http://www.reuters.com/article/2010/07/05/us-india-healthcare-feature-idUSTRE6640F120100705]. July 4, 2010.
8. Joydeep Nag, CFO of GE Healthcare South Asia, personal interview with Navi Radjou and Jaideep Prabhu, December 26, 2011.
9. Ibid.
10. Radjou, N., and Kaipa, P. 'Do Multinationals Really Understand Globalization?' *Bloomberg Businessweek*, August 6, 2010.
11. 'Scripps Study First to Validate Usefulness of Pocket Ultrasound Device; Could Significantly Reduce Cost and Inconvenience of Traditional Echocardiograms'. *PR Newswire*, July 4, 2011.
12. 'Healthymagination—2010 Progress Report'. GE website [http://www.healthymagination.com/progress/].
13. Comstock, B. 'A New Blueprint for Innovation'. [http://www.thedailybeast.com/articles/2011/01/27/ges-beth-comstock-a-new-blueprint-for-innovation.html]. January 27, 2011.
14. Employee Engagement Report 2011, BlessingWhite, [http://www.blessingwhite.com/EEE__report.asp].

15. Siegler, M. G. 'Schmidt Talks Wave's Death: 'We Celebrate Our Failures'.' *TechCrunch*, August 4, 2010.

16. Madhavan, N. 'Made in India, for the world'. [http://businesstoday.intoday.in/story/made-in-india,-for-the-world.html/1/5601.html]. May 30, 2010.

17. Jean-Philippe Salar, head of Renault's Design Studio in Mumbai, India, personal interview with Navi Radjou, January 24, 2011.

18. Dr Liu Jiren (see ch. 6, n. 16).

19. '3M's Open Innovation'. [www.strategy-business.com/article/00078?gko=121c3]. May 30, 2011.

20. Brown, M. 'OpenIDEO helps solve society's problems together'. [http://www.wired.co.uk/news/archive/2010-08/04/openideo-brainstorming]. August 4, 2010.

21. Heath, C., and Heath, D. *Made to Stick: Why Some Ideas Survive and Others Die*. New York, NY: Random House, 2007.

Chapter 9

1. Dickey, C. 'Citizens, It's Down to You'. *Newsweek*, September 11, 2011.

2. Dr Vivian Fonseca, Professor of Medicine, Tulane University, personal interview with co-authors, August 25, 2011.

3. 'About MyBnk'. [http://www.mybnk.org/about-mybnk.]

4. Anand, A. 'Start-up Generation Ready to Fix the Economy'. MSNBC.com, August 8, 2011.

5. Anderson, C. 'Q&A: Open Source Electronics Pioneer Limor Fried on the DIY Revolution'. *Wired*, April 2011.

6. 'Ada Byron, Countess of Lovelace'. [http://www.sdsc.edu/ScienceWomen/lovelace.html.]

7. Tanz, J. 'Kinect Hackers Are Changing the Future of Robotics'. *Wired*, July 2011.

8. '2011: Most Influential Women in Technology. Limor Fried'. *Fast Company*, 2011.

9. Thompson, C. 'How Khan Academy Is Changing the Rules of Education'. *Wired*, August 2011.

10. Ryan, T. 'Fostering A Love For Learning Through Game Mechanics [Future Of Gaming]' [http://www.psfk.com/2011/12/fostering-a-love-for-learning-through-game-mechanics.html]. December 8, 2011.

11. Levey, N. 'Pressing for Better Quality Across Healthcare'. *Los Angeles Times*, October 4, 2011.

12. 'BillFloat CEO Testifies "Too Scared to Lend" a Growing Problem in Consumer Lending'. *PR Newswire*, September 22, 2011.

13. 'Will Plastyc Encourage the Broke to Save More?' [http://www.prweb.com/releases/prwebNew_Generation/HIgh-Reward_Savings/prweb8802732.htm]. September 16, 2011.

14. 'Piggymojo, 'Impulse Saving"[http://cfsinnovation.com/financialcapability/Piggymojo].

15. Jason Rohrer, independent game developer, personal interview with Simone Ahuja, Navi Radjou, and Jaideep Prabhu, August 16, 2011.

16. Thompson, M. 'Playing God'. [http://www.hemispheresmagazine.com/2011/07/01/playing-god/].July 1, 2011.

17. Berman, J. 'Can D.I.Y. Supplant the First-Person Shooter?' *New York Times*, November 13, 2009.

18. 'Remarks by the President on Community Solutions Agenda'. [http://www.whitehouse.gov/the-press-office/remarks-president-community-solutions-agenda-6-30-09.] June 30, 2009.

19. 'Social Innovation Fund'. [http://www.nationalservice.gov/about/programmes/innovation.asp].

20. Sonal Shah, former director of the White House Office of Social Innovation and Civic Participation, personal interview with Navi Radjou and Simone Ahuja, September 12, 2011.

21. Huang, G. T. 'Desh Deshpande on Starting Merrimack Valley Innovation Centre—and Making a Global Impact from Massachusetts to India'. *Xconomy*, January 6, 2011.

22. Radjou, N., Prabhu, J., Kaipa, P., and Ahuja, S. 'The UK Could Rise to the Scarcity Challenge. Can Europe?' *Harvard Business Review* Blog, July 21, 2010.

23. 'Tax rise as UK debt hits record'. [http://news.bbc.co.uk/2/hi/8011321.stm]. April 22, 2009.

24. 'La mise en place de l'auto-entrepreneur: Bilan au 31 août 2011'. Press release from ACOSS, September 21, 2011.

25. Neuwirth, R. 'The Shadow Superpower'. *Foreign Policy*, October 28, 2011.

26. Polak, P. *Out of Poverty*. San Francisco, CA: Berrett-Koehler Publishers, 2008.

27. Professor James Patell, Stanford University, personal interview with Navi Radjou, May 20, 2011.

28. Colvin, B., Gandhi, M., Parker, J., and Zhang, W. 'Water Telemetry—Team Soochak'. [http://www.scu.edu/socialbenefit/programmes/frugalinnovation/upload/team_soochak.pdf].

29. Radha Basu, Director of Frugal Innovation Labs at Santa Clara University, personal interview with Jaideep Prabhu, Simone Ahuja, and Navi Radjou, September 2, 2011.

30. Ian Hosking, Senior Research Associate at the Engineering Design Centre, Department of Engineering, University of Cambridge, personal interview with Jaideep Prabhu and Navi Radjou, September 8, 2011.

31. Ibid.

32. Yuri Malina, founder of Design for America, personal interview with Navi Radjou, October 4, 2011.

33. Ibid.

34. 'Monitoring Hospital-Acquired Infections to Promote Patient Safety—US, 1990-1999'.[http://www.cdc.gov/mmwr/preview/mmwrhtml/mm4908a1.htm].

35. 'Our Mission'. [http://www.endeavor.org/model/ourmission].

36. Dr Rajiv Doshi, Executive Director, Stanford-India Biodesign Program, Stanford University, personal interview with Navi Radjou, September 6, 2011.

37. Alec Ross, Senior Advisor for Innovation to US Secretary of State Hillary Clinton, personal interview with Jaideep Prabhu and Navi Radjou, September 8, 2011.

38. 'CFSI Convenes Innovators for the First Bay Area Financial Capability Development Lab'. [http://cfsinnovation.com/news/article/440974]. September 26, 2011.

39. 'Future Group Creates "Khoj Lab" with National Innovation Foundation', Dec. 14, 2010. [http://www.nif.org.in/khojlab].

40. Kirkpatrick, D. 'Social Power and the Coming Corporate Revolution'. *Forbes*, September 26, 2011, p. 72.

41. Ibid.

42. Melin, E. 'Scott Monty in Kansas City: Ford's Approach to Social Media'. [http://www.spiral16.com/blog/2011/09/scott-monty-in-kansas-city-fords-appraoch-to-social-media/]. September 2, 2011.

43. Lawrence, J. 'The new shape of innovation'. [http://www.i-cio.com/features/july-2010/polycentric-innovation].July 19, 2010.

44. Radjou, N., Prabhu. J., Kaipa, P., Ahuja, S. 'How Xerox Innovates with Emerging Markets' Brainpower'. [http://blogs.hbr.org/cs/2010/08/how_xerox_innovates_with.html]. August 25, 2010.

Acknowledgments

They say it takes a whole village to raise a child. The same applies to writing a book. We couldn't have produced this particular book without the intellectual and practical support of several people. First, we wish to thank our agent, Bridget Wagner of Zachary Shuster Harmsworth. In late April 2011, Bridget wrote to us to ask if we'd be interested in writing a book about jugaad—a subject we had been researching and writing about for several years. Bridget had just returned to the US after a two-year stint working in India. Having witnessed jugaad innovation firsthand in India, Bridget felt strongly that jugaad was a big idea whose time had come, and she wanted to help us introduce it to corporate leaders worldwide—including in India—as a new management paradigm. Bridget worked with us tirelessly, and in just over five weeks and a dozen or so iterations, we had a winning proposal.

Next, we would like to thank the entire Random House India team for their fabulous support. Gaurav Shrinagesh, Managing Director, and Milee Ashwarya, Editorial Director, became huge fans of our book the moment they read our proposal. Milee offered creative ideas and crucial editorial input throughout the book development process. Radhika Marwah and Gurveen Chadha did a great job managing the whole editing process so beautifully. Finally, the PR team—Caroline Newbury, Shabnam Srivastava, and Sheeba Madan—pulled out all the stops to promote and market our book across India on very short notice.

We must thank Kal Patel, partner at VantagePoint Capital Partners, and former president of the Asia Region at Best Buy, for consistently sharing potent ideas and poignant insights on creativity and innovation, and for generously supporting the *Indique—Big Ideas from Emerging India* TV series, which led us to more deeply study jugaad; Dr R. A. Mashelkar, former director general of the Council of Scientific & Industrial Research (CSIR), for sharing his deep knowledge based on many years of dedication to the study of innovation; Dr Prasad Kaipa, CEO coach and senior fellow at the Indian School of Business, for his cutting-edge insights into how individuals from all walks of life can ignite the creative genius that lies within them; Eddie Bowman and Sarah Bogue at Ernst & Young, for introducing us to jugaad entrepreneurs in South America— including Gustavo Grobocopatel (Argentina); Fernando Fabre at Endeavor, for introducing us to the innovative business models of Enrique Gómez Junco (Mexico) and Heloísa Helena Assis (Brazil). We are also grateful for the ideas, comments, and case studies that were generously provided by Radha Basu, Dr Rajiv Doshi, Professor Carol Dweck, Ian Hosking, Reena Jana, Lakshmi Karan, Pradeep Kashyap, Joydeep Nag, Professor James Patell, V. Raja, Sonal Shah, and Ramesh Vangal.

We couldn't have writtren the book without the active input of all the Indian jugaad innovators mentioned in our book who generously shared their professional and personal stories. Their jugaad spirit continues to inspire us.

Finally, we are profoundly grateful to family members and friends who cared about what we were doing and offered us moral support throughout—support that has helped us maintain our sanity and produce the book you now hold.

A Note on the Authors

Navi Radjou is an independent thought leader and strategy consultant based in Silicon Valley. He is an internationally recognized voice of business innovation and leadership. Navi is also a fellow at Judge Business School, University of Cambridge, and a faculty member of the World Economic Forum.

Most recently, Navi served as executive director of the Centre for India & Global Business at Judge Business School. Previously, he was a longtime VP/analyst at Forrester Research in Boston and San Francisco, advising senior executives worldwide on breakthrough growth strategies.

Navi has been featured in the *New York Times, Wall Street Journal, Bloomberg Businessweek,* the *Economist,* and the *Financial Times.* He is a columnist on HBR.org and a sought-after speaker who has addressed the World Economic Forum, Council on Foreign Relations, The Conference Board, Harvard University, Asia Society, and more. A prolific writer, Navi has coined and popularized several business concepts, such as 'global innovation networks', 'polycentric innovation', and 'indovation'. Navi is also a co-author of *Smart to Wise,* a book on next-generation leadership (Jossey-Bass, 2013).

An Indian-born French national, Navi earned his master's degree in information systems from Ecole Centrale Paris and also attended the Yale School of Management. He lives in Palo Alto, California. Follow Navi on Twitter @NaviRadjou.

Dr Jaideep Prabhu is Jawaharlal Nehru Professor of Indian Business and Enterprise and Director of the Centre for India & Global Business at Judge Business School, University of Cambridge. He has held positions at Imperial College London, Tilburg University (the Netherlands), and UCLA. Jaideep has a Bachelor of Technology degree from IIT Delhi and a PhD from the University of Southern California.

Jaideep's research interests are in marketing, innovation, strategy, and international business. His current research is on the globalization of innovation, and the role of emerging economies in this process. He is particularly interested in how multinationals and domestic firms are using emerging markets as a lab to do affordable and sustainable innovation for global application.

Jaideep has published in and is on the editorial board of leading academic journals such as the *Journal of Marketing* and the *International Journal of Research in Marketing*. He has taught and consulted with executives from ABN Amro, Bertelsmann, BP, BT, GE, IBM, ING Bank, KPMG, Nokia, Philips, Roche, Shell, Vodafone, and Xerox, among others. Jaideep has appeared *on BBC News24* and *Bloomberg Businessweek*, and his work has been profiled in *Bloomberg Businessweek*, the *Economist*, the *Financial Times, Le Monde, MIT Sloan Management Review*, the *New York Times*, and the *Times*. He is a columnist on HBR.org.

Dr Simone Ahuja is the founder of Blood Orange, a marketing and strategy consultancy with special expertise in emerging markets and innovation, and content production capabilities.

Headquartered in Minneapolis, with teams in Mumbai, Blood Orange uses an agile, cost-efficient content production process built on principles learned through extensive work in India, including jugaad. Simone recently developed, produced, and directed the television series *Indique—Big Ideas from Emerging India*, for which she explored how innovation in India drives socio-economic development. Coupled with her own experience in leveraging the complementary skill sets of transnational teams, these meetings with CEOs of multinational corporations as well as grassroots entrepreneurs, heralding bottom-up, small-scale innovation gave her a holistic, on-the-ground look at the unique methods and mindset of innovation employed in India.

Ahuja has served as an advisor to the Centre for India & Global Business at Judge Business School, University of Cambridge, and as an associate fellow for the Asia Society in New York City. She provides advisory services and keynote presentations to trade delegations, academic institutions, and Fortune 100 companies including PepsiCo, Procter & Gamble, Honeywell, General Mills, ECOLAB, Colgate-Palmolive, and Best Buy. Ahuja regularly contributes to a *Harvard Business Review* blog on HBR.org.

To learn more about the authors and their research and consulting capabilities, visit: jugaadinnovation.com

A Note on the Type

Sabon is an old style serif typeface designed by the German-born typographer and designer Jan Tschichold (1902–1974). It was released jointly by the Linotype, Monotype, and Stempel type foundries in 1967. A unique feature of the typeface was that the roman, italic, and bold weights all occupied the same width when typeset—an unusual feature, but this meant that the typeface then only required one set of copyfitting data (rather than three) when compositors had to assess the length of a text prior to actual typesetting (a common practice before computer-assisted typesetting).